In Our Hands

Interpreter Education Series

CYNTHIA B. ROY, EDITOR

LAURIE SWABEY AND
KAREN MALCOLM, *Editors*

In Our Hands

Educating Healthcare Interpreters

GALLAUDET UNIVERSITY PRESS
Washington, D.C.

Interpreter Education
A Series Edited by Cynthia B. Roy

Gallaudet University Press
Washington, DC 20002
http://gupress.gallaudet.edu

Library of Congress Cataloging-in-Publication Data

Educating healthcare interpreters / Laurie Swabey and Karen Malcolm, editors.
    p. cm. — (Interpreter education)
    Includes index.
    ISBN-13: 978-1-56368-521-7 (hardcover : alk. paper)
    ISBN-10: 1-56368-521-3 (hardcover : alk. paper)
    ISBN-13: 978-1-56368-522-4 (e-book)
    ISBN-10: 1-56368-522-1 (e-book)
    1. American Sign Language.   2. Interpreters for the deaf—Training of—United States.
3. Deaf—Services for—United States.   4. Medical care—United States.   I. Swabey, Laurie.
II. Malcolm, Karen.
    HV2474.E38 2012
    419′.70071073—dc23
                                                                                2011042711

♾ The paper used in this publication meets the minimum requirements
of American National Standard for Information Sciences—Permanence of
Paper for Printed Library Materials, ANSI Z39.48-1984.

CONTENTS

To
Andy, Liz, and Eric,
with special thanks to
Ginger Thompson

LAURIE SWABEY AND
KAREN MALCOLM

Introduction

GIVEN THE importance of healthcare interpreting, both in terms of the high stakes involved and the fact that it affects almost all deaf individuals and their family members, it is time for our field to seriously expand the number of evidence-based publications that are accessible and available to educators, consumers, and students. As a contribution to that effort, this volume seeks to engage educators in building stronger courses in healthcare interpreting and to further engage the profession in the important work of preparing interpreters to facilitate full access to healthcare communication for Deaf people around the world.

Deaf Americans have identified healthcare as the most difficult setting in which to obtain a qualified interpreter (NCIEC, 2008). Despite the importance of healthcare interpreting services to the Deaf community, relatively little attention has been given to developing evidence-based curricula, textbooks, case studies, and other resources for educating healthcare interpreters. An equally glaring lack in the field of signed language interpreting is an agreed-upon standardized body of knowledge that all interpreters who work in healthcare settings should master before working unsupervised in these settings. Additionally, there is a lack of professional standards related to decision latitude, particularly in regard to the minute-by-minute decisions regarding boundaries and involvement that interpreters face during every healthcare encounter. Further, the field is in need of additional research on which to base curricula for teaching healthcare interpreters. As an example, relatively little research has been conducted on interpreted interactions between deaf patients and hearing healthcare professionals that are mediated by interpreters and even less empirical work on healthcare interactions in which Deaf interpreters are members of the healthcare team.

Our field has made many advances in the education of interpreters, from 6-week programs in the 1970s, to AA programs in the 1980s and the proliferation of BA programs in the 1990s and early 2000s. The latter period also saw the establishment of accreditation for interpreter education programs in postsecondary institutions, the requirement of a degree to apply for RID certification, an MA in teaching interpreting and a PhD in interpreting. Although a few institutions offer sequences of courses in healthcare interpreting, our field has yet to agree on standards of practice for healthcare interpreting and interpreting education. The domains and competencies for healthcare interpreters (chapter 1) is a step in the right direction, but further work needs to be done. Focus groups (CATIE center, 2007) indicate that experienced, certified interpreters still do not have agreed-upon standards for making decisions related to the highly personal and high-risk situations that full-time staff interpreters and freelance interpreters find themselves involved with in their daily work. As educators, we play a role in implementing changes in education and policy so that deaf patients can focus on their healthcare without the fear of having to make decisions based on information that was incorrectly communicated due to the interpreter's lack of competence.

One of the first records regarding the need for interpreting education, which was written in 1965 (Quigley & Youngs), recognized that haphazard approaches to training interpreters were not sufficient for interpreters either to attain certification or to meet the needs of consumers. Forty-five years after this initial book on interpreting was published, our field has made only incremental progress toward establishing healthcare interpreting as a specialty area based on education of significant scope and sequence.

An early notable effort in this direction occurred in 1983, when the first program specifically designed to educate healthcare interpreters was established in Minnesota on the St. Mary's Campus of the College of St. Catherine (now St. Catherine University).[1] Marty Barnum was instrumental in the development of the program, guiding it from a certificate program to a 3-year AAS program and finally a bachelor's degree. In 1985 Barnum was awarded a FIPSE grant to develop the first textbooks

---

1. When the Health Care Interpreting (HCI) program was established, Pauline Annarino was the director.

and video materials in signed language healthcare interpreting. With this funding, Sandra Gish, Beth Siebert, and Barnum published instructional manuals that changed the way educators and students approached health-care interpreting and healthcare interpreting education. Central to their approach was that the interpreter was a member of the healthcare team and was in fact a thoughtful decision maker. The goal was not invisibility but involvement in providing the best communication access for the patient and providers. This was a radical move away from the conduit approach, which was commonly practiced at that time.

Since then, other notable works useful in the education of signed language interpreters to work in healthcare settings have included video material on mental health interpreting, (Treehouse Video, 1997); Metzger's (1999) book, which examines the participant role of the interpreter in mock medical situations and dispels the myth of neutrality; the series of health-care interpreting CDs and DVDs with self-study guides developed under RSA funds awarded to St. Catherine University (2000–2005),[2] a training curriculum for healthcare interpreters in British Columbia (Humphrey & Harry, 2000);[3] the work of Dean and Pollard (e.g., 2001) and Dean, Pollard, and English (2004), which is related to the demand-control schema and decision latitude as applied to healthcare settings; and a website with resources for ASL-English healthcare interpreters and educators (www .healthcareinterpreting.org). Still, there are no widely recognized textbooks on ASL-English healthcare interpreting and relatively few journal articles on teaching healthcare interpreters who work between a signed language and a spoken language. In addition, despite the existence of research studies and journal articles in related fields, such as spoken language interpreting in healthcare settings, health communication, and applied linguistics, these sources seem underutilized in the education of ASL-English interpreters.

The general field of healthcare is expanding rapidly, and a variety of advances from new drugs and treatments to the provision of healthcare

---

2. The majority of these materials were developed by Doug Bowen-Bailey (Digiterp) and were initially coordinated by Paula Gajewski Mickelson and Richard Laurion (SLICES) through the Region V RSA grant at St. Catherine's, directed by Laurie Swabey. For further information see www.healthcareinterpreting.org.

3. This curriculum also included video materials developed by Nigel Howard, Karen Malcolm, and David Still.

at a distance via technology. The patient population is also shifting: The population of elders is growing, and the number of immigrants and refugees in the healthcare system is increasing. Policies on a wide range of topics from language access to insurance are being examined and changed. Spoken language interpreting organizations have mobilized and now have two national certifying bodies for healthcare interpreters working between spoken languages (see Downing & Ruschke, this volume). Yet the field of signed language interpreting seems relatively complacent in regard to healthcare interpreting education even amid the activity in these related areas. As stakeholders in this field, we must take active roles in examining both the work of healthcare interpreters and the research and resources available in our field and related ones. These areas should inform our work, and our goal should be the development and implementation of teaching and learning opportunities that foster the knowledge and competencies that are vital for healthcare interpreters. In that spirit, this volume presents the following chapters.

The first section of the volume features approaches to best practices for educating healthcare interpreters. We begin with the chapter by Swabey and Craft Faber, which discusses the development of domains and competencies for medical and mental health interpreters. Their discussion of the use of these documents during the first National Symposium on Healthcare Interpreting points us toward developing teaching methodology that addresses the knowledge, skills, and attitudes required for medical interpreting and mental health interpreting.

Following this, we read of a creative use of a discourse approach to preparing healthcare interpreters, one developed in Australia. Major, Napier, and Stubbe engaged students with discourse analysis techniques and worked with transcripts and recordings of actual healthcare interactions. Their activities can also be modified to work with interpreters using either a different signed language or a spoken language.

Next, Crump presents an overview of a model program in Alabama that prepares interpreters to work in mental health settings. She describes the many challenges that interpreters face in such venues and then outlines the Alabama program and the way it effectively prepares interpreters to work in this environment.

Two of the instructors in the Alabama program are the authors of our next chapter. Dean and Pollard detail the efficacy of their Demand-Control Schema (DCS) and show how it can be applied to preparing interpreters for healthcare settings, both medical and mental health. Their specific description of its use for educating healthcare interpreters is both timely and engaging.

A number of authors throughout this volume comment on the possibility that healthcare interpreters will experience vicarious trauma, making the next chapter apropos. Bontempo and Malcolm review the literature, describe the negative effects of vicarious trauma, and discuss strategies for educating students to avoid it or, if already affected, to manage their reactions in healthy and constructive ways.

Moving next in a new direction, we take a look at online education for healthcare interpreters. Bowen-Bailey describes the need for online educational opportunities that satisfy the criteria for effective education. He considers both Bloom's taxonomy and Vygotsky's approaches and applies these principles in his description of an online educational experience he designed.

Finally in this section, Moreland and Agan consider the education of interpreters working with deaf health professionals. While the number of deaf health professionals may be small at present, it is likely to continue to grow, making this chapter particularly relevant as we look to the future of the education of healthcare interpreters.

In the second section of this volume, we offer four unique perspectives on healthcare interpreting and healthcare interpreting education. In most of these cases, the areas of education discussed by the authors are relatively new; thus, the available studies on the topic are limited. For that reason, these contributions give more background than do the chapters in the first section, creating an important foundation for continued exploration of these relevant areas.

This section begins with an examination of the importance of the role of healthcare literacy in the doctor-patient interview. Many IEPs focus on educating students to work with college-educated, bilingual deaf adults. However, as this chapter points out, the deaf patients that educators are preparing interpreters to work with run the gamut from illiterate to highly educated. Written by a hearing signing physician (Kaufman) and a Deaf patient advocate (Hedding), this chapter realistically educates readers about the importance of understanding issues related to health literacy when thinking about patient access and care.

The next perspective focuses on the importance of the education of Deaf interpreters. Morgan and Adam examine their own pathways to becoming Deaf interpreters as well as documenting the important contributions Deaf interpreters have made and continue to make. Drawing on personal experience and current literature, they build a compelling case for the need for Deaf interpreters as well as professional training.

The third perspective is from two long-standing and active members of the National Council on Interpreting in Health Care and its Committee on Standards, Training and Certification, Downing and Ruschke. They take readers through the development of standards for training for spoken-language interpreters, specifically in the medical field. Our field is often quick to make comparisons with spoken-language interpreters, and this chapter gives educators an accurate insider's view about the challenges and successes of spoken-language interpreter education in the healthcare setting.

The final perspective is from Europe, specifically Great Britain, Italy, and the Netherlands. Three leading educators/interpreters/policymakers, Hema, Salami, and de Wit, describe the education of healthcare interpreters in their respective countries. With globalization, it is increasingly vital that educators and interpreters become aware of educational practices around the globe.

In closing, it seems timely to cite an incident that happened while editing this book. One of our Deaf colleagues stopped by to talk about a family member's illness. When we asked about a specific treatment option that we knew she was considering, she said, "I didn't ask the doctor about it this time, as the interpreter was already having difficulty with the more routine questions." She shrugged, indicating this is a common and frustrating experience. Given the severity of the medical issue facing this family, it is unfortunate that important questions went unasked and that potentially neither the doctor nor the interpreter had any inkling that the interpreter's lack of competence was a barrier to access to healthcare. Consumers and practitioners in the healthcare system face a variety of challenges, but, as educators, the one that is in our hands is the education of healthcare interpreters. May this book be one of the guideposts for significantly increasing the number of qualified interpreters who are well prepared to work in healthcare settings.

REFERENCES

CATIE Center, College of St. Catherine and NCIEC. (2007). Medical interpreting focus groups: Results for the background and experience survey. Retrieved November 15, 2011, from http://www.medicalinterpreting.org/PDF/FocusGroupSurvey.pdf

Dean, R. K., & Pollard, R. Q. (2001). Application of demand-control theory to sign language interpreting: Implications for stress and interpreter training. *Journal of Deaf Studies and Deaf Education, 6*(1), 1–14.

Dean, R. K., Pollard R.Q, & English, M. (2004). Observation and supervision in mental health interpreter training. In Elisa Maroney (Ed.), *CIT: Still shining after twenty-five years: Proceedings of the Fifteenth National Conference* (pp. 55–75). Washington, DC: Conference of Interpreter Trainers.

Duffy, K. & Veltri, D. (1997). *Interpreting in mental health settings.* DVD (50 minutes). Treehouse Video: Pleasant Hill, California.

Humphrey, J., & Harry, S. (2000). *Interpreting in medical settings: Curriculum guide.* Unpublished manuscript, Douglas College, Province of British Columbia. Ministry of Advanced Education, Training, and Technology.

Metzger, M. (1999). *The myth of neutrality.* Washington DC: Gallaudet University Press.

National Consortium of Interpreter Education Centers (NCIEC). (2008). *Phase one deaf consumer needs assessment: Final report.* Retrieved June 24, 2011, from http://www.nciec.org/resource/docs/FinalPhaseIDCReport.pdf

Quigley, S. P., & Youngs, J. P. (1965). *Interpreting for deaf people.* Washington, DC: U.S. Department of Health, Education, and Welfare.

CONTRIBUTORS

Robert Adam
Deafness Cognition and
Language Research Centre
University College London
London, United Kingdom

Todd Agan
Department of Medicine
The University of Texas Health
Science Center at San Antonio
San Antonio, Texas

Karen Bontempo
Department of Linguistics
Macquarie University
North Ryde, NSW, Australia

Doug Bowen-Bailey
Digiterp Communications
Duluth, Minnesota

Charlene Crump
Mental Health Interpreting
Alabama Department of
Mental Health
Montgomery, Alabama

Robyn K. Dean
Deaf Wellness Center
University of Rochester School
of Medicine
Rochester, New York

Bruce Downing
Program in Linguistics
University of Minnesota
Minneapolis, Minnesota

Quincy Craft Faber
Freelance Interpreter
Fridley, Minnesota

Teri Hedding
Deaf Access Program
Mount Sinai Hospital
Chicago, Illinois

Zane Hema
Freelance Interpreter
London, United Kingdom

Gary Kaufman, MD
Deaf Access Program
Mount Sinai Hospital
Chicago, Illinois

George Major
Department of Linguistics
Macquarie University
North Ryde, NSW,
Australia

Karen Malcolm
Program of Sign Language
Interpretation
Douglas College
New Westminster,
British Columbia, Canada

Christopher Moreland, MD
Department of Medicine
The University of Texas
Health Science Center
at San Antonio
San Antonio, Texas

Pamela Morgan
Freelance Interpreter
East Sussex, United Kingdom

Jemina Napier
Department of Linguistics
Macquarie University
North Ryde, NSW, Australia

Robert Q Pollard
Deaf Wellness Center
University of Rochester School
of Medicine
Rochester, New York

Karin Ruschke
International Language
Services, Inc.
Chicago, Illinois

Marinella Salami
Freelance Interpreter
Piacenza, Italy

Maria Stubbe, MD
Department of Primary Health
Care and General Practice
University of Otago Wellington
Wellington, New Zealand

Laurie Swabey
CATIE Center
St. Catherine University
St. Louis, Minnesota

Maya de Wit
Freelance Interpreter
Baarn, The Netherlands

In Our Hands

LAURIE SWABEY AND
QUINCY CRAFT FABER

Domains and Competencies for Healthcare Interpreting

Applications and Implications for Educators

THE NEED for sign language interpreters in healthcare settings has been identified as crucial by the deaf community in the United States. In a national needs assessment survey of deaf consumers conducted by the National Consortium of Interpreter Education Centers (NCIEC, 2008), respondents identified health care as the most difficult setting in which to obtain a qualified interpreter, followed by work settings. In terms of importance, deaf consumers ranked work-related settings as their top priority for interpreting services, followed by interpreting services in healthcare settings. Clearly, and not surprisingly, work and health are integral to one's quality of life, and communication access in these settings is essential.

Despite the importance of healthcare interpreting services to the deaf community, there is yet to be a model curriculum for educating medical interpreters. Very little research has been conducted on the practice of ASL-English interpreting in the medical setting (Swabey & Nicodemus, 2011), and the field is without an agreed-upon sequence of courses that are based on evidence in terms of scope, sequence, and outcomes. Furthermore, there has not been a national dialogue with stakeholders on signed language interpreting in healthcare settings, and perhaps most important of all, there is no shared understanding of the scope of the healthcare interpreter's role, particularly in medical settings.

These factors were the impetus for the CATIE Center at St. Catherine University to host the first National Symposium on Healthcare Interpreting

1

for signed language interpreters in July 2010. The final day of the symposium focused on the domains and competencies needed for medical and mental health interpreting, which served as the foundational documents for a curriculum map for healthcare interpreting education, developed with funding from the CATIE Center at St. Catherine University and the National Consortium of Interpreter Education Centers (NCIEC). In this chapter we describe the history and development of the domains and competencies, the applied educational activities presented during the symposium, the resulting key discussion topics, and, finally, implications for interpreter education.

FIRST NATIONAL SYMPOSIUM ON HEALTHCARE INTERPRETING

The first National Symposium on Healthcare Interpreting was held on July 19–21, 2010, on the campus of St. Catherine University in St. Paul, Minnesota. The symposium drew participants from the District of Columbia and twenty-two states; three attendees were from outside the country. According to the 110 participants that responded to the evaluation survey on the first day of the symposium, 88% indicated they were interpreters, 15% were interpreter educators, 10% were healthcare professionals, 4% were deaf consumers, 1% were deaf community health workers (CHWs), 1% were students planning to go into the healthcare field, and 1% were students planning to become interpreters.[1] The diversity of the participants provided a range of perspectives on the work interpreters do in healthcare settings.

   The keynote speakers at the symposium presented new research related to the deaf community and to the work of interpreters in healthcare settings. Chad Ludwig, MSW, and Matthew Starr, MPH, spoke on "Eliminating Health Disparities in Deaf Populations through Community-Based Participatory Research," reporting on their work with the National Center for Deaf Health Research (NCDHR) in Rochester, New York, bringing new information to participants, as well as the perspective of deaf

---

1. The sum of percentages listed here is greater than 100% because some individuals indicated more than one role.

researchers. Christopher Moreland, MD, MPH, a deaf physician, and Todd Agan, BS, CI/CT, interpreter, provided new information in their presentation, "Deaf Health Professionals and Designated Interpreters." On the third and final day of the symposium, participants were introduced to the medical and mental health interpreter domains and competencies through presentations and interactive learning activities. These activities are explained later in this chapter.

Background: Domains and Competencies for Healthcare Interpreting

The development of the domains and competencies was part of a larger project of the CATIE Center at St. Catherine University in collaboration with the NCIEC, which was tasked with developing effective practices for teaching interpreters in multiple specialties (www.healthcareinterpreting .org/new/educators/domains-competencies.html). The CATIE Center led the initiative that focused on the specialty area of health care. Although the long-range goal was to educate interpreters to work in specific settings, it was recognized that the setting-specific skills and knowledge sets needed by interpreters had to be determined before the appropriate curricula and educational resources could be developed. The following section focuses primarily on the development of the medical domains and competencies, although a similar process was followed by the Regional Interpreter Education Center at Northeastern University (NURIEC), under the leadership of Cathy Cogen, to document the domains and competencies needed for mental health interpreting

In 2006, after reviewing the literature and conducting preliminary interviews with medical interpreters and interpreter educators, Laurie Swabey and Marty Taylor convened a group of experts from across the United States and Canada to begin the process of identifying the domains and competencies for medical interpreting. Seven experts, with representation from each region of the country, were invited to St. Catherine University to participate: Marty Barnum, Glendia Boon, Lillian Garcia, Dan Langholtz, Karen Malcolm, Brenda Nicodemus, and Carol Patrie.

In advance of the expert meeting on medical interpreting, each participant reviewed several documents related to both spoken- and signed-language interpreting in healthcare settings. Documents on standard practices from the National Council on Interpreting in Health Care (NCIHC, 2005) and the California Healthcare Interpreting Association (CHIA, 2002) were particularly relevant. By the end of the 3-day meeting, a draft document of domains and competencies for medical interpreters had been created. The expert group participants returned to their region with the task of soliciting feedback on the first draft through a process of field interviews with healthcare interpreter practitioners.

With this additional input from practitioners across the county, a second draft of the domains and competencies document was created. However, it was clear that more in-depth input needed to be solicited from all regions of the country, as well as from stakeholders with diverse backgrounds. To meet this need, a total of 12 focus groups met in the spring of 2007 in Georgia, Illinois, Kansas, Maine, Minnesota, New Mexico, Oregon, and Texas. The participants in each group were certified interpreters with extensive experience in the medical setting. Each group was facilitated by an experienced interpreter who had been trained in the interview protocol for this project. A skilled notetaker was also provided for each group.

Before each focus group began, participants were asked to complete a 20-item survey (CATIE Center, 2007). Related to interpreter education, the results showed that 61% of interpreters did not feel appropriately prepared when they started interpreting in medical settings. When asked on the survey to identify the most important competencies for interpreters in a medical setting, they cited the following: a high degree of language competency in ASL and English, including specific competencies needed to function effectively in medical settings; a clear understanding of roles and boundaries; highly developed ethical and professional decision-making abilities; interpreting skills; and knowledge of healthcare systems. The most common barriers they listed on the survey in regard to interpreting in the medical setting included lack of knowledge (anatomy, physiology, medical terms, medical practices, prescription drugs, interview structure), lack of common protocol followed by interpreters, uncertainly about how to skillfully navigate difficult or sensitive issues, and an aversion to blood and/or needles.

Facilitators were responsible for organizing and managing the focus group process, probing whenever necessary to go beyond what interpreters believe they are "supposed" to say about their work. This was included as part of the protocol because previous interviews with medical interpreters supported one of the findings in the literature: that what interpreters say they do and what they actually do in a situation may be quite different (Wadensjö, 1998).

In the focus groups, many interpreters reported feeling conflicted when they have to choose between following what they still perceive to be a rule-based code of ethics and truly serving the communication needs of a deaf patient in a healthcare setting. Although the professional organization of interpreters, the Registry of Interpreters for the Deaf (RID), moved from a rule-based code of ethics to its Professional Code of Conduct in 2005, many practitioners still feel bound by the "rules" they were taught in their interpreter education programs, based on a previously accepted paradigm that interpreters were "invisible" and that to add anything to the situation would be unethical (Swabey & Gajewski Mickelson, 2008). Even though research has shown the fallacy of this perception of the interpreter's role (Metzger, 1999; Roy, 2000; Wadensjö, 1998), there has been a lack of agreed-upon standard practices in the highly personal and potentially high-risk setting of health care.

During the focus groups, interpreters revealed their angst over decisions they have made while interpreting in medical settings, as the following quotes show. In interview Excerpt 1, one interpreter made a decision to do what she calls "stepping out of role." In Excerpt 2, another interpreter related her decision to follow what she perceived as the narrowly defined standard of the field. The fact that interpreters believed for years that they could not talk about their work in an honest, professional way that still protected the privacy of the patient has held back the development of the interpreting field. In not dialoguing about our work—again, not about the patients but the work—practitioners unwittingly created some false perceptions of the complex work and decision making that are required in healthcare settings. The domains and competencies were developed as an additional resource to aid interpreters in moving beyond rule-based thinking.

INTERVIEW EXCERPT 1

I have acted as an advocate. I thought that I had to because I'm like—
this is dangerous stuff, you know. They're not getting it. I would do
it again. It was like, wow, I really stepped out of my role. I could have
been called big time for stepping out of the role, but I felt like I had
to do it just to be able to sleep at night.

INTERVIEW EXCERPT 2

I've been beaten over the head that we [interpreters] don't get to say
anything. That boundary is like a cement wall, and nothing happens
. . . I didn't say anything in the situation because it was at that time
when it was, like, the interpreter can't say anything. You don't do
anything, and I left, and I was, like, I can't do this job. I still don't
know what happened to the woman, but it probably wasn't good.

The results of the focus group discussions brought to the fore topics that
needed to be considered in the revision of the domains and competencies
document. Topics included the following:

- The active nature of the interpreter's role and the constant need to make
  in-the-moment decisions related to language, culture, and interactional
  dynamics.
- The role and function of power in the interpreted interaction.
- The intimacy and personal nature of the medical setting as two examples
  of factors that make interpreting in the medical setting different from
  interpreting in other settings.
- When, how, and why interpreters may need to provide support or advocacy in the medical setting.
- The lack of widely accepted standards of practice for ASL-English interpreters working in medical settings.
- The lack of curriculum, textbooks, and other resources for teaching medical interpreting.
- The need for consistent support for observation, mentoring, and internship opportunities for medical interpreters and students.

Within and across focus groups, staff interpreters at medical facilities and private-practice interpreters had different perspectives on roles, boundaries, support, and advocacy. In general, full-time staff interpreters in health care reported seeing themselves as part of the healthcare team with a commitment to patients' health and well-being. Freelance or private-practice interpreters reported seeing themselves as facilitating the communication in the moment, without a strong sense of being part of the healthcare team. In practical terms, according to focus group participants, this results in differing views on roles and boundaries, particularly related to when support or advocacy may be appropriately provided.

Related to educating interpreters to work in the medical setting, participants agreed that theory and application were both important and that structured mentorship opportunities were needed in order for interpreters new to the healthcare setting to apply the competencies and knowledge learned in a classroom. Participants agreed that both deaf and hearing interpreters need both specialized training prior to working in the healthcare setting and ongoing professional development. The topic of education for consumers, both healthcare providers and deaf patients, was also seen as crucial.

Unexpectedly, participants stated that the focus group format was beneficial because it provided a place where they could discuss their work in a professional manner with their peers. Medical interpreting can be taxing cognitively, physically, and emotionally, and interpreters have long believed that confidentiality prevented them from having professional dialogue about their work. One participant summarized this complexity well:

> I had a female audiologist from India with a strong accent and parents who are from Mexico and don't speak English and their deaf child, plus the Spanish interpreter and me [the ASL interpreter]. Four different cultural backgrounds in one small room, plus gender and power issues. It gets complicated quickly.

With the input from the focus groups, as well as a review of the literature, another version of the domains and competencies for medical interpreting was drafted. This version was reviewed by 25 deaf and hearing stakeholders around the country, and after their input was incorporated, the final version was created. The domains and competencies are viewed as a "living" document that will be reviewed on a regular basis and will change as the profession moves forward. The document in its current form was finalized in the fall of 2008 (http://healthcareinterpreting.org /new/educators/domains-competencies.html). It has 13 general domains: healthcare systems, multiculturalism and diversity, self-care, boundaries, preparation, ethical and professional decision making, language and interpreting, technology, research, legislation, leadership, communication advocacy, and professional development. Under these 13 domains are a total of 80 different competencies.

One of the areas of discussion throughout the development of this document was the amount of foundational knowledge that should be included. Some experts and reviewers believed that the domains and competencies for medical interpreting should not contain any information that was already in the NAD-RID Code of Professional Conduct. The assertion was that anyone interpreting in medical settings should be RID certified and well versed in the tenets and guidelines of the Code of Professional Conduct. The other view articulated by experts and stakeholders was that because interpreters with varying degrees of education and certification interpret in medical settings, it was beneficial for the field and for consumers to have the domains and competencies include information that was also covered in the Code of Professional Conduct.

The participants in the expert group believed that interpreters are more likely to take medical interpreting jobs without having previous training in medical interpreting than they are to take mental health or legal interpreting jobs without training in those specialty areas. Potential explanations for this include the perception that medical interpreting may be low risk and routine, whereas legal and mental health settings are less likely to be so. An additional factor discussed was that since most interpreters have more personal experience with the medical system than the mental health or legal system, they are more comfortable accepting work in the medical setting, which is more familiar to them.

In contrast to the medical interpreting domains and competencies, the mental health interpreting domains and competencies were developed with the assumption that the NAD-RID Code of Professional Conduct (CPC) is the base standard and that the mental health interpreting domains and competencies articulate what is needed beyond the CPC

(http://healthcareinterpreting.org/new/prof-development/mental-health
-resources/domains-a-competencies.html). Moreover, the medical and
mental health domains and competencies documents are not formatted
alike. Different conventions are used (roman numerals, uppercase letters,
lowercase letters) to indicate a domain and the various competencies associated with it. A future project may be to integrate the domains and
competences for medical interpreting and mental health interpreting into
one document, thereby standardizing the content and the format.

The Domains and Competencies as a Foundation for Curriculum Development

After the current version of the medical interpreting domains and competencies was created, it was used for a specific purpose: to serve as one
of the foundational pieces for the development of curriculum for teaching
medical interpreting. The next step in the process was to hire a curriculum developer (Karen Malcolm) to use the domains and competencies
documents, as well as other published resources (Angelelli, 2006; Dean &
Pollard, 2005; Metzger, 1999; Shaw, Collins, & Metzger, 2006), to develop
a concept map for online interpreter education modules for healthcare
interpreters.

By this time in the grant cycle, it had become apparent that the NCIEC
medical interpreting work team (led by the CATIE Center) and the NCIEC
mental health interpreting work team (led by NURIEC) should pool their
efforts and resources and move forward as one team. In the beginning, the
work to develop domains and competencies was so intensive that it was
determined that the two efforts should be conducted independently. However, with the overlap between the two specialty areas and the potential
benefits of shared resources, the teams joined forces in 2008 to move on
to the next task: curriculum development.

Using the resources and references identified and created to date, the
curriculum consultant (Malcolm) developed an outline for a sequence of
modules to teach interpreters to work in healthcare settings. The concept
map for healthcare interpreting education included the following eight
modules: orientation/overview of mental health/medical interpreting, conditions and treatments, language use in mental health/medical settings,

ethics and boundaries, interpreting skills, interpersonal skills, self-care, and professional and research skills.[2]

It should be noted that, in this project, we were not investigating the use of interpreters for deaf medical students or deaf healthcare professionals. However, as more people became aware of the CATIE Center's work in medical interpreting, we received an increasing number of inquiries about the education and availability of interpreters to work with deaf health professionals and deaf students in graduate healthcare programs. This is an additional area for investigation into interpreting practices and education. Although some work has been done, this is still an area of need, particularly as the number of deaf people pursuing postgraduate degrees in healthcare-related fields increases (Moreland & Agan, this volume; Hauser, Finch, & Hauser, 2008; Swabey, Nicodemus, & Moreland, 2010).

Although the domains and competencies served their purpose as a foundational document for curriculum development, they were also disseminated more widely. The final day of the first National Symposium on Healthcare Interpreting focused on these documents, with the goal of facilitating professional discussion about the challenges of working in the healthcare setting and ways in which stakeholders can use the document as a resource. The next section of this chapter explains the structure of the symposium presentation and is followed by a section on implications for educators.

APPLIED EDUCATIONAL ACTIVITY

Participants were encouraged to become familiar with the domains and competencies documents prior to the symposium. To facilitate this process, each participant received an email link to the documents and had access to a printed version in the program book. After a short presentation on the final day of the symposium, participants met in small, facilitated groups to observe simulated doctor-patient interviews and then discuss applications to the everyday work of healthcare interpreters.[3]

---

2. This document may be accessed at www.healthcareinterpreting.org.

3. Doug Bowen-Bailey, Karen Malcolm, and Laurie Swabey facilitated the third morning of the symposium. They, along with Richard Laurion, also developed the program for this day.

At the symposium, four simulated interpreted encounters were presented, each representing different settings or healthcare topics: the emergency room, psychotherapy, oncology, and cardiology. These settings were chosen because of the frequency with which these types of appointments occur and because of the challenges these specialty areas pose to healthcare interpreters. The actors for each simulation were identified prior to the symposium and matched the characters they portrayed, including licensed physicians and psychotherapists as healthcare providers, certified deaf and hearing interpreters as healthcare interpreter practitioners, and deaf individuals as patients. The actors met the day before the activity to prepare, and the content of each simulation was provided to each of them on a note card. These cards described the situation for each character and served as a launching point for their understanding of the context and creation of the scenarios as they prepared with the other actors assigned to their specialty. (See appendix I for brief role-play descriptions.)

Each of the four groups had a moderator who introduced the actors and the scenario. Following each simulated interpreted interview, the moderator facilitated a discussion on the domains and competencies related to the simulation. Later, each group broke into smaller sections and continued to dialogue about what they saw in the simulation and how it related to the medical and mental health interpreting domains and competencies. As time allowed, the participants engaged in an additional role play. They were provided a different scenario and instructed to enact it, then engage in a discussion of applying the domains and competencies to yet another situation.

EXAMPLES OF KEY TOPICS AND RELATIONSHIP TO DOMAINS AND COMPETENCIES

This section does not offer solutions to the conflicts and issues presented in the simulated interpreted interviews; rather, it summarizes some of the topics raised and various perspectives of the symposium participants.

The topic of the role and necessity of certified deaf interpreters (CDIs) in medical settings was discussed in depth after the simulation that was set in an emergency room (ER). Many symposium participants identified medical interpreter domain 7, language and interpreting, in this context and specifically highlighted 7G as an issue in their professional practice. This competency states the following:

> The interpreter demonstrates skills in working as part of a team with CDIs and spoken language interpreters.

Participants acknowledged their lack of experience in working with CDIs. Numerous questions were raised regarding placement, communication between the deaf and hearing interpreting team, and a way to explain to healthcare professionals the rationale for using a CDI. Participants also expressed frustration with the small number of working CDIs in specific geographic areas. Some asserted they felt confident with medical interpreter domain and competency 2D:

> The interpreter assesses and accommodates varied levels of language competency, knowing when to call in a specialist such as a CDI or deaf community health worker (CHW).

However, in many instances the participants stated that there were no CDIs within hours of their location. The simulation and discussion assisted the group in identifying medical domains and competencies related to the issues of accessing CDIs and gaining knowledge in order to effectively work as a deaf/hearing interpreting team of practitioners.

The second theme that surfaced during the ER group discussion was related to medical interpreting domain 6, ethical and professional decision making. Participants discussed the issue of whether an interpreter should disclose pertinent information with an ER physician if the patient had not shared the information. Various perspectives were considered, and attention was given to the interpreter's role in the situation, as related to medical interpreting domain and competency 6C:

> The interpreter demonstrates knowledge that the decision-making processes and the expectation to disclose and/or report certain information may be different between staff interpreters and freelance interpreters (e.g., staff interpreters may have more access to pertinent information and make different decisions than freelance interpreters).

During the discussion, the deaf patient in the simulation stated her view on the scenario: She believed that the interpreter could prompt the patient or tactfully elicit the information from the patient, allowing the patient to share directly with the doctor. The experienced ER doctor in the simulation, however, urged interpreters to share information with the physician in a life-or-death situation because the physician is an expert and is aware of the triggers or symptoms of medical conditions. These comments relate to medical interpreting domain and competency 6D:

> The interpreter has advanced decision-making skills and knows when ethical dilemmas need to be resolved in collaboration with the patient and healthcare provider in order to lead to the best outcome for patient treatment and recovery.

This part of the discussion highlighted the complex role of the interpreter in a healthcare setting and the importance of understanding what it means to work as a part of an interdisciplinary team. It also prompted discussions of the active nature of the interpreter in this type of setting and the fact that it is far removed from that of the mythical invisible interpreter.

The psychotherapy role play and discussion specifically incorporated the mental health interpreting domains and competencies. This simulation stimulated discussion on many of the mental health domains and competencies, including domain 2, therapeutic dynamics. In this domain, the symposium participants in this group focused on mental health interpreting competency 2 B.1, which reads as follows:

> The interpreter will demonstrate ability to establish appropriate rapport and boundaries with the consumer.

Within the framework of the symposium discussion, participants were advised to discuss boundaries openly and politely at the beginning of the first meeting between the interpreter and the deaf consumer. Instead of awkwardly avoiding the topic and hoping that no information will be shared before the therapeutic session begins, the interpreter in this type of setting was encouraged to purposefully set clear boundaries.

Also highlighted during the discussion was domain 3, and, under that domain, competency 3B was emphasized for interpreters working in this type of setting:

> The interpreter will demonstrate skills in providing linguistic and cultural equivalences to mirror the therapeutic interaction.

Symposium participants suggested that mirroring the therapeutic interaction may be done by purposefully interpreting vague language from therapist to consumer or not interrupting the flow of therapy to clarify information with the deaf consumer. Also, mental health interpreting domain and competency 3D was identified as imperative:

> The interpreter will demonstrate ability to identify and respond effectively to the presence of a variety of dysfluency patterns and symptoms.

This topic of detecting dysfluent language use by the deaf consumer in a mental health setting was discussed at length by the symposium participants. Strategies discussed to effectively communicate with the therapist included incorporating first- and third-person narratives and descriptions (reflected in mental health interpreting domain and competency 3D.2).

In exploring the communication between the therapist and the interpreter, the symposium participants discussed mental health interpreting domain 4, the interpreter as a professional, and specifically highlighted mental health interpreting domains and competencies 4D.1–3. In numerical order, these state the following:

> The interpreter will communicate with mental health providers about working effectively with interpreters.

> The interpreter will develop team relationship/collaboration with providers.

> The interpreter will appropriately advocate/consult around language and culture issues (culture broker) that could lead to misdiagnosis.

Considering these competencies, the participants agreed that discussing the interpreting process with the therapist was imperative and that this meeting would ideally occur before the initial therapy appointment. They also agreed that it is most effective when interpreters provide ongoing consultation regarding language and culture to the therapist during both pre- and postsession meetings.

In the discussion of the oncology appointment simulation, there were several interesting threads that can be organized by domain. One prominent theme was the decision regarding the use of fingerspelling if the interpreter believes that the patient will not understand the term in English. Several interpreters strongly advocated for fingerspelling and signing the concept. Others advocated for signing only, specifically recommending the use of classifiers and other visual aids. Within this debate, interpreters cited anecdotal reports from deaf patients expressing frustration over interpreters' overuse of fingerspelling in medical settings. Still other interpreters advocated for fingerspelling technical terms and then allowing the patient and the provider to negotiate the meaning. The physician in the simulation, along with a participant with a background in public health, strongly believed that the technical terms or diagnoses should be written down either by the patient, the provider, or the interpreter. They believed this gives the patient more information, particularly in terms of sharing specifics with family members or finding out more information online.

The domains and competencies do not specifically address the topic of fingerspelling, although the idea of how best to convey a medical concept or term comes up repeatedly. For example, under domain 1, health care systems, both competency "B" and "C" focus on the knowledge of medical terms and procedures, as well as bilingual competency with these terms. Under domain 8, technology, competency "A" states the following:

> The interpreter demonstrates knowledge of medical technology necessary to accurately interpret a procedure (e.g., use of classifiers for colonoscopy).

Under domain 5, preparation, competency "B" speaks to the interpreter as having the background knowledge and skills to effectively represent procedures and treatments visually.

The decision about when and why to use fingerspelling in a medical interview generated strong and diverse opinions from the group, particularly related to health literacy, communication access, and the linguistic resources used in ASL to convey medical terms. This type of discussion again highlighted the interpreter's active role in terms of constantly making decisions about aspects of the communication. This specific question about when to fingerspell, as well as the larger topic of communicating technical medical concepts, could be further explored, potentially examining the literature related to health literacy (Margellos-Anast, Estarziau, & Kaufman,

2006) and conducting focus groups with healthcare providers, deaf patients, and interpreters. Although input for the current version of the domains and competencies was solicited across the country from interpreting professionals (both hearing and deaf), one weakness of the document is that less input was gathered from deaf consumers and even less from healthcare providers. Including more input from these particular groups of stakeholders would strengthen the document and should be addressed in the next version.

The other main topic of discussion related to the oncology simulation was the appropriateness of the interpreter briefly suggesting a resource to the physician regarding communication access through interpreting services. During the interaction the interpreter made the recommendation, using spoken English and sign language at the same time. Neither the doctor nor the deaf patient in the simulation found the short recommendation to be problematic; they both agreed it was helpful. However, several participants voiced concerns during the discussion about whether such an addition was appropriate for the interpreter to provide. Medical interpreting domain 12, communication advocacy, was discussed, particularly competency 12I:

> The interpreter provides healthcare providers with information about interpreting and refers providers to deaf, hard of hearing, and deaf-blind people who can discuss deaf culture, deafness, blindness, and how the needs of individuals from these communities can be best met in the healthcare system.

Many of the interpreters present had, in fact, made such referrals in their own practice, although they had previously not been confident that this was considered part of the interpreter's role. Participants in general agreed that the way the interpreter handled the referral in the simulation was professional, appropriate, and beneficial to the consumers involved. Furthermore, it was noted that observing the simulation and then discussing the choices made by the interpreter in light of the domains and competencies was beneficial, particularly more so than discussing it hypothetically. The group also reported that having a healthcare provider and a deaf person playing the role of a patient was helpful and that watching experienced healthcare interpreters "working" allowed them to consider options in the situation from a greater number of perspectives. Furthermore, the interpreter's active role was once again highlighted, allowing participants to see "in action" applications of the findings of researchers such as Metzger (1999), Roy (2000), and Wadensjö (1998), who describe the interpreter as a discourse participant.

Implications for Interpreter Education

Given that the majority of deaf individuals have multiple interactions with the healthcare system during their lives, it is surprising that relatively little attention has been devoted to educating interpreters to work in this setting.

In regard to higher education in general, Hutchings and Shulman (1999) wrote about advancing the profession of teaching, claiming that it needed to become "something other than a seat-of-the-pants operation, with each of us out there making it up as we go." Mikkelson and Mintz (1996) have also used similar phrasing to talk about the profession of spoken-language community interpreting, saying that it is made up of bilingual individuals who, in many cases, have learned interpreting by the seat of their pants. Although not a phrase that we commonly think of in regard to teaching or interpreting, the definition has some truth to it regarding how healthcare interpreters are educated "based on or using intuition and experience rather than a plan or method; improvised" (*American Heritage Dictionary*, 2009).

The medical and mental health domains and competencies documents described in this chapter are part of an effort by the NCIEC to establish best practices for interpreting and interpreter education. A commitment to using best practices in any field is a commitment to using all of the knowledge and technology at one's disposal to ensure success. In this section, suggestions for using the domains and competencies are presented. Fundamentally, they provide a resource that can be used by students, interpreters, educators, consumers, and stakeholders to further understand the depth and breadth of the healthcare interpreter's role. However, because of the format and function, they serve mainly as reference documents and are not the type of documents that are easily digested in a single reading. Here are some suggestions offered for educators to use these documents in meaningful ways:

• Curriculum development: The domains and competencies provide a solid foundation on which to build a program or a series of workshops or courses. As an example, educators are directed to the curriculum map developed by Malcolm (2008) as one way this document was applied to the development of a module sequence.

- Interpreter education (within interpreter education programs, or IEPs): The domains and competencies are a resource that students can be directed to as part of their IEP. It demonstrates the potential complexities of the work of healthcare interpreting and can serve as a guide to developing a plan for acquiring the knowledge and skills to work effectively in a healthcare setting. Students working on assignments in IEPs related to ethics, decision making, roles, boundaries, and skill development could find this document helpful.
- Mentoring: Both mentors and mentees who are working in the area of health care may find the domains and competencies useful as they pursue activities such as self-assessment and the creation of a professional development plan for a specific skill or particular knowledge. Referring to it in preparing for or debriefing after observation or supervised practice may also be of benefit.
- Observation and supervision: Observation and supervision have been documented as effective practices for teaching healthcare interpreting (Dean & Pollard, 2009). As students or working interpreters observe and engage in discussions about their observations, they could employ the domains and competencies documents as additional resources.
- Educating health professionals and/or employers: This may be a tool for interpreters to use with employers to explain the complexities of the interpreter's work and/or to develop a job description. Similarly, there may be opportunities to share this document with healthcare providers in educational or continuing education settings. Having providers and patients who are well informed about the work of interpreters further increases the chances of a successful interaction.

Participants at the National Symposium on Healthcare Interpreting suggested the following three ways in which the domains and competencies could be useful to interpreters at various levels. A new interpreter stated that they gave her a whole new respect for working in healthcare settings and particularly for the wealth of information and knowledge that more experienced interpreters bring to the work. An experienced interpreter talked about how the domains fit many situations she has found herself in over the past several years. Furthermore, she felt the document validated her work and provided her with a framework and a more productive approach for talking about her work. An educator described how the document fits with her teaching, particularly observation and supervision. She also stated that, after students became familiar with the document, aspects of it might come up during think-aloud protocols (TAPs), as students responded to simulations of healthcare interpretations.

CONCLUSION

Over the past five years, the CATIE Center has taken the lead on the healthcare interpreting initiative of the NCIEC. Along with partner institutions, the CATIE Center has surveyed the literature, conducted focus groups, brought together expert panels, drafted domains and competencies for healthcare interpreting, and revised these documents with input from interpreters and stakeholders across the nation. As the 2005–2010 grant cycle closed, the National Symposium on Healthcare Interpreting brought together educators, researchers, practitioners, and other stakeholders to address topics identified as germane to healthcare interpreting. This is a step in the right direction, but much remains to be accomplished in the areas of research, education, practice, and public policy in order for deaf patients and deaf healthcare providers to have full access to the healthcare system.

The healthcare setting is complex. Challenges range from meeting the needs of increasingly diverse patients to negotiating the latest trends in treatment and healthcare delivery. Still, although other settings (e.g., legal or educational venues) may require specialist credentials for interpreting, that is not yet the case for health care. The demand for services has always overshadowed the demand for research in this area. One of the fundamental issues in our field is the persistent lack of evidence-based research on the practice of ASL-English interpreting in the healthcare system in the United States (Swabey & Nicodemus, 2011). Moreover, there is little peer-reviewed research on the effectiveness of healthcare interpreter education for interpreters working between a signed language and a spoken language.

The domains and competencies for medical and mental health interpreting are a foundational piece for developing evidence-based curricula for healthcare interpreting education. However, more work needs to be done on these documents as well. Specifically, the medical and mental health domains and competencies could be combined into one document, with reconsideration given to moving beyond the NAD-RID Professional Code of Conduct, therefore eliminating some of the competencies that are currently included in the medical interpreting document. Further, the domains and competencies were last reviewed in 2008; now, 3 years later, there is additional literature that needs to be considered.

It is our goal that the work of the CATIE Center and the NCIEC, including the domains and competencies documents, will contribute to improving access to communication in healthcare settings for deaf patients. Deaf and hearing healthcare providers, deaf and hearing interpreters, deaf and deaf-blind consumers, researchers, educators, administrators, and policy makers need to join forces to examine the barriers to healthcare communication access and set a course of action to stimulate positive change. As educators, we have a responsibility to facilitate learning environments in which students and working interpreters develop the core competencies needed to work effectively in healthcare settings. The process of developing the competencies to interpret effectively in a specialized area such as health care takes both time and guidance. In this regard, it seems fitting to end with a quote from Witter-Merithew (2010):

> Specialization is a process of professional maturity—an intentional/deliberate deepening of knowledge, skills, and expertise associated with a particular setting over a period of time and from a broad range of experiences that enable a practitioner to manage multiple and complex factors effectively.

ACKNOWLEDGMENTS

We recognize and thank Richard Laurion and Rosa Ramírez of the CATIE Center for their work in planning and coordinating the first National Symposium on Healthcare Interpreting. Without their efforts, the symposium would not have taken place.

The CATIE Center is funded by a grant from the U.S. Department of Education, Rehabilitation Services Administration, Grant # H160A050008 (2005–2010) and Grant # H160A100003 (2010–present).

REFERENCES

American Heritage Dictionary of the English Language, The. (2009). S.v. "seat-of-the-pants." Boston: Houghton Mifflin.

Angelelli, C. (2003). The visible co-participant: The interpreter's role in doctor-patient encounters. In M. Metzger, S. Collins, V. Dively, & R. Shaw (Eds.), *From topic boundaries to omission: New research on interpretation* (pp. 3–26). Washington, DC: Gallaudet University Press.

Angelelli, C. (2004). *Revisiting the interpreter's role: A study of conference, court, and medical interpreters in Canada, Mexico, and the United States.* Philadelphia: John Benjamins.

Angelelli, C. (2006). Designing curriculum for healthcare interpreting education: A principles approach. In C. Roy (Ed.), *New approaches to interpreter education* (pp. 23–45). Washington, DC: Gallaudet University Press.

California Healthcare Interpreters Association (CHIA). (2002). *California standards for healthcare interpreters: Ethical principles, protocols, and guidance on roles & intervention.* Sacramento, CA: Author. Available at http://www.chiaonline.org/?page=CHIAStandards.

CATIE Center, College of St. Catherine and NCIEC. (2007). Medical interpreting focus groups: Results for the background and experience survey. http://www.medicalinterpreting.org/PDF/FocusGroupSurvey.pdf.

CATIE Center, College of St. Catherine and NCIEC. (2008). Medical interpreter: ASL-English domains and competencies. Retrieved June 25, 2011, from www.medicalinterpreting.org/Interpreting/ProfDevelopment/Resources/DomainsCompetencies.html.

Dean, R., & Pollard, R. (2005). Consumers and service effectiveness in interpreting work: A practice profession perspective. In Marc Marschark (Ed.), *Interpreting and interpreter education* (pp. 259–82). New York: Oxford University Press.

Dean, R., & Pollard, R. (2009). Effectiveness of observation-supervision training in community mental health interpreting settings. *REDIT E-Journal on the Didactics of Translation and Interpreting, 3,* 1–17.

Hauser, P. C., Finch, K. L., & Hauser, A. B. (Eds.). (2008). *Deaf professionals and designated interpreters: A new paradigm.* Washington, DC: Gallaudet University Press.

Hutchings, P., & Shulman, L. (1999, September/October). The scholarship of teaching: New elaborations, new developments, In *Change 31:* 5,10–15. Retrieved from http://www.carnegiefoundation.org/elibrary/scholarship-teaching-new-elaborations-new-developments#article.

Malcolm, K. (2008). Concept map for mental health/medical interpreting education. Retrieved June 24, 2011, from http://healthcareinterpreting.org/new/educators/curriculum-ideas/concept-map.html.

Margellos-Anast, H., Estarziau, M., & Kaufman, G. (2006). Cardiovascular disease knowledge among culturally deaf patients in Chicago. *Preventive Medicine 42*, 235–39.

Mental Health Interpreting Domains and Competencies. 2007. Retrieved June 24, 2011, from http://www.asl.neu.edu/riec/projects_activities/national_projects /mental_healthcare/documents/MHSA_Domains_Feb2007.pdf.

Metzger, M. (1999). *Sign language interpreting: Deconstructing the myth of neutrality.* Washington, DC: Gallaudet University Press.

Mikkelson, H., & Mintz, H. (1997). Orientation workshops for interpreters of all languages: How to strike a balance between the ideal world and reality. In S. E. Carr, et al. (Eds.), *The critical link: Interpreters in the community : Papers from the First International Conference on Interpreting in Legal, Health and Social Service Settings.* (pp. 55–63). Amsterdam & Philadelphia: John Benjamins. Available at http://works.bepress.com/holly_mikkelson/24.

National Consortium of Interpreter Education Centers. (2008). Phase one deaf consumer needs assessment: Final report. Retrieved June 24, 2011, from http:// www.nciec.org/resource/docs/FinalPhaseIDCReport.pdf.

National Council on Interpreting in Health Care (NCIHC). (2005). *National Standards of Practice for Interpreters in Health Care.* Washington, DC: Author. Retrieved June 24, 2011, from http://data.memberclicks.com/site/ncihc /NCIHC%20National%20Standards%20of%20Practice.pdf.

Roy, C. (2000). *Interpreting as a discourse process.* New York: Oxford University Press.

Shaw, R., Collins, S., & Metzger, M. (2006). MA to BA: A quest for distinguish-ing between undergraduate and graduate interpreter education, bachelor of arts in interpretation curriculum at Gallaudet University. In C. Roy (Ed.), *New approaches to interpreter education* (pp. 1–21). Washington, DC: Gallaudet University Press.

Swabey, L., & Nicodemus, B. (2011). Bimodal bilingual interpreting in the U.S. healthcare system: A critical linguistic activity in need of investigation. In B. Nicodemus & L. Swabey (Eds.), *Advances in interpreting research: Inquiry in action.* Amsterdam: John Benjamins.

Swabey, L., Nicodemus, B., & Moreland, C. (2010). *An examination of deaf physician–deaf patient discourse: Implications for interpreting practice.* Paper presented at the Conference of Interpreter Trainers, San Antonio, TX.

Swabey, L., & Gajewski Mickelson, P. (2008). Role definition: A perspective on forty years of professionalism in signed language interpreting. In C. Valero Garces & A. Martin (Eds.), *Crossing borders in community interpreting: Definitions and dilemmas.* Amsterdam: John Benjamins.

Wadensjö, C. (1998). *Interpreting as interaction.* London: Longman.

Witter-Merithew, A. (2010). Conceptualizing a framework for specialization in ASL-English interpreting: A report of project findings and recommenda-tions. Retrieved June 24, 2011, from http://www.nciec.org/projects/docs/Legal -ConceptFrameworkSpecialization.pdf.

APPENDIX I

Role-Play Descriptions

The role-play scenarios presented at the National Symposium on Healthcare Interpreting are listed in this appendix. It is important to note that each role-play participant received only the paragraph correlating to the participant's assigned part before the activity. Please feel free to duplicate and integrate these materials into your curriculum as desired.

EMERGENCY ROOM ROLE PLAY

Deaf Patient

You have gone to the ER because of shortness of breath, and you are afraid you may be having a heart attack. You are bipolar but recently stopped taking your meds because they make you feel tired all the time. You are feeling very anxious and have been hearing voices that tell you the people on TV are trying to plant messages in your mind. You keep getting confused by the voices when you are trying to talk to people.

EMERGENCY ROOM ROLE PLAY

Hearing Physician

You are an emergency room doctor meeting with a patient who is complaining of shortness of breath. You want to find out what her symptoms are and whether she is taking any medications. You started to interview the patient with a hearing interpreter, and then the hearing interpreter requested permission to bring in a deaf interpreter, so you are now recommencing the interview.

EMERGENCY ROOM ROLE PLAY

Deaf and Hearing Interpreters

The hearing interpreter was called to the hospital to interpret for a patient complaining of shortness of breath. The hearing interpreter was unsure of correctly understanding the deaf patient and has texted a deaf interpreter, who has now arrived.

PSYCHOTHERAPY ROLE PLAY

Deaf Client

You have been seeing this therapist for several months and trust and like her/him. In fact, you would like to be better friends with her/him, but it seems to you that the therapist is not all that friendly. You ran into her/him at Starbucks one weekend and were surprised and hurt that she/he didn't stay and chat with you, so you want to address that today.

PSYCHOTHERAPY ROLE PLAY

Hearing Therapist

You have been seeing this client for several months, and therapy has been progressing well. You ran into the client at Starbucks one weekend, and, as is customary for you, you replied and said hello when the client greeted you but did not stay and talk. You are starting to feel that the client wants more of a personal connection with you, which you think would be counterproductive to the therapy.

PSYCHOTHERAPY ROLE PLAY

Interpreter

You have been interpreting for this client and therapist weekly for several months, and they seem to have good rapport. You are not sure what the session today will focus on.

ONCOLOGY ROLE PLAY

Deaf Patient

You have had a cough and chest pain for several months, and you have been feeling fatigued. Your doctor sent you for a chest X-ray, and you are now meeting with the doctor to find out the results. You are very anxious that it might be cancer.

ONCOLOGY ROLE PLAY

Hearing Physician

You are meeting with a patient who was complaining of a cough, chest pain, and fatigue. You sent the patient to get a chest X-ray. The results show a mass, so you are meeting with the patient to explain next steps:

• Have a CT scan to better determine where the mass is.
• Have a bronchoscopy to do a biopsy and see whether the mass is malignant or benign.

If the biopsy is malignant but the condition has been identified in an early stage, it may be treated first with surgery and then chemotherapy. Another possibility is radiation, but these decisions will be made after more is known.

ONCOLOGY ROLE PLAY

Interpreter

You are interpreting for a Deaf patient meeting with a family doctor. Several months ago, the patient was complaining of a cough, chest pain, and fatigue. The doctor sent the patient for a chest X-ray. Today the patient will get the results.

CARDIOLOGY ROLE PLAY

Deaf Patient

You have an appointment with your family doctor. For the past 2 months, you have been experiencing some shortness of breath when you walk upstairs or try to exercise. In general, you have been healthy before this point. You did not really want to visit the doctor, but your partner finally convinced you to come. You have high blood pressure, which is controlled by taking the medication Monopril. You think it is probably nothing serious, and you don't really want to make any changes, such as stopping smoking or cutting out salt.

CARDIOLOGY ROLE PLAY

Hearing Physician

You are a family doctor seeing a patient who has no history of cardiovascular issues but has high blood pressure, which is controlled by Monopril. You want to find out whether the patient has any chest pain. You are planning on having lab work done to check the patient's cholesterol level. You may end up having to refer the patient to a cardiologist to have an angiogram. In the meantime, you will encourage your patient to stop smoking and to reduce salt intake. You may need to emphasize that these factors can lead to heart disease, which could lead to heart attack or stroke.

CARDIOLOGY ROLE PLAY

Interpreter

You are an interpreter in private practice who is called to interpret for an appointment between a deaf patient and a family doctor. This is the first time you have worked at this clinic and with this patient.

GEORGE MAJOR, JEMINA NAPIER,
AND MARIA STUBBE

"What Happens Truly, Not Textbook!"

Using Authentic Interactions in Discourse Training for Healthcare Interpreters

HEALTHCARE INTERPRETING is a high-consequence setting in which accuracy is an interpreter's most important objective (Napier, McKee, & Goswell, 2010). At the same time, there are often other challenges to deal with: anxious patients, sensitive topics, busy doctors, and difficult healthcare terminology, to name just a few. Being aware of how and why participants are using language in context can help interpreters to better predict the direction of interaction, likely topics, terminology, and potential communication challenges. According to Metzger (2005, p. 100), "one cannot deny that the basic work that interpreters engage in on a daily basis is the comprehension and manipulation of discourse." Interpreters are essentially discourse analysts: when they enter assignments, they immediately assess the discourse being used, salient contextual features, and make interpreting decisions as a consequence of their understanding of the goals of the interaction, the power dynamics, and interpersonal relationships among the participants. Although interpreters are arguably experts when it comes to managing the talk of themselves and others, this is not always a conscious skill; they may not realize that what they are doing is actually analyzing the discourse in situ. We believe that learning basic techniques of discourse analysis can aid interpreters—from new students to very experienced practitioners—in learning how to better utilize those skills to improve their interpreting.

This chapter explores an innovative technique for preparing interpreters to work in healthcare settings by exposing them to discourse analysis techniques and, most important, to transcripts and recordings of authentic, same-language healthcare interaction. We provide an overview of the discourse analysis procedure and walk readers through the step-by-step process of the teaching activity, concluding with discussion of the benefits of using such an approach to train healthcare signed-language interpreters. Although we focus specifically on the training and education of signed-language healthcare interpreters in Australia, we are confident that the teaching activity is applicable to the teaching of healthcare spoken- and signed-language interpreters worldwide.

Australia has approximately 300 Australian Sign Language (Auslan)/English interpreters who are active and regularly available (ORIMA, 2004; Napier, Bontempo, & Leneham, 2006) to serve a signed-language-using deaf population of approximately 6,500 (Johnston, 2006). Auslan/English interpreters receive their "license to practice" (accreditation) from the National Authority for the Accreditation of Translators and Interpreters (NAATI) by either passing a NAATI test or completing a NAATI-approved course of study. Accreditation is available at both the paraprofessional or the professional level. Paraprofessional-level accreditation is an entry-level certification that assesses interpreters as being "safe to practice," although the professional level is regarded as the ideal minimum level of competence. Australia is one of the few countries in the world that accredits spoken-language and signed-language interpreters through the same system (Napier, 2005a). Demographic surveys of Auslan/English interpreters in the last decade have found that approximately 70% are accredited at the paraprofessional level, and approximately 30% at the professional level (Bontempo & Napier, 2007; Napier & Barker, 2003). The same surveys also note that Auslan/English interpreters are typically female (80:20 female:male) and work part-time.

Auslan/English interpreters are provided in various healthcare contexts through different booking agencies depending on the type of appointment and the state in which the deaf person lives. The general model is that interpreters are provided in public healthcare settings via the state government–funded Healthcare Interpreting Service (HCIS) in a particular state, and interpreters for private healthcare consultations are provided through the federally funded National Auslan Interpreter Booking and

Payment Service (NABS).[1] A survey of 491 deaf Auslan users (ORIMA, 2004) revealed that the purpose for which most (almost 70%) deaf people required professional interpreting services in the 12 months preceding the survey was to see a doctor or a specialist. The demand for healthcare interpreting is high; thus, high-quality training for healthcare signed-language interpreters in Australia is imperative.

Both HCIS and NABS book only interpreters that have NAATI accreditation, and both organizations encourage interpreters on their registers to participate in professional development training for healthcare interpreting, although it is not mandated. In addition, HCIS provides medical terminology workshops, and NABS has developed a series of DVDs for interpreting practice that focus on different aspects of healthcare terminology (e.g., anatomy, mental health). The only discourse-based healthcare interpreter training currently available for Auslan/English interpreters is a module offered at Macquarie University as part of the postgraduate diploma in Auslan/English Interpreting.[2]

In this chapter we focus on teaching discourse analysis skills to healthcare interpreters and healthcare interpreting students, although the techniques that we explore here could be replicated in any interpreting setting. Learning and teaching about healthcare discourse is not a completely novel idea; discourse-focused training and professional development courses on this topic exist in Australia and around the world (Napier, 2006b). However, these courses tend not to be based on analysis of authentic (real-life) interaction because very little data exist that have been tailored for use in interpreter education. We believe that the method presented in this chapter is innovative, first, because it is based on authentic interaction data and, second, because we focus on monolingual healthcare interaction. This method allows students to step back from interpreting and learn to first

---

1. NABS was established as a consequence of the ORIMA (2004) report, when the Australian government decided to fund a national healthcare interpreting service to fill gaps in the provision of interpreting assistance for private healthcare appointments that were not covered by state-based public healthcare interpreting services.

2. Macquarie University offers the only postgraduate university signed-language interpreter education program in Australia. The goal of the program is to upgrade accredited paraprofessional interpreters to the professional level. For more information about the training of signed-language interpreters in Australia generally see Napier (2004) and Bontempo and Levitzke-Gray (2009). For information about the structure and delivery of the Macquarie University program see Napier (2006a).

identify features of healthcare discourse involving a general practitioner (GP) and a patient who share the same language and then to learn basic discourse analytical skills that can later be applied to interpreting practice.

DEVELOPMENT OF THE METHOD AND TRAINING RESOURCES

The development of this method was the result of collaboration between the Applied Research on Communication in Health (ARCH) Group, University of Otago, Wellington (New Zealand), and the Medical Signbank team at Macquarie University in Sydney (Australia). In order to give a context for the development and delivery of the activity, we first provide a summary of how the collaboration came to fruition. The remainder of the chapter then explores how and why we created the discourse analysis activity for practicing interpreters and interpreting students.[3] We envisage that this description will encourage greater discussion and collaboration between interpreter educators and healthcare communication researchers in the future, further bridging the gap between research and practice in interpreting.

Our collaboration began with the need to find interesting and engaging materials for teaching healthcare interpreting workshops, as part of the Medical Signbank project based at Macquarie University.[4] As part of our data collection for this project, we held discussions with practicing interpreters in Perth, Melbourne, Sydney, Newcastle, and Brisbane in 2009. As well as collecting important data from interpreters for the Medical Sign-

---

3. In this chapter we refer mainly to "the activity," which is the interactive discourse analysis exercise that we created originally for use in the interpreter training workshops that we conducted around Australia. The ARCH Group has also generously supplied other excerpts of texts that have been used in the curriculum for the Master of Translating and Interpreting program at Macquarie University.

4. "Medical Signbank: Sign language planning and development in interpreter-mediated medical health care delivery for deaf Australians" (LP0882270), Australian Research Council (Scheme: Linkage Projects) 2008–2011. Chief investigators: Professor Trevor Johnston and Associate Professor Jemina Napier. Research assistants: George Major and Lindsay Ferrara. Medical Signbank is a bottom-up approach to creating an online database of medical and mental health information. We have spent considerable time talking to deaf people and interpreters in Australia and collecting signs used in the community. We have also elicited their views on medical interpreting in general. For more information about the Medical Signbank project itself see Johnston and Napier (2010).

bank project,[5] we wanted to make the most of this opportunity and also provide interpreters with useful professional development materials. To this end, we incorporated a 20-minute data-collection session into a 3-hour interactive workshop that focused not only on terminology but also on healthcare discourse.

We planned workshops that included activities on terminology and an interactive role play; additionally, we wanted to include an interactive discourse analysis activity based on empirical research. The reason for this is that there are many steps to learn when it comes to healthcare interpreting (or there are numerous things that can be revisited in development for already experienced healthcare interpreters). Authentic interaction is never as "clean" as created script examples; the discourse is filled with hesitations, repairs, repetition, laughter, and many other features that make up real-life talk but are often forgotten when we report our experiences of communication. One step that is arguably lacking in many education programs is to step back from healthcare interpreting, discuss the nature of healthcare discourse, and ask questions such as these:

• How do people use language in health care?
• What are the differences between practitioners' and patients' talk in health care?
• What strategies do participants use to achieve their own goals or agendas?
• What characteristic features or patterns in healthcare discourse do we notice?

At the time of devising materials for our workshops, we were not aware of any existing materials based on authentic interaction data, so we turned to the ARCH Corpus of Health Interactions. The ARCH Group is based in the Department of Primary Health Care and General Practice, University of Otago, Wellington, New Zealand,[6] and consists of researchers from a

---

5. See Napier, Major, and Ferrara (in press) for details about the Medical Signbank interpreting workshops and Auslan/English interpreter perspectives on interpreting in healthcare settings.

6. All of the data in the ARCH Corpus were recorded in New Zealand and thus predominantly consist of interactions in New Zealand rather than Australian English. While the ideal would clearly be to use local interactional data whenever possible, in this case, any differences between the two varieties were unimportant for the purposes of the workshop activity described here.

variety of clinical and social science backgrounds in primary health care, public health, sociolinguistics, psychology, and sociology. Members of the ARCH core group have been collecting and analyzing video recordings of naturally occurring interactions between health practitioners and patients since 2003, using a range of qualitative methods such as conversation analysis, interactional sociolinguistics, and thematic content analysis.[7] These recordings have been digitally archived along with various related data and, together with a custom-designed information management system, now comprise the ARCH Corpus of Health Interactions, currently the only dataset of its kind in New Zealand and Australia. At the time of writing, the ARCH Corpus holds audio and video recordings of more than 400 videotaped health interactions and associated data collected from approximately 350 participants at 33 different clinical sites.

This collaborative project came about as a result of the various authors' involvement with the ARCH Group and/or with interpreter education. Before moving to Australia, one of the authors, George Major (a qualified New Zealand Sign Language interpreter), had worked as part of the ARCH Group as a summer research scholarship holder and subsequently as the corpus data manager. In 2006 and 2007, she conducted a study of lifestyle talk in doctor-patient interactions, based on the general practice section of the ARCH Corpus, which at that time included audio and video recordings of 58 consultations with 7 GPs. The lifestyle talk project used an interactional sociolinguistics framework to explore the discourse of lifestyle talk and advice in these interactions, and a preliminary description was developed (for further details see Stubbe & Macdonald, 2010; Dew et al., 2008; Major, 2007; Major et al., 2007). The ARCH Group generously gave us access to a text that had been analyzed as part of this project. This proved valuable as we could report patterns identified through an analysis of discourse that had already been completed, based not only on that one recording but on an entire corpus of authentic GP-patient interactions. Jemina Napier, one of the chief investigators for the Medical Signbank project, established the Auslan/English Interpreting program at Macquarie University, and Maria Stubbe, a senior founding member of the ARCH

---

7. See Dowell et al. (2007) for further details of the methodology developed by the ARCH Group and an early explanation of how this has been applied to the study of clinical communication.

group, codirects the ARCH Corpus of Health Interactions. This combined expertise gave us the perfect opportunity to collaborate on designing a teaching activity for research-based discourse analysis. We were fortunate to have a preexisting relationship of this kind with a research team, although there is no reason that interpreter educators could not approach healthcare communication research groups to build new and mutually beneficial relationships.

WHAT DO WE KNOW ABOUT HEALTHCARE DISCOURSE AND HEALTHCARE INTERPRETING?

The large body of research on communication in healthcare consultations dating back to the 1960s falls into two broad traditions of research. The first set of approaches is based on the quantifiable description and categorization of interaction in consultations at a fairly general level and uses standardized coding systems designed to produce an overview of high-level constructs, such as the degree of empathy or patient-centeredness displayed by doctors. The second set of approaches focuses much more closely on the localized content and context of health discourse and uses ethnographic and microanalytic approaches to study in detail the various ways in which doctors and patients jointly construct their interactions moment by moment.

Early coding approaches to doctor-patient interaction were based on the "interaction process analysis" coding scheme developed by Bales (1950), which was originally used to classify roles and behavior in small-group, task-focused interactions. A foundational study by Byrne and Long (1976), *Doctors Talking to Patients*, used this framework to code 2,500 audio recordings of primary-care consultations. This analysis determined the phases of interaction and described in broad terms how doctors communicated in each interaction to provide a framework for evaluating the degree of doctor- or patient-centeredness in clinical decision making. A more recent and refined development of this approach is the Roter Interactional Analysis System (RIAS), which remains very influential in health communication research and education (e.g., Roter & Frankel, 1992; Roter & Larsen, 2002). This classification system codes the content of health interactions according to 39 predefined socioemotional and task-oriented categories.

While coding systems such as these have been widely used in research and have produced some interesting and useful results, this approach does not offer us much insight into the specifics of how doctor-patient communication actually works, because the content and context of healthcare encounters tend to be "washed out" in the analysis (Heritage & Maynard, 2006, p. 7). Such approaches are therefore of limited value for our purpose here, which is to help interpreters enhance their awareness of the subtleties of healthcare discourse, namely, the precise ways in which patients and doctors talk and interact to develop a mutual understanding (or not).

By contrast, microanalytic approaches to healthcare discourse use a variety of "bottom-up" interpretive methodologies to unpack the "background orientations, individual experiences, sensibilities, understandings, and objectives that inhabit the medical visit" (Heritage & Maynard, 2006, p. 4). An early and still compelling example of the usefulness of this approach is Elliot Mishler's (1984) influential work *The Discourse of Medicine*, which demonstrates the ways in which doctors and patients often pursue quite different agendas in the history-taking phase of the consultation. Mishler showed that, in pursuing their biomedical agenda, doctors consistently suppressed patients' expressions of their "lifeworld" concerns and circumstances even though these often had a real bearing on their medical problems and outcomes (Mishler, 1984).

The past two decades have witnessed an explosion of research on authentic healthcare discourse using the microanalytic methodologies of interactional sociolinguistics and conversation analysis. Researchers using these approaches pay very close attention to localized context and the ways in which discursive practices and activities are constructed sequentially as an interaction gradually unfolds turn by turn. This type of analysis makes it possible to put the spotlight on common "interactional dilemmas" (Gill & Maynard, 2006) posed by the inevitable importing of ordinary sociocultural norms of interaction into the institutional context of the health encounter. Such microanalysis of discourse thus allows us to better understand "the inexplicit tactics by which patients approach physicians on various topics and the taken-for-granted ways by which physicians deploy their specialized knowledge through conversational means whose effects they may not fully comprehend . . . [and] to lay bare the multiple paradoxes and dilemmas that inhabit the medical interview" (Heritage & Maynard, 2006, p. 20).

The majority of communication training in healthcare settings relies on methods such as role plays based on constructed scenarios, often working with actor patients, or video feedback based on the kinds of process coding discussed earlier. However there is increasing recognition of the value of incorporating examples of authentic interactions into training and educational materials for healthcare professionals—a technique pioneered in (nonhealthcare) workplace communication training (e.g., Stubbe & Brown 2002a, 2002b; Jones & Stubbe, 2004; Stokoe, 2010, 2011). Initial attempts have been made to apply the findings and tools of microinteractional analysis to professional training and education in medical, nursing, and mental health professional education (e.g., Malthus, Holmes, & Major, 2005; Parry, 2005; Petersen, Ladefoged, & Larsen, 2005; Collins et al., 2007; Stubbe et al., 2006; Dowell et al., 2007). Some researchers are also experimenting with different kinds of reflective videoethnography, working with healthcare teams to help them evaluate their own communication processes and identify areas they would like to improve (e.g., Carroll, Iedema, & Kerridge, 2008).

By comparison, research on interpreter-mediated healthcare communication is in its infancy. The majority of the published work in this area has been on spoken-language healthcare interpreting, and many of these studies have been based on reported or elicited data, such as role plays (e.g., Dubslaff & Martinsen, 2005; Cambridge, 1999), interviews (e.g., Baker, Hayes, & Puebla Fortier, 1998), surveys (e.g., Karliner, Pérez-Stable, & Gildengorin, 2004; Kuo & Fagan, 1999; Leman, 1997), and observations (e.g., Fagan et al., 2003). In the last decade or so, however, researchers have begun examining linguistic aspects of authentic interpreter-mediated healthcare interactions, many focusing on the role of the healthcare interpreter. Metzger's (1999) pioneering study examined the discourse of an American Sign Language/English interpreter-mediated pediatric consultation and illustrated the complexity of discourse management work done by the interpreter. Her analysis of authentic data revealed that interpreters are active participants in interaction and that the previously idealized notion of interpreter "neutrality" is a myth. Subsequent studies based on authentic data by spoken-language researchers have explored the role of structural and contextual factors (i.e., patients' and employers' expectations) that may help us understand linguistic choices made by interpreters (e.g., Tebble, 2003; Angelelli, 2004; Davidson, 2001; Bolden, 2000).

Although Roy (2000), Napier (2006b), and Winston (2005) have discussed the importance of using a discourse-based approach to interpreter training, and Metzger (2000) has written about the use of role plays in interpreter training, to date there is little evidence of the application of authentic data in the training of signed-language interpreters for healthcare purposes. Our approach to teaching interpreters about healthcare discourse complements the use of role plays by first exposing students to examples of real-life doctor-patient talk so that they can identify discourse characteristics of healthcare interaction for themselves. There have been calls for (both spoken- and signed-language) interpreter education to be informed by interpreting research (Hale, 2007; Napier, 2005b; Turner, 2005), as research provides a deeper understanding of linguistic and cultural issues, the interpreter's role, and the interpreting process, which interpreter educators can draw upon to enhance their teaching. This link feeds into a cycle of research-education-practice (Napier, 2005b, in press), which is crucial to enhancing the quality of interpreting in any setting. Now that we have established the reasoning behind the design of our activity, the remainder of this chapter focuses on describing how the activity proceeds.

How Do We Teach Signed-Language Interpreters about Healthcare Discourse?

The data that ARCH permitted us to use consisted of an audio recording and a transcript of a consultation that took place in New Zealand using New Zealand English. Although a video exists and was used in the 2007 lifestyle project, it could not be shared with students for reasons of privacy and confidentiality. Due to ethical protocols, we were also permitted to share only excerpts of the data with students, never the full audio recording or transcript. We created an interactive activity based on a short excerpt from this interaction, which we then used in our workshops around Australia. This activity and other similar exercises based on authentic healthcare interaction have also been conducted in several classes as part of the Postgraduate Translation and Interpreting and Auslan/English Interpreting programs with spoken- and signed-language interpreting students at Macquarie University. We have found it to be a fun and engaging way to teach discourse analysis methods to interpreting students and experienced practitioners alike.

In this section we demonstrate and discuss the activity step by step. It is our hope that others might replicate this method—not necessarily with the same excerpt but based on this approach. The activity involves a mix of guided analysis (to develop students' confidence in doing their own discourse analysis), prediction work, and finally discourse analysis tasks in pairs or small groups.

We begin by giving students some background information about the excerpt, such as where it is from and who the participants are. It is useful to emphasize that the students will listen to a real doctor and a real patient—not actors or role-play participants. The excerpt we used to create this activity involves a GP and a patient, both of whom are New Zealand European males who are between 50–54 and 55–59 years of age, respectively, and they have not met each other previously. The duration of the entire consultation is 23 minutes and 12 seconds, and the selected excerpt runs for 2 minutes and 16 seconds. The patient has come to see the GP because he would like a general checkup, and the excerpt we examine begins approximately 10 minutes into the consultation. Earlier in the consultation the patient had initiated lifestyle talk, saying he had felt dizzy after a night out smoking and drinking. The GP has spent quite some time advising the patient to quit smoking and is now turning to the topic of alcohol.

For this activity, we decided to focus broadly on strategies participants use to talk about alcohol and also on their use of discourse devices. Alcohol use (especially misuse) can be a difficult topic for both patients and GPs to talk about. Aira et al. (2003), for example, conducted an interview study with GPs in Finland and found that practitioners were reluctant to ask about alcohol use because it is such a sensitive topic, more so than others. In order to convey this important message in an encouraging way, the GP in this excerpt uses many strategies to make his questioning and advice seem less harsh. As Tebble (1999, pp. 191–92) notes, doctors can use even seemingly trivial discourse markers to express empathy while delivering serious news, and it is important for interpreters to learn to capture not only what is said but how the message is conveyed.

The excerpt is revealed to students in three parts (as shown later). Splitting the excerpt into chunks allows students to practice predicting what might come next—an important skill in interpreting (Napier, McKee, & Goswell, 2010)—and to focus on drawing detailed meaning from a small piece of text. We focus mainly on the opening of this topic (part 1) and the advice the GP gives to the patient (part 3). Students are asked to think about the different strategies the participants are using to talk about this sensitive topic.

Part 1: Opening of Alcohol Talk

To begin with, the audio recording of part 1 is played. Students can listen to and/or read a transcript of the talk.[8] Transcription conventions can be seen in the Appendix. For this first chunk, students are asked to consider specific strategies that the patient is using to make his drinking seem less problematic than it might actually be.

```
GP:  um ((exhales)) alcohol you regular drinker or
PT:  yes to be honest um reasonable yes no not [(too)] regular
GP:                                             [so  ]
GP:  how how many times a week would you go out (.) most most days
PT:  yeah quite a bit on my way home
GP:  yep
PT:  it's it's like a habit [it's like] on coronation street i suppose
GP:                         [sure   ]
GP:  ((laughs)) yeah okay
PT:  little clubs not pubs generally
GP:  yep
PT:  little clubs for a couple of hours go home for tea
GP:  right okay
PT:  that's it (      )
```

This can be played more than once, and a group discussion is then conducted. Students are asked to identify interesting strategies that the patient is using. If volunteers are not forthcoming, it can be a good idea to start

---

8. This activity can be tailored to the makeup of the group. If deaf interpreters or deaf students are present, they can watch the interpreter or read the transcript. In many countries (especially the United States) deaf people work as interpreters in various capacities. In healthcare settings this would typically be in a "relay" role involving a hearing signed-language interpreter and a deaf patient who uses a different (foreign or indigenous) signed language or other linguistic challenges. See Boudrealt (2005) or Forestal (2005) for more information on deaf interpreters.

the discussion by drawing the participants' attention to the first question-answer pair. The doctor asks, "alcohol you regular drinker or," to which the patient replies, "yes to be honest um reasonable yes no not too regular," which in itself may be evidence that this is not an easy topic to talk about. Students will probably notice that the patient contradicts himself here with his use of "yes . . . yes no." It could also be pointed out that constructions like "yes to be honest" often indicate that what is coming next should perhaps *not* be interpreted literally. They may also notice that the patient goes on to relate drinking to the routine of going home, mentioning it twice in fact—"quite a bit on my way home" and "for a couple of hours go home for tea." Perhaps he is distancing his type of drinking from the type that involves being out on the streets all night. A drink or two on the way home may be a more socially acceptable routine. Along similar lines, he also relates drinking to a well-known British television show—"it's like a habit it's like on coronation street i suppose." Again, this may be a strategy to normalize his habit—many people (such as those we see on popular soaps) drink daily and are not portrayed as having a problem with it.

It is important to acknowledge that without talking to the patient himself, we cannot say with complete certainty that we are interpreting his talk as he intended—if these are even conscious strategies on his part. However, for our purposes, the important thing is to slow down the interaction (i.e., talking about it, splitting it into chunks, listening to it, discussing it) to the point that students notice discourse patterns for themselves. This noticing is a key skill for interpreters to learn and practice.

Students are then asked to predict what will happen next, and it is not difficult to guess: the GP asks more questions.

Part 2: Information Gathering

With the second chunk we encourage students to listen and make remarks about anything they find interesting. If students are not confident in doing this, it is valuable to point out that their answers are not necessarily right or wrong; rather, it is just that different people notice different interesting things about talk. The important thing is that students be able to support their ideas with examples from the text.

GP: so what would you do three four four five or
PT: what
GP: ((laughs)) drinks
PT: yes but measure?
GP: um [you tell me]
PT: [(   )   ]
GP: beer beer or
PT: it's essentially beer
GP: yeah
PT: occasionally i might have a (.) probably rarely a wine
GP: yeah
PT: rarely a wine and um occasionally a (.) a spirit
GP: right but most of the time you'd be [(   )   ]
PT: [most of the time] it's beer
GP: okay
PT: and it's a um it's not not usually the bottled
GP: okay
PT: variety it's it's the draught variety
GP: right   draft - 牛ヒ-ﾉV
PT: from the tap
GP: so halves or pints or
PT: yeah pints basically
GP: yeah okay [(   )   ]
PT: [so we're talking oh]
GP: three or four
PT: yeah
GP: okay yeah
PT: maybe lavishly six
GP: right   好ﾑ よく
PT: that's about that's about it

With regard to part 2, students may note that, after the GP asks, "so what would you do three four four five or," the patient does not immediately give a direct answer. At first he responds with "what," and when the GP laughingly clarifies, "drinks," the patient then follows up with "yes but measure?" We cannot say for certain, but the patient may be stalling because it is an uncomfortable topic to talk about, or perhaps he is just gaining some extra time to consider his answer. Whatever the reason, he clearly does not want to answer immediately.

We can also see that the GP gives constant feedback throughout this part (e.g., "yeah," "okay," "right," "okay yeah"). This seems to be evidence of good listening skills, although we can also hazard further guesses about why the GP keeps his contributions minimal during this phase. Does his minimal feedback help the patient to feel at ease and more confident in talking about this sensitive topic? Or is the GP indicating in places that the patient has not given him enough information to continue and that he is waiting for more? Notice that at the end of this chunk, the GP does receive an answer to his original question, that being the number of drinks the patient has per day.

Again, students are asked to predict what is coming next. And again, it is not difficult for them to predict that next will be some lifestyle advice from the GP.

Part 3: Advice about Drinking

The main focus of our activity is on the third chunk; students, having been guided though analysis of the first two parts, now have some basic discourse analytical tools and are ready to tackle analysis themselves. This portion of the activity is ideal for pair or small-group work. Students are asked to listen to the excerpt once or twice as a class and then work from the transcript to identify the following:

a. The actual pieces of advice (e.g., how much of the GP's talk is actual advice and how much is "other stuff"?)
b. Ways in which the GP hedges or softens his advice. Students are asked to identify specific softening devices (words and phrases that make the advice seem less offensive) and to discuss the GP's choice of words (e.g., why did he say it that way at that time?)

> GP: totting that up through the week ((exhales)) um ((voc)) in terms of the recommended alcohol levels now and and dose if you like it's a bit over [not a lot]
> PT: [of course] yeah
> GP: but what i'm saying is not not a lot
> PT: yeah
> GP: that um added up probably you would be they they measure it by units of alcohol and you'd probably be doing somewhere between sort of twenty

> eight and thirty units over the course of a week where the recommended
> level for a for a man would be twenty
> PT: uh huh
> GP: so
> PT: (   )
> GP: it probably means that if it was three or four and on a good night five or six
>   you peg that back to sort of two or three and on a good night [four   ]
> PT: [three or four]
> GP: um and i think
> PT: yes
> GP: you know with that and the smoking i mean it
>   [that that's the main kind of lifestyle things   ] sure and but then
>   that that=
> PT: [well it comes to a level of responsibility for yourself]
> GP: =means that you build on the good shape that you are in
> PT: yep

Students are given 10–15 minutes to work on their analysis, and a guided class discussion then ensues. Identifying the core pieces of advice can be challenging, but we can paraphrase them in these two short statements:

a. You drink too much alcohol.
b. You need to reduce the amount of alcohol you drink.

This leads smoothly into a discussion of discourse devices (e.g., if the preceding statements represent the core lifestyle advice, then what role do all of the other words and phrases play?).

The GP uses many softening words and phrases in his talk, such as "if you like," "a bit," "probably," and "sort of." To illustrate their impact, the students can be asked to read a sentence aloud without these "extra" words. For example, compare a modified "in terms of the recommended alcohol levels and dose it's over" with the GP's actual words—"in terms of the recommended alcohol levels now and dose if you like it's a bit over not a lot." The second sentence in this pair is a lot more reassuring and also less immediately face threatening. It also implies that a less radical change is required, perhaps making it more realistic for the patient to follow the doctor's advice—and therefore more likely for this to be acted upon.

Students may also notice that the GP uses some phrases that we would associate with everyday talk rather than medical talk: "totting that up," (adding that up) "peg that back" (reduce that slightly). Even though we cannot say for sure why he chose these phrases, it can be useful to discuss with students what some possible reasons might be. For example, the GP may be accommodating to the patient's way of talking to build rapport between them, or he may be trying to make the medical advice sound less severe so as to further encourage the patient to follow his advice.

At several points, the doctor attributes the medical advice to an outside body or to other people: "in terms of the recommended alcohol levels," "they measure it by units of alcohol," "the recommended level for a man." Why is this? It may be that the GP is again distancing himself from the potentially face-threatening act of telling someone that the person has a problem with alcohol (i.e., it is not the GP personally saying this but rather the health authorities). At the same time, this strategy may add weight to the advice because it is not just the GP's individual opinion; rather, "they" are an authoritative source of (scientific) information and evidence.

Finally, notice that the doctor finishes giving his advice on a positive note: "that means that you build on the good shape that you are in." Recall that in the original lifestyle talk project, this same pattern was found in other consultations as well: Doctors regularly had to state harsh facts about unhealthy lifestyle choices but often framed their advice in a positive way and ended the sequence in alignment with the patient, sometimes by using strategies like humor to do so (Major, 2007; Stubbe & Macdonald, 2010). At the end of the discussion, we replay the entire clip so students can listen to it again and reflect on some of the sociolinguistic strategies at play.

At the end of the activity, the basic discourse analysis tools the students have just learned can be related once again to interpreting. We do this with a discussion on how these tools can help interpreters both during and after interpreting assignments. First, a better understanding of some typical patterns and unique challenges of this setting can help interpreters to keep the big picture in mind. Thinking about *how* language is used can help interpreters understand what participants are trying to achieve in the interaction. For example, the discourse analysis activity has shown that the GP in this interaction is trying to give lifestyle advice to the patient and encouraging him to take it to heart while at the same time positively managing his relationship with the patient, which in this context is likely to be an ongoing one. The patient, on the other hand, is trying to avoid presenting himself as a "bad" patient (i.e., he is trying to minimize the severity of what the GP has identified as a problem, one that carries certain social attitudes and moral overtones). Both participants are negotiating their way through this sensitive topic. If this had in fact been an interpreter-mediated rather than a monolingual interaction, simply having an idea of the participants' different agendas would help the interpreter predict the shape of the interaction, possible discussion points, and areas of tension. Again, we are not suggesting the interpreter can always predict exactly what will happen, but understanding likely patterns, topics, and terminology can lessen the processing demands and allow the interpreter more mental space in which to attend to the important "extra" aspects such as affect.

Interpreters can also use these tools for self-analysis after assignments. After a challenging job, for example, they can use these skills to reflect on the interaction and their own interpretation. Some useful reflective questions include the following:

a. What do you think each participant was trying to achieve?
b. How do you know this? That is, what linguistic strategies were they using that give you some clues?
c. Do you think you captured all of this in your interpretation?
d. If not, was this a strategic choice you made, or was there something you would do differently next time?

We have also created a small extra activity to help students reflect on how discourse analysis relates directly to interpreting and think more critically about their interpreting choices.

We have used this and similar activities with interpreting students from non-English–speaking backgrounds, and it is interesting to review their feedback on similarities and differences between the healthcare talk they see in this example and what they would expect to encounter in their home countries.

EXTRA ACTIVITY

Below are some example pairs; each consists of a made-up example, followed by an example taken from the data. While they mean virtually the same thing, there are some noticeable linguistic differences in the English used.

Interpret the sentence pairs from English into Auslan (or other working language), paying attention to capturing the intent of each utterance. It might be helpful if you record or gloss your interpretations. Then compare your interpretation of sentence one with sentence two—what are the linguistic differences between them, now that you have translated them into the target language? For example, did you interpret the softening devices literally, or have you used other strategies to capture the same intent in the target language?

- You are drinking too much alcohol
- *In terms of the recommended alcohol levels now and and dose if you like it's a bit over not a lot*

➤ You are drinking between 28 and 30 units of alcohol per week
➤ *That um added up probably you would be they they measure it by units of alcohol and you'd probably be doing somewhere between sort of twenty eight and thirty units over the course of a week*

❖ You need to reduce the amount of alcohol you drink
❖ *So it probably means that if it was three or four and on a good night five or six you peg that back to sort of two or three and on a good night four*

WHAT DO STUDENTS LEARN?

We found that this and similar exercises based on authentic monolingual healthcare interaction have been ideal materials for interpreter education and professional development. We have received much positive feedback that students found the activity and discussion interesting, fun, and not as daunting as they had expected. At the same time, the exercise is also engaging for those students who have prior discourse analysis experience, which

---

1. Information learned / take home messages

(a) General

Informative. Raised some interesting points that I hadn't considered before.
Definitely makes me think about how I interpret things and the choices I make.
A new angle—refreshing.
Gave me food for thought.
Good examples of true life, what happens truly, not textbook!

(b) Specific

Reinforces 'management' of situation as imperative.
I was interested in the aspect of linguistic softening and how to convey the intent of the language chosen.
Built on what we have been taught—to consider the objectives of those involved, and the way they are expressing it.
Motivated me to re-read interpreting and linguistic books to further improve.

2. Evaluation of the workshop

(a) Process

Moved along quite smoothly and quickly considering it was 3 hours.
Awesome, learned so much.
Great mix of interactive discussion and information giving.
Kept people engaged and awake!

(b) Content / interest

Interesting and informative.
The discourse analysis was great.
Interesting and fun.
Very useful for the future!

Figure 1. Workshop evaluation comments.

likely has much to do with using a rich and authentic piece of dialogue rather than role plays or created examples. Figure 1 shows examples of student evaluation comments.

Authentic language is, of course, all around us, and interpreters encounter authentic interactions every day. The value of gaining access to recordings of authentic language data for interpreter education, however, is that one can slow the text down to an extremely detailed level and look at it closely multiple times and from different perspectives. This allows students to gain firsthand experience in discourse analysis by identifying features of discourse, looking for supportive evidence in the text, and later relating these patterns to the task of interpreting. A better understanding of discourse analysis enables interpreters to recognize important patterns and features of participants' talk. Ultimately, this broader understanding of interaction is crucial for an interpreter's ability to convey not only what people are saying but also how they are saying it to each other.

CONCLUSION

In conclusion, this chapter has highlighted our suggestion that, for the purpose of interpretation analysis, interpreter educators ought to recognize that interpreting is a discourse process (Roy, 2000) and that interpreters and students need to consider the discourse features of healthcare communication and thus the influence of these factors on their interpreting decisions.

As Napier states, "Interpretation does not take place within a vacuum; it is a living, evolving, and changing entity, in much the same way as language" (2005c, p. 135). Interpreters need to be aware of the sensitivities involved in healthcare communication and of the fact that particular politeness strategies and discourse markers are used for specific purposes. Encouraging students and practitioners to engage in a discourse activity such as the one we have designed will enable interpreters to develop critical thinking skills. Interpreting students need to develop critical thinking skills generally (Winston, 2005) but particularly in relation to language use. As stated earlier, interpreters are essentially discourse analysts, and this activity provides them with a structured approach to developing their discourse analytical skills.

We recommend that this type of discourse analysis activity be applied by spoken- and signed-language interpreter educators in a variety of contexts, including health care. We encourage interpreter educators who do not have existing relationships with communication researchers to actively search out potential opportunities for collaboration. We see great potential for future discourse-based healthcare interpreter training using this technique and believe that sharing this approach will pave the way for more collaboration between interpreter trainers and healthcare communication researchers.

REFERENCES

Aira, M., Kauhanen, J., Larivaara, P., & Rautio, P. (2003). Factors influencing inquiry about patients' alcohol consumption by primary health care physicians: Qualitative semi-structured interview study. *Family Practice, 20*(3), 270–75.

Angelelli, C. (2004). *Medical interpreting and cross-cultural communication.* London: Cambridge University Press.

Baker, D. W., Hayes, R., & Puebla Fortier, J. (1998). Interpreter use and satisfaction with interpersonal aspects of care for Spanish-speaking patients. *Medical Care, 36*, 1461–70.

Bales, R. F. (1950). *Interaction process analysis.* Reading, MA: Addison-Wesley.

Bolden, G. B. (2000). Toward understanding practices of medical interpreting: Interpreters' involvement in history taking. *Discourse Studies, 2*(4), 387–419.

Bontempo, K., & Levitzke-Gray, P. (2009). Interpreting down under: Sign language interpreter education and training in Australia. In J. Napier (Ed.), *International perspectives on sign language interpreter education* (pp. 149–70). Washington, DC: Gallaudet University Press.

Bontempo, K., & Napier, J. (2007). Mind the gap! A skills analysis of sign language interpreters. *Sign Language Translator and Interpreter, 1*(2), 275–99.

Boudrealt, P. (2005). Deaf interpreters. In T. Janzen (Ed.), *Topics in signed language interpreting* (pp. 323–56). Philadelphia: John Benjamins.

Byrne, P., & Long, B. (1976). *Doctors talking to patients: A study of the verbal behaviors of doctors in the consultation.* London: Her Majesty's Stationery Office.

Cambridge, J. (1999). Information loss in bilingual medical interviews through an untrained interpreter. *Translator, 5*(2), 201–19.

Carroll, K., Iedema, R., & Kerridge, R. (2008). Reshaping ICU ward round practices using video-reflexive ethnography. *Qualitative Health Research, 18*(3): 380–90.

Collins, S., Britten, N., Ruusuvuori, J., & Thompson, A. (2007). *Patient participation in health care consultations.* Maidenhead, UK: Open University Press.

Davidson, B. (2001). Questions in cross-linguistic medical encounters: The role of the hospital interpreter. *Anthropological Quarterly, 74*(4), 170–78.

Dew, K., Plumridge, E., Stubbe, M., Dowell, T., Macdonald, L., & Major, G. (2008). "You just got to eat healthy": The topic of CAM in the general practice consultation. *Health Sociology Review.* [Special issue]. *Integrative, Complementary, and Alternative Medicine: Challenges for Biomedicine? 17*(4): 396–409.

Dowell, A., Macdonald, L., Stubbe, M., Plumridge, E., & Dew, K. (2007). Clinicians at work: What can we learn from interactions in the consultation? *New Zealand Family Physician, 34*(5): 345–50.

Dubslaff, F., & Martinsen, B. (2005). Exploring untrained interpreters' use of direct versus indirect speech. *Interpreting, 7*(2), 211–36.

Fagan, M. J., Diaz, J. A., Reinert, S. E., Sciamanna, C. N., & Fagan, D. M. (2003). Impact of interpretation method on clinic visit length. *Journal of General Internal Medicine, 18*(8), 634–38.

Forestal, E. (2005). The emerging professionals: Deaf interpreters and their views and experiences on training. In M. Marschark, R. Peterson, & E. A. Winston (Eds.), *Sign language interpreting and interpreter education: Directions for research and practice* (pp. 235–58). New York: Oxford University Press.

Gill, V., & Maynard, D. (2006). Explaining illness: Patients' proposals and physicians' responses. In J. Heritage & D. Maynard (Eds.), *Communication in medical care: Interactions between primary care physicians and patients* (pp. 115–50). Cambridge: Cambridge University Press.

Hale, S. (2007). *Community interpreting.* New York: Palgrave Macmillan.

Heritage, J., & Maynard, D. (2006). Introduction: Analyzing interaction between doctors and patients in primary care encounters. In J. Heritage & D. Maynard (Eds.), *Communication in medical care: Interactions between primary care physicians and patients* (pp. 1–21). Cambridge: Cambridge University Press.

Johnston, T. (2006). W(h)ither the Deaf community? Population, genetics, and the future of Auslan (Australian Sign Language). *Sign Language Studies, 6*(2), 137–73.

Johnston, T., & Napier, J. (2010). Medical Signbank: Bringing deaf people and linguists together in the process of language development. *Sign Language Studies, 10*(2): 258–75.

Jones, D., & Stubbe, M. (2004). Communication and the reflective practitioner: A shared perspective from sociolinguistics and organisational communication. *International Journal of Applied Linguistics, 14*(2), 185–211.

Karliner, L. S., Pérez-Stable, E. J., & Gildengorin, G. (2004). The language divide: The importance of training in the use of interpreters for outpatient practice. *Journal of General Internal Medicine, 19*(2), 175–83.

Kuo, D., & Fagan, M. (1999). Satisfaction with methods of Spanish interpretation in an ambulatory care clinic. *Journal of General and Internal Medicine, 14*(9), 547–50.

Leman, P. (1997). Interpreter use in an inner-city accident and emergency department. *Journal of Accident and Emergency Medicine, 14*, 98–100.

Major, G. (2007). *Lifestyle talk and advice in clinical consultations.* Unpublished summer studentship paper. Wellington: Wellington School of Medicine and Health Sciences, Otago University.

Major, G., Stubbe, M., Dew, K., Macdonald, L., Dowell, T., & Plumridge, E. (2007). *Preventing illness and promoting wellness: Lifestyle talk in GP consultations.* Paper presented at the New Zealand Discourse Conference, AUT University, December 6–8.

Malthus, C., Holmes, J., & Major, G. (2005). Completing the circle: Research-based classroom practice with EAL nursing students. *New Zealand Studies in Applied Linguistics, 11*(1), 65–89.

Metzger, M. (1999). *Sign language interpreting: Deconstructing the myth of neutrality.* Washington, DC: Gallaudet University Press.

Metzger, M. (2000). Interactive role-plays as a teaching strategy. In C. Roy (Ed.), *Innovative practices for teaching sign language interpreters* (pp. 83–107). Washington, DC: Gallaudet University Press.

Metzger, M. (2005). Interpreted discourse: Learning and recognizing what interpreters do in interaction. In C. Roy (Ed.), *Advances in teaching sign language interpreters* (pp. 100–22). Washington, DC: Gallaudet University Press.

Mishler, E. G. (1984). *The discourse of medicine: Dialects of medical interviews.* Norwood, NJ: Ablex.

Napier, J. (2004). Sign language interpreter training, testing, and accreditation: An international comparison. *American Annals of the Deaf, 149*(4): 350–59.

Napier, J. (2005a). Training sign language interpreters in Australia: An innovative approach. *Babel, 51*(3): 207–23.

Napier, J. (2005b). Linguistic features and strategies of interpreting: From research to education to practice. In M. Marschark, R. Peterson, & E. A. Winston (Eds.), *Sign language interpreting and interpreter education: Directions for research and practice* (pp. 84–111). New York: Oxford University Press.

Napier, J. (2005c). Teaching interpreters to identify omission potential. In C. Roy (Ed.), *Advances in sign language interpreter education* (pp. 123–37). Washington, DC: Gallaudet University Press.

Napier, J. (2006a). Educating signed language interpreters in Australia: A blended approach. In C. Roy (Ed.), *New approaches to interpreter education* (pp. 67–103). Washington, DC: Gallaudet University Press.

Napier, J. (2006b). Effectively teaching discourse to sign language interpreting students. *Language, Culture, and Curriculum, 19*(3), 252–65.

Napier, J. (in press). If a tree falls in the forest, does it make a noise? The merits of publishing interpreting research. In B. Nicodemus & L. Swabey (Eds.), *Moving forward in interpreting studies: Methodology and practice revisited.* Philadelphia: John Benjamins.

Napier, J., & Barker, R. (2003). A demographic survey of Australian Sign Language interpreters. *Australian Journal of Education of the Deaf, 9,* 19–32.

Napier, J., Bontempo, K., & Leneham, M. (2006). Sign language interpreting in Australia: An overview. *VIEWS* (April), 1, 7, 8, 45.

Napier, J., Major, G., & Ferrara, L. (in press). Medical Signbank: A cure-all for the aches and pains of medical sign language interpreting? In L. Leeson, M. Vermeerbergen, & S. Wurm (Eds.), *The sign language translator and interpreter.* Manchester: St. Jerome.

Napier, J., McKee, R., & Goswell, D. (2010). *Sign language interpreting: Theory and practice in Australia and New Zealand* (2nd ed.). Sydney: Federation Press.

ORIMA (Organisational Improvement and Market Research). (2004). *Supply and demand for Auslan Interpreters across Australia.* Canberra: Australian Government Department of Family and Community Services.

Parry, R. (2005). *Offering the movement experts some new perspectives: In-service training on communication for physiotherapists.* Paper presented at the Conference on Training the Health Professions: Applying Interaction Research in Health

Educational Settings, University of Southern Denmark, Odense, October 20–22.

Petersen, M., Ladefoged, J., & Larsen, D. (2005). *Teaching doctor-patient communication by using authentic video data.* Paper presented at the Conference on Training the Health Professions: Applying Interaction Research in Health Educational Settings, University of Southern Denmark, Odense, October 20–22.

Roter, D., & Frankel, R. (1992). Quantitative and qualitative approaches to the evaluation of the medical dialogue. *Social Science and Medicine, 34*(10), 1097–1103.

Roter, D., & Larson, S. (2002). The Roter Interaction Analysis System (RIAS): Utility and flexibility for analysis of medical interactions. *Patient Education and Counseling, 46*(4), 243–51.

Roy, C. (2000). *Interpreting as a discourse process.* Oxford: Oxford University Press.

Stokoe, E. (2010). *Application without compromise? Using conversation analysis to evaluate and develop new types of role-play training.* Paper presented at the International Conference on Conversation Analysis, Mannheim, July 4–8.

Stokoe, E. (2011). Simulated interaction and communication skills training: The 'Conversation Analytic Role-play Method.' In C. Antaki (Ed.), *Applied conversation analysis: Changing institutional practices.* Basingstoke: Palgrave Macmillan (ISBN: 9780230229969).

Stubbe, M., & Brown, P. (2002a). *Let's get real: Natural interactions as a resource for language learning.* Plenary address, ALANZ Symposium, Hamilton, New Zealand, November 23.

Stubbe, M., & Brown, P. (2002b). *Talk that works: Communication in successful factory teams: A training resource kit.* (Video and handbook). Wellington: School of Linguistics and Applied Language Studies, Victoria University of Wellington.

Stubbe, M., Dowell, T., Dew, K., Plumridge, E., & Macdonald, L. (2006). *Interaction under the microscope: Talk at work in the general practice consultation.* Workshop for the Royal New Zealand College of General Practitioners Conference, August 10, Auckland, New Zealand.

Stubbe, M., & Macdonald, L. (2010). *Preventing illness and promoting wellness: Lifestyle talk in New Zealand general practice consultations.* Paper presented at EACH 2010, Verona, Italy, September 5–7.

Tebble, H. (1999). The tenor of consultant physicians: Implications for medical interpreting. *Translator, 5*(2), 179–200.

Tebble, H. (2003). Training doctors to work effectively with interpreters. In L. Brunette, G. Bastin, I. Hemlin, & H. Clarke (Eds.), *The critical link 3: Interpreters in the community. Proceedings of the Third International Conference on Interpreting in Legal, Health, and Social Service Settings, Montreal, Canada 2001* (pp. 81–95). Amsterdam: John Benjamins.

Turner, G. H. (2005). Toward real interpreting. In M. Marschark, R. Peterson, & E. A. Winston (Eds.), *Sign language interpreting and interpreter education:*

Directions for research and practice (pp. 29–56). New York: Oxford University Press.

Winston, E. A. (2005). Designing a curriculum for American Sign Language/ English interpreting educators. In M. Marschark, R. Peterson, & E. A. Winston (Eds.), *Sign language interpreting and interpreter education: Directions for research and practice* (pp. 208–34). New York: Oxford University Press.

Appendix I

Transcription Conventions

((laughs)) *yeah*	Non-linguistic features that carry on over talk
(.)	Short pause (one second or less)
((voc))	Vocalization
A ..[...]... B: [...]	B overlaps while A is talking
A ..[...]...= B: [...] A: =.....	= shows that A's talk continues on the next line, while B's overlap is shown on the line in between
( )	Unclear utterance that cannot be transcribed

CHARLENE CRUMP

Mental Health Interpreting
Training, Standards, and Certification

THE AMERICANS With Disabilities Act (ADA) sets the benchmark standard for the qualifications of an interpreter. The standard set forth, according to the ADA is as follows: "A qualified interpreter is one that is able to communicate, expressively, and receptively, using any specialized vocabulary" (Americans With Disability Act, 1990).

The Southern District Court in Florida ruled in *Tugg v. Towey* that providing mental health services through an interpreter was not providing equal access. The court went on to order the Florida Department of Health and Rehabilitation Services to provide mental health services to the Deaf using signing clinicians (*Tugg v. Towey*, 1994). The landmark *Tugg* case notwithstanding, a significant segment of mental health services are still provided by primary care physicians or mental health therapists who are not Deaf and are also nonsigners with rudimentary knowledge of or, more often, no experience at all in working with Deaf individuals. Exacerbating the obvious problem this creates, these clinicians are often paired with interpreters who have limited or no experience working in mental health settings.

Mental health interpreting is a unique and highly specialized field in which technical vocabulary and words in general carry great weight. Pollard and Dean (2003) explain that "Psychiatry is unique among the medical fields in that most of the symptoms are conveyed by or through communication, and communication also is the primary method and nature of treatment." No one seriously disputes the view that therapeutic services provided directly by a practitioner sharing the same linguistic and cultural framework is preferable. It is axiomatic that "something is lost in the translation." The work of therapy in a counseling session using an interpreter

54

will never be the same as work that is done when both the therapist and the client speak the same language (Hamerdinger & Karlin, 2003).

Traditional interpreter training and historical relationship dynamics between interpreters and members of the Deaf community have not adequately prepared either interpreters or consumers for the overt and covert challenges of providing effective access in mental health environments. Some of the challenges that are present for interpreters include alliances, technical vocabulary, working as a member of a clinical team, unusual or unexpected behavior, stress caused by secondary or vicarious trauma, and working with consumers who may have extreme language dysfluency. Such dysfluency may be a result of singular or multiple causes, including developmental delays, mental illness, medical or neurological complications that may also have been a contributing factor to the cause of deafness, or a combination of the aforementioned reasons. Treatment methodologies vary according to a multitude of factors, including the diagnosis of the consumer, discipline, the practitioner's clinical orientation, and even the funding stream that renders payment for the services. Interpreters who are not knowledgeable about these factors may be less effective and even countertherapeutic in the clinical milieu.

Currently there is no nationally based certification for sign language interpreters working in mental health. Only within the past two decades has the interpreting field begun to specialize as more and more people have come to understand the uniqueness of interpreting in various clinical/professional realms. The Registry of Interpreters for the Deaf (RID) has established a specialty certification for legal interpreting. Some states have addressed certification for medical interpreting, but it is mostly from the perspective of spoken-language interpreters. The need for in-depth training in mental health interpreting remains particularly acute.

In addition, there are also currently no nationally based program-level certificates for sign-language interpreters working in mental health. A number of states and programs have attempted to address the need for training in highly specialized fields, including mental health interpreting. With the exception of Alabama's Mental Health Interpreter Training project, most attempts have consisted of a series of ad hoc workshops, not a systemic approach guided by specific standards, learning objectives, and learning outcomes. In 2007 RID published a practice paper for mental health interpreting, which serves as a standard of best practices, but the recommendations are not tied to any specific activities that need to be pursued to achieve measurable outcomes. The lack of standards generally means that there are no guidelines for what should or should not be included in any training. This results in interpreters' having widely divergent concepts of what "mental health interpreting" is, even those who have attended various training opportunities.

Clinicians who are not used to working with Deaf people have little concept of just how differently one interpreter works from another. These clinicians are unaware of the impact of divergent interpreters' thought worlds on their behavioral and linguistic output. Thought worlds are the interpreters' own perspectives based on the sum of their own life experiences. These perceptions, or thought worlds, are brought into the mental health setting. Interpreters who have witnessed or experienced trauma or abuse themselves will bring their subconscious reactions and defenses to that experience and consequently may over- or undercompensate.

In one scenario, for example, an interpreter grew up with deaf parents (such a child is often referred to as a child of deaf adults, coda) and, as a child, had been sexually abused by a neighbor. This interpreter contracted for a forensic-based assignment where a Deaf male consumer accused of sexual predation was being interviewed for a court-ordered evaluation. The Deaf person started the session by discreetly asking the interpreter whether she was a coda. He stated that she must be a coda because she signed so well. She nodded affirmatively. This set the stage for alliances in the session. None of this information was voiced to the clinician as the interpreter viewed it as typical introductory relationship building and identification. Before long, the Deaf consumer again started a side conversation with the interpreter and stated that she was pretty and suggested that the two of them go out on a date. The interpreter started explaining to the Deaf consumer that she did not want to date him. Within a few seconds, the two of them were having a conversation that not only did not include the clinician but was pertinent to the evaluation.

In another example, after a therapy session the male Deaf consumer asked the interpreter whether she was a coda. When she said no, he replied, "That's why I didn't understand you." Indications through dialogue and responses were that the consumer had indeed understood the interpreter.

However, at the next appointment, a coda was utilized. After the assignment, the Deaf consumer asked this interpreter, too, whether she was a coda. When she said yes, the consumer replied, "Odd. I wonder why I didn't understand you." Indications through dialogue and response again implied that the consumer had indeed understood the interpreter. Several other interpreters were subsequently hired to work for his appointments with similar outcomes. This occurred at a time in his therapy when he was beginning to reveal childhood sexual abuse and was attempting to avoid discussing these issues. The conversations with the interpreters were happening outside of the therapy session. None of the interpreters realized what had transpired prior to their involvement, and the therapist was not privy to the conversations that were occurring after the session.

Sometimes the examples are not as explicit. An interpreter may have had previous experiences in which a Deaf consumer misunderstood questions or suffered consequences because the interpreter's decision was based on insufficient knowledge. This interpreter may work to ensure that Deaf consumers are fully aware of their options and the intrinsic meanings of question. Instead of asking, "What is the date?" an interpreter may ask "TODAY WHAT?" which may still be too vague. The interpreter might therefore expand on the question in this manner: "TODAY MONDAY, TUESDAY, WEDNESDAY, WHAT?" This is, however, probably more directive and specific than the clinician wanted.

Many interpreters have come to believe that when there is a communication problem, the source is poor skills on the part of the interpreter. This is connected to the idea that "the consumer is always right" (or always fluent) and also to a desire to present Deaf people in their best light. This makes interpreters reluctant to reveal language or social problems. Interpreters may fear that, when the Deaf person is not presented in the best possible light or when the outcome is an undesirable one, they will be blamed by the Deaf person and, by word of mouth, the Deaf community for their perceived lack of skills or inappropriate attitude.

An interpreter's personality can also impact the establishment and subsequent measurement of baselines unless the interpreter and therapist are aware of this phenomenon and take steps to ensure that the interpreter's own individuality is filtered. Simply put, one interpreter whose natural personality is bubbly and gregarious could make a Deaf person seem to be exhibiting manic symptomology, whereas the next interpreter, whose innate tendency is to be reticent, could make the same Deaf person sound flat, if not depressed, especially when compared to the previous baseline. This change in interpreters can confound diagnosis or medication monitoring.

The effect is not limited to how the clinician views the Deaf consumer. How the clinician and the interpreter view each other's work is also highly dependent on who was exposed to what information. Interpreters do not understand what clinicians are trying to do, and clinicians do not understand the mental gymnastics interpreters are required to perform. The lack of exposure to the demands on the other may cause each professional to misperceive and misconstrue variances. Thus, trust is not readily forthcoming, and professional collaboration between interpreters and clinicians is not as common as it is among psychiatrists and social workers.

In an attempt to improve this situation, the state of Alabama has codified standards for mental health interpreting that outline the qualifications for state certification as "qualified" (Alabama Department of Mental Health and Mental Retardation Administrative Code, 2003). The standards were developed as part of a settlement to a lawsuit filed by the Alabama Association of the Deaf and Verna Bailey. Bailey alleged that her son had been inappropriately served for several years by programs funded by the Alabama Department of Mental Health. Among other charges, the lawsuit stated that the Department of Mental Health (DMH) failed to "provide qualified interpreters, and physicians, psychologists, social workers, caseworkers, nurses, and support staff who are fluent in American Sign Language and by failing to provide adequate culturally and linguistically appropriate mental health services" (Bailey v. Alabama Department of Mental Health, 2002).

The lawsuit, which was settled in 2002, resulted in the establishment of the Office of Deaf Services within the Division for Mental Illness. As a part of the settlement, DMH agreed to develop training and standards for interpreters working with Deaf people with mental illness. This gave rise to the Alabama Mental Health Interpreter Training (MHIT) Program.

The program is based on the preliminary work by Steve Hamerdinger, Wayne Elrod, Jay Wolfe, Kelley Clark, and Ben Karlin while they were working for the Missouri Department of Mental Health (Hamerdinger, Karlin, & Clark, 2000). Borrowing from that model, the Alabama Department of Mental Health proposed rules to codify standards describing the necessary skill set, which would be quantified and measured in an objective way. This would enable the establishment of required training and a formal process for certification. The DMH held a series of stakeholder meetings with the Interpreter Licensure Board, the state chapter of RID, and the Alabama Association of the Deaf. The goal of these meetings was to seek input to establish minimum competencies for interpreters working in mental health settings.

The new standards, which define what constitutes a "qualified mental health interpreter," were entered into the Administrative Code of Alabama as section 580-3-24 in December 2003. This became the basis for both the curriculum of MHIT and the certification of Qualified Mental Health Interpreter (QMHI).

A portion of the definitions included in these standards, which outline competencies and knowledge, is listed in appendix A. Additional competencies are listed in the following section.

PROFESSIONAL COMPETENCIES/KNOWLEDGE

In order to effectively provide interpretation from one language to another in mental health settings, certain levels of fluency and knowledge are necessary. The interpreter shall demonstrate professional competencies/ knowledge and the level indicated.

1. Sign language interpreters must be licensed as interpreters in Alabama or otherwise eligible to work at an equivalent level as set forth in the Administrative Code of Alabama (34-16-5-10). The interpreter must demonstrate understanding of mentoring and supervision.
2. Interpreters working in other languages shall hold an appropriate certification in their field, if one is available. If no certification is available for the language(s) the interpreter is working in, it is expected that the interpreter will successfully pass a screening test approved by the Office of Deaf Services.
3. Interpreters must demonstrate interpreting methods and appropriate use of simultaneous (first-person and third-person), consecutive (first-person and third-person), and narrative (third-person) interpreting.

4. Interpreters must demonstrate familiarity with mental health issues and treatment options in Alabama.
   a. Mental illness services
      1. The interpreter must be able to accurately interpret specialized vocabulary used in psychiatric settings in both the source and the target languages.
      2. The interpreter must be aware of psychopathologies, including knowledge of the names of the major mental illnesses treated by the Department of Mental Health in both the target and source languages and familiarity with symptomology of major mental illnesses experienced by the consumers of services provided by the Department of Mental Health as presented within the psycholinguistic context of the target language group.
      3. The interpreter must demonstrate familiarity with assessment methods and understanding of the impact of interpretation when interpreting assessments.
      4. The interpreter must have exposure to treatment approaches and demonstrate awareness of how cultural influences might impact treatment.
   b. Substance abuse services
      1. The interpreter must be able to accurately interpret specialized vocabulary used in addiction treatment in both the source and the target languages.
      2. The interpreter must have familiarity with addiction theory and issues involving addiction.
      3. The interpreter must have familiarity with assessment methods and how cultural influences might impact assessment.
      4. The interpreter must have exposure to treatment approaches and demonstrate awareness of how cultural influences might impact treatment.
5. The interpreter must be familiar with inpatient settings, with the various staff that will be working in those settings, and how interpreting and cultural differences can influence therapeutic relationships in those settings.
6. The interpreter must be familiar with outpatient settings, with self-help and support groups, the specialized vocabulary used in those groups,

and how interpreting and cultural differences can influence therapeutic relationships in those settings.

   c. Mental retardation services

     1. The interpreter must have exposure to issues involving mental retardation and developmental disability and the role culture and language play in providing services to people with mental retardation.

     2. The interpreter shall be aware of the difference between interpreting and communication assistance/language intervention.

7. The interpreter shall be able to identify care providers, identify mental health disciplines, and be familiar with milieus and settings.

8. The interpreter must be able to explain the role of an interpreter as a professional consultant.

9. The interpreter must understand professional boundaries and must be able to explain confidentiality and privilege, including, at a minimum, abuse reporting, the duty to warn, and protections specific to Alabama statute.

CULTURAL COMPETENCIES/KNOWLEDGE

The interpreter must demonstrate cross-cultural competencies.

1. The interpreter must be able to explain the impact of stereotypes on mental health service delivery.

2. The interpreter must understand cultural views of mental illness, mental retardation, and addiction specific to the populations the interpreter works with and must be aware of various constructs of Deafness and hearing loss relative to majority/minority cultures and pathological models.

3. The interpreter must demonstrate understanding of the sociological impact of cross-cultural mental health service provision and the impact of an interpreter on the therapeutic dyad.

CONDUCT COMPETENCIES/KNOWLEDGE

1. The interpreter must demonstrate knowledge of personal safety issues, including an understanding of at-risk conduct and personal boundaries as they apply to mental health interpreting work and an awareness of de-escalation techniques and universal precautions.

2. The interpreter must demonstrate professional boundaries and judgment particularly in professional collaboration through pre- and post-conferencing.
3. The interpreter must demonstrate the ability to assess effectiveness of communication.
    a. The interpreter must demonstrate the ability to appropriately match the interpreting method with the consumer and the setting and must understand the impact of emotionally charged language.
    b. The interpreter must demonstrate the ability to discuss unusual or changed word or sign selection.
    c. The interpreter must demonstrate the ability to discuss linguistic dysfluency or any marked change in linguistic fluency within a psycholinguistic context.
        1. The interpreter must demonstrate the ability to convey information without alteration, emotional language without escalation, and ambiguous or emotionless language.
        2. The interpreter must demonstrate the ability to isolate peculiar features of eccentric or dysfluent language use.
4. The interpreter must demonstrate the ability to read consumer case documentation and record appropriate documentation of linguistic significance.
    a. The interpreter must demonstrate knowledge of confidentiality as defined by state and federal law.
    b. The interpreter must understand the difference between personal records and records shared with other interpreters and other professionals. The interpreter must understand the ramifications of keeping personal records and must demonstrate knowledge of what records may and may not be kept pertaining to consumers.
5. The interpreter must be aware of personal mental health issues and maintenance.
    a. The interpreter must understand how personal issues may impact the interpreting process.
    b. The interpreter must be aware of counter-transference in the interpreter and must be familiar with transference to the clinician or to the interpreter.

Having codified minimum competencies for interpreters, DMH developed the training curriculum based on these standards, which, in turn, is being used at the annual Mental Health Interpreter Institute. The forty-hour training offered at the institute focuses primarily on mental illness and the unique dynamics that are present when Deafness and interpreting intersect.

The annual training provides foundational mental health skills to highly skilled interpreters who have already obtained national interpreting certification status through RID. The training includes lectures, demonstrations, exercises, evaluation, and discussions to enhance interpreters' knowledge, skills, and resources. Additionally, participants take a pre- and posttest to demonstrate what they have learned and the impact of the training. The core of the curriculum includes topics such as the following:

• Mental health systems and treatment approaches
• Diagnostic criteria and disorder types according to the DSM-IV
• Sources of language dysfluency and techniques for interpreting
• Interpreting as a practice profession
• Demand Control Schema in mental health settings
• Confidentiality and collegiality
• Secondary trauma stress/vicarious trauma, self-care, and safety
• Psychopharmacology
• Simulation of auditory hallucinations
• Certified deaf interpreters working in mental health settings
• Clinician's panel on the clinician and interpreter working relationship

In developing and conducting the training, DMH sought leaders in the field of mental health interpreter training as instructors. Robert Pollard, Robyn Dean, Roger Williams, Steve Hamerdinger, Charlene Crump, Brian McKenny, Shannon Reese, and others have been longtime instructors in the program. The program is rounded out by a pharmacist, a substance abuse specialist, and clinicians who work regularly with interpreters (such as psychiatrists, psychologists, and social workers).

The curriculum is not static. Each year it is carefully reviewed, and new technology, techniques, and practices are incorporated in the training. Since the faculty members are leaders in the field of mental health interpreting, the Interpreter Institute is often the first place new ideas are introduced. The most recent revision to the curriculum included the topics of "what clinicians expect from competent mental health interpreters," "specialty settings," and "sources of dysfluency," and previously taught courses are continually updated. Because of the frequent revisions that occur within the curriculum, around 10% of any given class consists of people who have taken the training before.

Interpreters are screened for acceptance into the training based on a combination of criteria, including educational status, certification level, years of experience, involvement in mental health settings, and previous training in the field. The purpose of the screening is to ensure a cohort of participants who are able to both understand the material presented and to create a synergistic discussion of issues in the field. A maximum of 50 interpreters are accepted annually. The limited class size provides each interpreter an opportunity to receive individualized attention and creates a manageable group for various activities and discussions.

Since its inception in 2003, 342 interpreters from 48 states and 2 foreign countries have been trained. In 2010, 26 states were represented. Additionally in the same year, two students from the state's Interpreter Training Program participated as student representatives. These students, along with five others, are being supported by full financial scholarships from the Alabama Department of Mental Health. Since these students will be working in mental health settings upon graduation, having access to this specialty training allows them to apply this information early in their academic course of study.

The training package has two parts: the classroom work and a 40-hour field practicum. Each interpreter who completes the classroom work is eligible to participate in the supervised practicum, which can take place at a specialized psychiatric hospital unit serving Deaf people and in community mental health settings. During the practicum, interpreters are given an opportunity to work with not only consumers who are Deaf and have mental illness but also Deaf professionals who work in those environments. Alabama requires that the practicum be completed within 1 year of completion of the 40 hours of classroom instruction in order to ensure application of the most current practices without retaking the entire sequence.

The practicum has two parts: observation and fieldwork. Upon scheduling the practicum, the interpreter is responsible for conducting 10 hours of observation in the interpreter's own state, writing case studies for each event using an environmental, interpersonal, paralinguistic, and intrapersonal (EIPI) perspective based on the observation supervision and demand control models developed by Robyn Dean and Robert Pollard (Dean &

Pollard, 2004a). The case studies are submitted to the practicum supervisor for discussion. Once the case studies have been completed, the supervisor begins a dialogic process with the practicum interpreter. The discussion examines the dynamics of the case studies to prepare the practicum interpreter for the experiences, which will be encountered on-site, and to assist the interpreter in developing a greater synthesis of mental health settings. The resulting discussion initially focuses on the practicum interpreter's identification of demands and controls and subsequent demands. The supervisor then leads the practicum interpreter to identify additional areas that have not been noted. This process is designed to broaden and strengthen the practicum interpreter's ability to critically analyze interactions. It also helps the interpreter to begin actually putting into practice the concepts of interpreting as a practice profession (Dean & Pollard, 2004b).

Supervision supplements experiential opportunities with reflection on case studies and dialogue with the practicum supervisor. The qualifications of the practicum supervisor are defined by the practicum guidelines (Alabama Department of Mental Health and Mental Retardation Administrative Code, 2003, Alabama Department of Mental Health, 2010), which state that an approved supervisor is a staff interpreter who is assigned to the Office of Deaf Services or a DMH facility and who is certified as a Qualified Mental Health Interpreter, a QMHI with extensive experience in mental health interpreting, or an interpreter or Deaf professional who also has a terminal degree in psychology, clinical social work, psychiatry, or counseling and has participated in MHIT. Additionally, all supervisors must complete training in Robyn Dean's observation-supervision method of guidance and mentoring.

Practicum sites must be primarily clinical in nature and are approved by the DMH practicum coordinator, who is different from the practicum supervisor. Acceptable assignments at a given site include counseling, testing, group therapy, treatment team meetings, emergency room intake, and psychosocial education classes. Because clinically based settings are used, the practicum helps to ensure that principles and practices taught in the classroom are reinforced in the field. Moreover, the work is expected to be direct clinical interpreting work and not social or interactive time. With prior approval, a practicum experience can include some 12-step groups. Unacceptable assignments include platform interpreting for workshops, interpreting professional-level meetings that are not directly related to treatment planning, social activities, or interpreting assignments that are primarily educational in nature, with the exception of psychosocial education.

The practicum provides a way to apply academic understanding, analysis, and an approach on which to base and validate the interpreter's work product. Case studies are a vital part of the practicum experience because they allow interpreters to learn not only how to focus on the content of the message but also how to usefully analyze discourse situations. Subsequent discussions with the supervisor help the interpreter to encompass a clinical perspective in addition to a Deafness worldview. Interpreters leave the program with more awareness of the clinical thought world, and they are better able to collaborate with the clinical team than they would otherwise have been. They are able to predict functional linguistic and behavioral outcomes based on diagnostic criteria. They also learn to empower the clinician to make more effective determinations and to enhance treatment. In short, they learn to align with the treatment process rather than with the Deaf consumer.

Feedback is important in the development of skills. Guided by rubrics developed by the MHIT staff, it covers a variety of settings and situations that include professional conduct, chart review, live and remote interpreting, clinical meetings, working with various disciplines, interpreting for sign-fluent professionals and consumers who are not fluent in sign, interpreting with a team, interpreting with a Deaf interpreter team, communication assessments, and other situations. Guiding all of the feedback is the desire to produce interpreters who are comfortable in clinical settings and who can operate with a clinician's perspective while respecting and communicating what is happening in the consumers' point of view.

THE PRACTICUM EXPERIENCE

Mental health interpreters learn that approaches to interpreting must match the diagnostic and linguistic or communication profile of the Deaf consumer and also be an appropriate match for the clinical techniques being used. Since consumers, both providers and individuals with mental illness, are extremely heterogeneous, interpreters need to be forearmed with as much background information as possible. As such, one element of the practicum has the interpreters review consumer/patient files to become familiar with the information in them before meeting with the consumers. They and their supervisor discuss how to use this knowledge to guide and shape interpreting (linguistic, behavioral, relationship, etc.) choices. The interpreter is provided the following list of questions to consider when examining each file:

• Where was the patient educated? For how long?
• How might the age of the consumer impact communication abilities and socialization as well as impact interpreting style/choices?
• What relationship does the consumer have with family members? How might this impact the consumer's ability to communicate and socialize?
• Are there any language notes regarding unusual language exhibited by the consumer?
• What do we know about the consumer's current or previous language usage?
• What fund of knowledge deficits might be present?
• Does the consumer have any known cognitive deficits?
• What is the etiology of Deafness, and how can this impact language?
• What are the current diagnosis and course of treatment? What is known about this diagnosis (symptoms, language impact, etc.)?
• What is the consumer's level of familiarity with this environment and the other individuals?
• What current medications is the consumer taking? Are there any potential issues regarding language (blurry vision, shaky hands, involuntary movements, lethargy, etc.)?
• Are there any medical conditions that might hamper the consumer's ability to communicate effectively (diabetes, vision problems, stroke, cerebral palsy, Parkinson's, etc.)?
• Are there any personal issues that may arise for the interpreter working with this consumer related to specific issues (victim of domestic violence, substance abuse issues, death in the family, personal/moral beliefs, family history/personal history with mental illness, etc.)?

- Are there any professional issues that may arise for the interpreter when working with this consumer (boundary issues, interpreter's previous relationship with consumer, male/female relationships, etc.)?
- Who are the other professionals working with this case? Who might the interpreter expect to be working with, and what issues would be pertinent?
- Have there been cases of incident reports, medication interventions (used to control behavior), seclusions or restraints that might occur and hinder communication? Are there indicators that signal when the consumer might be escalating? What should the interpreter do in situations if an escalation occurs? What is the communication policy in these cases?
- Is there a communication assessment completed on the consumer? How can this benefit the interpreter?

COMMUNICATION ASSESSMENT

The communication assessment is such an important tool in working with Deaf consumers that it is now part of the program standards for all mental health service providers in Alabama. The report is conducted by a trained staff member such as an interpreter, communication specialist, or clinician. Assessments of consumers who have atypical or dysfluent language are often administered by a team. The report considers the following elements:

Hearing Loss

- What is the extent of the hearing loss, and how was the information obtained? What observations were made in regard to the consumer's hearing loss and communication abilities? What impact can the etiology of hearing loss have on language use, treatment, and functioning level?

Educational Status

- Describe the consumer's educational achievements and communication strategies used/not used during school. How can this impact the consumer's fund of knowledge and language use? How can the educational status impact the consumer's ability to understand the current clinical environment?

Communication with Family/Friends

• Describe the consumer's communication strategies used with family/ friends. How can this impact treatment or daily communication? What type of linguistic support system does the consumer have?

Literacy

• Describe the consumer's ability to use written English. What is the approximate reading level (grade level)? How can written English be utilized/not utilized in treatment or daily communication? Would there be negative clinical consequences if these were used inappropriately? To what extent?

Auditory/Verbal/Speechreading Ability

• What usable/functioning auditory, verbal, or speechreading ability does the consumer seem to have? To what extent can this be utilized/not utilized in treatment or daily communication? Would there be negative clinical consequences if these were used inappropriately? To what extent?

Use of Sign Language

• What usable/functioning sign language ability does the consumer seem to have? What strengths and weaknesses does the consumer exhibit? How fluent in sign language is the consumer? To what extent can this be utilized in treatment or daily communication?
• How well does the consumer communicate directly? With an interpreter?
• Are there any uses of dysfluent or idiosyncratic language?
• Are there any expressive or receptive differences?
• Are there any physical or mental complications related to language?

- At what age did the consumer learn to sign?
- What type of grammar is identified within the consumer's language?

Recommendations

- Preferred communication modality of the consumer
- Modifications for treatment related to language (direct therapy by a signing therapist, one-on-one communication, eye contact, confirmation of information, interpreter, certified deaf interpreter, or visual-gestural communication specialist, etc.)
- Environmental considerations
- Ability to use modifications or accommodations
- Additional considerations

When possible, practicum interpreters are given an opportunity to complete a communication assessment profile on consumers. This allows them to develop familiarity with the communication assessment profile and gain experience in applying the information to the work.

The practicum interpreters also maintain a communication log, which is used to document the consumers' language use. In addition, interpreters are also required to utilize a checklist to document linguistic behaviors to address during treatment-team or postsession meetings with clinicians or the communication team. In Alabama, this information becomes part of the consumer's clinical record. Although not a universally accepted practice, it is becoming increasingly recognized as a critical part of the consumer's chart.

Practicum interpreters are provided documents to help them develop a portfolio that can be utilized as a resource for future interpreting assignments. They are encouraged to tailor the information to their specific needs and develop additional materials that best fit the local circumstances. This portfolio includes the following:

- The interpreter's credentials
- State law and policies
- Lawsuits related to mental health and deafness
- Federal laws and policies
- Professional competencies, ethics, and position statements
- Interpreter resources while working in mental health settings
- Contact information

- Therapist resources when working with individuals who are Deaf
- Materials for dysfluent consumers

EXAMINATION

After an interpreter successfully completes the practicum segment, based on the practicum supervisor's evaluation and the recommendation of the practicum committee, the interpreter moves to the next phase, which is the comprehensive examination. This test examines the interpreter's knowledge of material presented in the training and the practicum experience, as well as the interpreter's ability to apply the information to test-case scenarios. The written examination, which takes 4–6 hours to complete, is designed to assess the interpreter's comprehension and ability to synthesize and apply knowledge of mental health interpreting. Examples of questions that a candidate might encounter are the following:

1. Describe transference and countertransference within a therapeutic setting and how this is complicated by the presence of a third party (i.e., interpreter).
2. Compare and contrast how you approach interpreting for a Deaf consumer exhibiting each of the following:
   a. Extremely dysfluent language
   b. Deficit in consumer's fund of knowledge
   c. Presence of atypical nonmanual markers
   d. Bizarre language content
3. Discuss the challenges of interpreting family or group therapy.
4. Explain the presence and manifestations of auditory hallucinations in a prelingually Deaf adult.

The preceding examples can have more than one right answer. The interpreter must not only be able to give a solution (and sometimes more than one) but also be able to defend that solution using a demand-control framework.

Passing this test results in the award of certification as a Qualified Mental Health Interpreter. In Alabama, this certification is tied to a higher rate of compensation for contract interpreters and is a job requirement for staff interpreters working in mental health.

Once an interpreter successfully passes the comprehensive written examination and is recognized as a Qualified Mental Health Interpreter, 40 hours of continuing education and work experience annually in mental health are required to maintain the QMHI certification status. This ensures that the QMHI will spend at least 1 hour a week, on the average, in mental health work or training. Most QMHIs greatly exceed this amount as demonstrated by documentation submitted at renewal time.

Ongoing training is also recommended for interpreters to continue to develop their understanding of specialized settings in mental health. They are encouraged not only to expand their knowledge of elements of the core curriculum but also to acquire a sufficient knowledge base in areas not covered extensively during the 40-hour training period, areas such as interpreting in competency-based settings with language-dysfluent consumers, domestic violence, interpreting in play therapy, and interpreting in emergency responder situations. Quarterly training sessions are recommended for more in-depth learning opportunities. To facilitate such instruction, DMH provides training for interpreters online, which is thus also accessible to interpreters who do not live in Alabama.

Training interpreters in mental health is only one part of maximizing services for Deaf individuals who are mentally ill. A service-delivery system must also consider the working relationship of the therapist and the interpreter. This includes clinicians who are sign fluent and those who are not. Working through a third person is very different from working one-on-one with a client (Hamerdinger & Karlin, 2003). Interpreters and clinicians must not only be trained in their respective fields and have cross-training in or at least a base knowledge of each other's field but also have instruction in how to work together effectively. Additionally, administrators who oversee clinical programs and frontline staff who work with Deaf consumers must also be trained in the unique needs of Deaf individuals seeking mental health services.

Interpreters who are Deaf, often referred to as Deaf interpreters (DI) or certified deaf interpreters (CDI), must also be trained beyond MHIT on the unique role of functioning as a Deaf interpreter in mental health. At times, the CDI may be hired in what is considered the typical role of a CDI and at other times as a language coach or consultant. Hearing and Deaf interpreter teams also need instruction in working together to collaborate effectively in mental health settings, including dealing with more than the usual expectation of transparency during the process.

In a typical setting involving a hearing interpreter and a CDI, the hearing interpreter will translate a spoken message to ASL, and the CDI will break the message down to a language that is more readily understood by the consumer. The message may be delivered through atypical signs and gestures, in shorter segments, or through connections based on intimate knowledge, for example. Once the consumer responds, the CDI will formulate a response in ASL, and the hearing interpreter will interpret the message in spoken English. The clinician is interested in how the consumer uses language in order to draw appropriate conclusions regarding issues like mental status, competence, language competence, fund of information, or thought processes. As such, how the question is arrived at and how the response is formulated are integral parts of the session. In the typical scenario just described, hearing interpreters are often silent while the CDI is working, which deprives the clinician of critical information. Alabama's training program prepares interpreters to accommodate this need by techniques such as providing a third-person narrative of the interpreted process between the CDI and the deaf consumer.

The addition of two interpreters may change the dynamic into something clinicians are very unprepared to deal with. Issues of alliances, transference, and countertransference will arise. The clinician and both interpreters must be aware of these challenges and be prepared to address them honestly and openly and without hidden agendas or issues of control. Acknowledging the tenuous balance of power between the interpreters and the "us vs. them" dynamics at play, both the "Deaf vs. hearing" dynamic and the "signing vs. non-signing" one will be vital to ensuring that the sessions are therapeutic for the consumer.

The following is a case in point of how an interpreter's alliance can be detrimental in mental health settings. A certified interpreter, untrained in mental health work, contracted with a hospital that provided interpreting services for consumers with mental illness. The patient was a consumer in extended care. Whenever the treatment team met to assess the consumer's care, the interpreter would spend time arguing with the team, stating that "they didn't understand Deaf people" and "they were against Deaf people." When the treatment team met and recommended that the patient cease smoking and cut down on sweets (concerns related to the patient's severe medical needs), the interpreter, who disagreed with the decision on "human rights" grounds, regularly purchased candy and cartons of cigarettes, gave them to the patient, and instructed the patient to hide them in his room. While this may be an extreme example, interpreters without training are more apt to side with the Deaf consumer, which can disrupt the therapy.

In their evaluative reports, interpreters who have completed this extensive certification program report that they become more comfortable in dealing with dysfluent language by understanding the various roles of mental health professionals, common diagnosis, interview questions, and clinical objectives and by using various interpreting techniques, such as third-person descriptive interpreting. Trained interpreters are less likely to be defensive when questioned and also less likely to explain away unusual behaviors or language and more likely to align with the program of therapy.

In addition, QMHIs are more apt to cooperate with the therapeutic process in order to focus on the consumer's recovery. This, in turn, means better outcomes for the consumer, a therapist who feels better about the therapy process, and interpreters who feel their contributions to the therapy were effective.

The cadre of interpreters who are qualified to work alongside clinicians provides services that are conducive to the therapeutic environment. Clinicians have commented in consumer satisfaction surveys that interpreters who are trained and certified to work in this setting are better prepared to match the goals of therapy and to be able to dialogue about what is occurring within the communication arena by capturing critical clinical information.

Further studies are needed to determine the efficacy of Mental Health Interpreter Certification, including evidence-based practices, consumer recovery, and clinical effectiveness.

REFERENCES

Alabama Department of Mental Health. (2003). *Chapter 580-3-24, Mental health interpreter standards.* Retrieved June 26, 2011, from http://www .alabamaadministrativecode.state.al.us/docs/mhlth/3mhlth24.htm.

Alabama Department of Mental Health. (2010). *Mental health interpreter training practicum experience.* Montgomery, AL. Retrieved from http://www.mhit.org /supportingdocuments/supportingdocuments.html.

Americans With Disabilities Act. *ADA title III technical assistance manual covering public accommodations and commercial facilities.* (1990). Retrieved from http://www .ada.gov/taman3.html.

Bailey, Verna, v. Alabama Department of Mental Health. (2002). 99-A-1321-N.

Dean, R. K., & Pollard, R. Q. (2004a). Consumers and service effectiveness in interpreting work: A practice profession perspective. In M. Marschark, R. Peterson, and E. Winston (Eds.), *Interpreting and interpreter education: Directions for research and practice* (pp. 259–82). New York: Oxford University Press.

Dean, R. K., & Pollard, R. (2004b). Observation-supervision in mental health interpreter training. In L. Swabey (Ed.), *Proceedings of the 14th National Convention of the Conference of Interpreter Trainers.* St. Paul, MN: CIT Publications: 55–76.

Hamerdinger, S., & Karlin, B. (2003). Therapy using interpreters: Questions on the use of interpreters in therapeutic settings for monolingual therapists. *Journal of American Deafness and Rehabilitation Association 36*(3), 12–30.

Hamerdinger, S., Karlin, B., & Clark, K. (2000). *Minimum competencies for interpreters in mental health settings: Report to the Missouri Board of Certification of Interpreters.* Retrieved from http://www.mhit.org/images/Minimum_Competencies.pdf.

Pollard, R. Q., & Dean, R. K. (2003). Interpreting/translating in mental health settings: What clinicians and interpreters need to know. Grand rounds presentation, Rochester Psychiatric Center, Rochester, NY, February 24.

Registry of Interpreters for the Deaf. (2007). *Interpreting in mental health settings.* RID Standard Practice Paper. Retrieved from http://www.rid.org/UserFiles /File/pdfs/Standard_Practice_Papers/Mental_Health_SPP.pdf.

Tugg v. Towey. (1994). 864 F. Supp. 1201 S.D. Fla.

APPENDIX A: DEFINITIONS

Definitions included in the standards outlining competencies and knowledge are the following:

Exposure: having some knowledge of a field's existence and its place in the setting and possibly some of the vocabulary used in the field

Demonstration (or compliance): showing that a skill has been learned and incorporated into the interpreter's practice

Familiarity: having actual experience with a field and/or practitioners in that field

Awareness: insight that goes beyond familiarity in that it includes beginning to internalize information about a field and to grasp how it affects one's professional and personal behavior. It does not necessarily include having resolved particular issues.

Understanding: having sufficient knowledge of a field to be able to explain the discipline, including its limits and its relationship to other disciplines

ROBYN K. DEAN AND
ROBERT Q POLLARD

Beyond *"Interesting"*

Using Demand Control Schema to Structure Experiential Learning

PROBLEM-BASED LEARNING, cooperative learning, and service learning are all terms associated with the active learning or student-centered learning movement that gained momentum in the 1960s (McKeachie, 1999). The literature in interpreter education over the last several years shows a growing interest in and use of these and other experiential learning approaches (e.g., Bentley-Sassaman, 2009; Dean et al, 2003, 2004a, 2009b; Dean, Pollard, & English, 2004; Peterson & Monikowski, 2005; Winston, 2005). While there are obvious benefits to the use of these methods in interpreter education, McKeachie (1999) warns of potential pitfalls: "All too often, experiential learning is entered into as something obviously valuable without enough consideration of the values to be achieved" (p. 156).

New learning or the acquisition of knowledge per se is not always *educational* in a practical sense. It is therefore the job of educators to balance student independence and teacher control in the goal of employing experiential learning to foster meaningful development (McKeachie, 1999). Teachers overestimate students' abilities to draw relevance from an experiential learning opportunity (Mercer, 2000); the connection between a given experience and one's future work performance must be modeled by the teacher. Palmer (1998) cautions against what appears to be a problematic pendulum swing from teacher-centered educational approaches to student-centered ones. Instead, he recommends a *subject-centered* philosophy. This would require interpreter educators to provide students and practitioners with learning experiences that build a sense of competence and demonstrate how concepts, principles, and skills are directly applicable and generalizable to various subjects relevant to interpreting work (McKeachie, 1999). That is, it is not enough for learning experiences to be interesting; they must also be relevant.

Experiential learning and reflective learning practices have been the primary method we have employed in our medical and mental health interpreter training activities (Dean et al 2003; Dean & Pollard, 2004, 2005, 2009b, 2009c). Our educational approach has been driven by our position that interpreting is a practice profession rather than a technical profession (Dean & Pollard, 2004, 2005, 2011). Accordingly, we believe that the interpreting profession should educate students and working professionals in ways that are similar to those used in other practice professions, that is, through early and extensive exposure to in-vivo practice realities. In developing our experiential learning approaches, we have taken great care to *structure* the exposure, analysis, and discussion of the practical experience.

Our DC-S approach to the conceptualization and teaching of interpreting work (Dean & Pollard, 2001, 2004, 2005, 2006, 2008a, 2008b, 2009b, 2009c, 2011; Dean et al, 2003, 2004; Dean, Pollard, & English 2004) has proved valuable not only in providing structure during the experiential portion of such learning activities (helping interpreting students and practitioners know what they should be looking for) but also during the analysis portion of the experience (fostering generalizability of what is learned). In this chapter we argue for the use of such deliberate structure in experiential learning and illustrate how educators can use DC-S in this regard and thus "close the educational loop" between practical experiences and *relevant* educational outcomes—what Turner (2005) refers to as "real interpreting." Given that the medical and mental health arenas are our content areas of greatest expertise, as well as the theme of this volume, examples of our use of DC-S methods in experiential learning in medical and mental health settings will be employed hereafter. However, it should be noted that the underlying ideas apply to any interpreting setting or content area.

Why Structure and Terminology Matter

Over the past decade of investigating and reporting on the effectiveness of DC-S (Dean et al. 2003; Dean & Pollard, 2001, 2004a, 2004b, 2009b;

Dean et al., 2004; Dean, Pollard, & English 2004; Pollard & Dean, 2008), we sometimes hear from interpreter educators comments such as "We have always taught DC-S concepts—we just don't use that vocabulary" or "We recognize the novelty and value of DC-S, but we don't use your specific terminology." While such reactions were not of great concern to us initially, over the years we have seen significant benefits in student and practitioner learning outcomes when DC-S nomenclature is maintained along with its broader constructs.

As with any taxonomy system, DC-S terminology will necessarily be artificial and manifest limitations in the ability to adequately encapsulate complex and nuanced ideas. Yet, after considerable experience and observation regarding how we and others employ DC-S (with or without its nomenclature), we now maintain that the benefits of the formal structure and nomenclature outweigh any artificiality or limitations these constructs involve. The structure of DC-S—whether the basic theoretical construct (demands and controls and their respective categories; Dean & Pollard, 2001, 2005, 2008a, 2011; Dean et al., 2004) or the dialogic work analysis aspect of DC-S (demand-control-consequence-resulting demand, or DCCRD; Dean & Pollard 2006, 2008a, 2011)—provides inexperienced interpreters with a concrete method for thinking about their work and work decisions and encourages experienced interpreters to replace intuitive or habitual work processes with conscious and deliberate ones.

Most people familiar with our schema recognize the benefit of using the DC-S dialogic work analysis method (DCCRD) in discussions about interpreting because it is an accessible and effective decision-making tool. By providing needed structure through which one can analyze the complexities and nuances of interpreting work, it fosters the development of professional judgment and "scaffolds" one's critical thinking within an ethical frame. We have addressed the use of DCCRD in interpreter education and its benefits in other publications (Dean & Pollard, 2006, 2008b, 2009b, 2009c, 2011; Pollard & Dean, 2008). However, since the need for the structure provided by the more fundamental, theoretical construct aspects of DC-S (i.e., demands and controls and their respective categories) appear less evident to some interpreter educators, we herein describe the ways in which the theoretical construct can be used to optimize subject-centered learning outcomes.

Demands are defined as any factor in the work setting that rises to a level of significance that impacts, or should impact, interpreting work (Dean & Pollard, 2001, 2005, 2008a, 2011; Dean et al., 2004). Using the term "demand" in reference to an aspect of the work environment is to assert that this aspect *matters*. This may seem simplistic, but given the prevailing technical focus of the interpreting profession (Dean & Pollard, 2001, 2005, 2011), many interpreters either perceive or have been told that aspects of the work environment that are not directly related to the interlocutor's utterances and meaning fall outside the boundaries of their professional role and, therefore, outside the boundaries of their concern or responsibility. Countering that message by employing the term "demand" affirms that other aspects of the work environment beyond utterances alone often do matter, which, in turn, places an expectation on the interpreter to respond—even if the response is merely giving due consideration to their presence and significance.

Similarly, using the term "controls" conveys that the broad array of skills, knowledge, characteristics, and behaviors of the interpreter, including but not limited to one's technical skills, also matter in the work of interpreting. Acknowledging and appreciating this broad array of controls allows for a more critical and insightful appraisal of one's work effectiveness, in part because we always frame this array of controls in both the affirmative and the negative, that is, by addressing what resources one brings *and* does not bring to interpreting practice.

Educators can infuse DC-S structure into experiential learning opportunities both prior to (or during) the experiential event, as well as in later analysis of the event. The event can be structured by asking students to employ the four demand categories (Dean & Pollard, 2001, 2005, 2008a, 2011; Dean et al., 2004)—environmental, interpersonal, paralinguistic, and intrapersonal (EIPI)—to collect relevant data. Subsequent to the experience, educators can use these and other elements of DC-S structure to denote overtly *what* the students have learned and *why* it is relevant to their (future) work as interpreters.

Illustrations from Medicine and Psychiatry

Imagine that a student returns from observing a computer-assisted tomography (CAT) scan appointment and has recorded in the following environmental demand category on the observation form (or in a journal, report, etc.):

> The CAT scan table stood 3½ feet from the floor, situated in the center of the room; the lighting was very dim, and there was an observation window with pale green curtains.

While all of these aspects of the environment indeed are "factors" (a term we commonly see used in lieu of "demands"), they are not all demands of interpreting as we define them. In a discussion with the student, one would need to point out that the height of the table and the central positioning of the equipment, along with the presence of curtains and their color, are probably not demands of interpreting because they fail to rise to a level of significance that impacts an interpreter's work.[1] However, the presence of the observation window and the dimly lit room do constitute environmental demands. The dim room would affect visual communication, and the observation room is where the technician would go during the scan. This latter point, perhaps not obviously a demand to some, can lead to a further discussion of *potential* interpersonal and paralinguistic demands: What if the deaf person tries to communicate in ASL during the exam while the interpreter is in the observation room, or what if the technician usually uses an intercom to communicate with patients during the scan? This simple example illustrates how an educator can sift through material generated from a student's learning experience and use DC-S constructs (in this case, the meaning of the term "demand") to make the experience directly relevant to interpreting practice.

The next example, drawn from experiential learning within mental health settings, shows how the construct of demands can help focus attendees and the discussion on the most relevant interpreting topics, not just those that happen to catch the attendee's attention. In our mental health interpreter trainings, we frequently show videos of clinicians conducting mental health evaluations of (hearing) patients with various mental health symptoms. The videos we use (Films for the Humanities and Sciences, 1994) were originally designed to improve the interviewing and diagnostic skills of (hearing) clinicians. In one particular interview, a clinician is interviewing a

---

1. However, these might constitute demands if the deaf patient were in a wheelchair or the machine were positioned in a way that compromised sight lines.

woman in her 40s with major depressive disorder who has been hospitalized because of significant suicidal ideation. The interview is about 10 minutes long, but we divide the interview into a number of shorter segments so that we can draw out certain teaching points relevant to interpreting practice. The following dialogue is from a segment that elicits from the patient a significant list of her depression symptoms:

> Clinician: I want to understand more about what you mean by feeling depressed. What does depression mean to you?
>
> Patient: [long pause] Physically, I am lethargic to the point of not wanting to get out of bed.
>
> Clinician: Mm-hmm.
>
> Patient: Not wanting to shower. When my kids are in college, I will stay in bed for a couple of days on and off—if I am not working and can do that. I feel like my arms are so heavy I cannot lift them.
>
> Clinician: How do you feel about yourself?
>
> Patient: Oh, I hate me. I hate the way I look, I hate the way I feel. [pause] I hate the way I talk to other people.
>
> Clinician: Do you find yourself feeling guilty about things?
>
> Patient: All the time. I do everything wrong.
>
> Clinician: Do you find yourself feeling guilty about things that are far in the past . . . that are way past doing anything about?
>
> Patient: Yeah, like 20, 30 years ago . . . something I said to somebody, something that hurt their feelings that I didn't mean to do.
>
> Clinician: When you're feeling that way, do you have much hope for the future? Is there any hope in your view, or is that gone?
>
> Patient: [long pause, looking away from clinician] Ummm, the only hope that I had, the only thing I was hanging on to all these years was, I was waiting for my children to get through college. So that I could be done. Done. I felt that that was kind of a goal I wanted to get to . . . and it's done [smiling], and I don't know what else to do. I have to find something else to do with me—'cause there isn't anything else to do [becomes tearful] . . .
>
> Clinician: So you feel like . . .

> Patient: [interrupts] Really hopeless.
> Clinician: Not much of a purpose.
> Patient: Yeah. Nothing.
> Clinician: There's no purpose.
> Patient: Right.

At the end of this segment, we ask the audience to identify demands that would have been present during this interview if the patient had been deaf. Initially, most mention things that are relevant to the work of clinicians but not to that of interpreters. Attendees eventually learn to make relevant connections between the video stimuli and demands of interpreting, but this process is not immediate and requires much modeling. The following are some typical responses to this video segment and how our use of the terms "demands" and "controls" helps attain the desired educational outcomes:

> Attendee: I'd be concerned about the patient. The patient is at the place that she has been working toward—her kids in college . . . and now she is there. She even says she is "done."
> Educator: Right, and what is the interpreting demand here?

This attendee is noting something of significance, but it is not yet identified as an interpreting demand. Experiential learning activities are designed to heighten the learners' interest or draw them into the subject. This is purposeful (hence the term "active learning"), but this benefit also can lead to distraction. Indeed, the temptation in this mental health learning activity is to play "armchair psychologist." Unlike the earlier example, where the educator needs to draw out relevant interpreting topics from the student's list of mundane aspects of the CAT scan, in this example the need is to scale down and focus the conversation only on what is relevant to interpreting.

Here is how an educator might use the structure of DC-S to accomplish that. The attendee's comment points out that the patient's elevated suicide risk is a demand for interpreters in that the patient's suicide risk is an important part of the clinician's "thought world" (Namy, 1977; Dean & Pollard, 2005, 2009b). Further, the patient's suicide risk is likely to be referenced during the clinician's further dialogue, for example, during an explanation of his plan for treatment (e.g., to admit her to the hospital). Noting that suicide risk assessments are common in psychiatric evaluations

is one way to generalize from this specific case to mental health evaluations in general. Educators could elaborate on the components of a suicide
risk assessment, which would include discussion of the suicide plan, the
lethality of any identified suicide method, and the opportunity the patient
has to effect a specific plan (e.g., does the patient own a gun?). Another
way to generalize from this specific case would be to discuss how this case
example might be different from others (e.g., a suicide risk assessment in
which the patient might have vague suicidal thoughts but no specific or
imminent plan).

Consider another comment an attendee made at the conclusion of this
same interview segment:

> Attendee: I thought it was strange that she smiled while she was
> talking about something that was really sad. Seems like
> inappropriate affect.
>
> Educator: Inappropriate affect is something clinicians look for, but
> how, in this instance, is that a demand?

The educator's question directs the interpreter away from whether or
not this observation is evidence of inappropriate affect (which, if true,
would be of interest to the clinician) and toward the topic of how the patient's smile constitutes a demand in interpreting. This shift allowed the
discussion to evolve into a consideration of how facial expressions (or lack
thereof) that are detected by the interpreter and do *not* have grammatical
significance but may have *affective* significance could be passed along to the
clinician. The attendees discussed how the interpreter's responsibility to
reveal such potentially relevant information should not be confused with
opining on the affective significance or meaning of the facial expression—
that responsibility ultimately lies with the clinician.

We frequently use simple and direct questions such as "What is the
interpreting demand here?" or "How is that a demand for interpreting?"
with students and practitioners who are responding to simulated interpreting experiences. No matter how obvious the link between the observed
phenomenon and an interpreting demand may be to an educator, the student or practitioner cannot be presumed to recognize what is relevant in
their observational data nor understand how to properly articulate it as
an interpreting demand. Learners often have good reason to be noting
something as relevant (as in the preceding example), but they frequently

struggle to articulate that final connection to interpreting practice. The educator must be prepared to steer the dialogue away from a superficial or tangential focus on what the learner found interesting and toward more relevant and generalizable content. Asking "How is that a demand?" often facilitates that conversation.

In terms of controls, it is worthwhile to point out what new controls the attendees now have after engaging in an experiential learning activity such as watching the video described earlier. That particular video segment was heavier on mental health content than mental health dynamics. In this regard, an educator might point out that the video facilitates *appreciation* for the ways depression can be manifested, *knowledge* of some of the symptoms of depression (guilt, hopelessness, etc.), and an *understanding* that clinicians frequently ask questions in an open-ended manner to elicit as much data from patients as possible. When controls are understood only as "responses" (another term we often see used in lieu of the term "controls"), then these important control resources (appreciation, knowledge, and understanding) may go unrecognized and therefore not be "harvested" from the learning experience. Another control that could be highlighted is the "concern" the earlier attendee mentions, which could be highlighted as another important control. Concern, better phrased in a mental health context as "empathy," indeed is an important control for interpreting work in general and in mental health settings specifically.

This video segment offers many other potential learning opportunities, some of which are addressed later in this chapter. Yet even these brief examples illustrate the inherent value of experiential learning. Instead of a mere listing of major depression symptoms presented in an article or by a content expert, the relevant information is *discovered* by the attendees. Perhaps more important, the depression symptoms are presented in a real-life context that allows the educator to generalize learning points to numerous other interpreting practice realities, leading the attendees toward a more sophisticated and nuanced appreciation of the demands of mental health work.

Like many educators, we opt for practical, experience-based teaching (Dean et al, 2003; Dean & Pollard, 2001, 2005, 2008a, 2009b; Dean, Pollard, & English 2004) and regularly use the video series of clinician-patient diagnostic interviews to teach introductory mental health material. In essence, this experiential learning activity is an alternative version of our observation-supervision (O-S) approach (Dean et al, 2003; Dean &

Pollard, 2005, 2008a, 2009b; Dean et al., 2004; Dean, Pollard, & English 2004). Like most experiential learning approaches, learners are first exposed to some form of stimulus that is relevant to professional practice (simulated or real), followed by a reflective analysis of that experience (Fogarty, 1997; Kolb, 1984). In O-S we employ in-vivo observations of interactions between hearing interlocutors exclusively. Learners complete observation forms that facilitate a structured documentation of EIPI demands. Subsequently, educators lead discussions among small groups of learners to ensure that the relevant information has been identified and to foster broader, generalizable learning.

Professional practice stimuli can originate from many sources: actual interpreting assignments (i.e., case presentations), a picture of a simulated interpreting assignment from which EIPI demands can be elicited, videos, a hypothetical scenario or devised case analysis, or an observed interpreted situation. Most recently, we have begun to collaborate with our medical school's Simulated Patient Program. Interpreting students and practitioners observe second- and third-year medical students interviewing simulated patients (actors playing the role of patients with specific illnesses). These interviews may focus on differential diagnosis, explaining a procedure, delivering bad news, and so on,[2] all of which are relevant to interpreting practice in healthcare settings.

Real-life or simulated practice material allows for rich learning opportunities for students and practitioners, but, as with anything, opportunities can be taken or missed. It should not be assumed that educational goals will be reached via experiential learning without significant help from the trainer or teacher in both the design of the experience and its analysis stage. We maintain that the structure provided by DC-S fosters effective facilitation of these educational goals in both these stages. In the long run, once the process of deriving relevant learning from structured observation and analysis of practice material is thoroughly instilled, the ability to derive benefits from reflective learning via any stimulus (including one's own work) continues throughout one's career.

---

2. The most recent application of this method is our collaboration with the National Technical Institute for the Deaf and its department of American Sign Language and Interpreter Education. Together we are developing the curriculum for a Certificate in Healthcare Interpreting: http://www.ntid.rit.edu/aslie/heathcare_interpreting.php.

DC-S Observation Forms

In discussing experiential learning methods, McKeachie (1999) recommends a balance between students' learning independence and teacher control. Palmer (1998) conveys that same balance by employing the term "subject centered" (rather than student centered or teacher centered) when discussing these learning approaches. One of the ways the teacher in an experiential learning event can assert this necessary control is to require the student to report on the learning experience in a structured manner. The student's structured report (not merely recollections or a "story" of the event) then serves as the central focus of the discussion and helps the entire class to benefit (albeit vicariously) from the student's experience. Such reports should be rigidly observational in nature, not reflections on or analyses of the student's experience because these reports must serve as the teacher's source material for centering and facilitating the discussion of the relevant educational material for the entire class.

Assigning a reflection paper following an experiential learning event can be beneficial but is quite different in this regard. Students and practitioners who have not been taught overtly (through modeling or otherwise) how to identify and document relevant observational material will not automatically provide the "clean data" the teacher needs. Rather than presenting a compilation of practice-relevant data useful to the whole class, they often return with an *interpretation* of their experience, which benefits only that student. The observation forms we use in our O-S teaching (Dean et al, 2003; Dean & Pollard, 2005, 2008a, 2009b; Dean et al., 2004; Dean, Pollard, & English 2004) offer one such type of report structure; many other educators have created DC-S forms for use with picture analyses and other classroom exercises (see appendix A for an example).

These observations and other DC-S structured forms typically focus on the theoretical construct level of DC-S (Dean & Pollard, 2001, 2008a; Dean et al., 2004): environmental, interpersonal, paralinguistic, and intrapersonal demands and preassignment, assignment, and postassignment controls. Various observation forms have been created for different interpreting practice content areas (e.g., K–12, medical, legal, and mental health settings). Content area distinctions usually manifest in the interpersonal and paralinguistic sections of the form, where questions are geared toward setting-specific issues (e.g., "what were the chief complaints the patient brought?"). For the purposes of the remainder of this chapter, when examples from observation forms are presented, they are drawn from our medical and mental health observation forms.

While it is a relevant point that properly categorizing EIPI demands matters less than identifying distinct demands in the development of interpreters' decision-making skills, doing so does help develop the analytical skills of students and practitioners. This initial analytical phase is the first step in any teleological, or consequences-based, ethical process (Cottone & Claus, 2000; Cesna & Mosier, 2005; Dean, 2009; Dean & Pollard, 2006, 2011; Mandelbaum, 1955; Niebuhr, 1963). On the other hand, when working at the dialogic work analysis level of DC-S (Dean & Pollard, 2006, 2011; Dean et al., 2004), the construct of EIPI categories is supplanted by the constructs of main and concurrent demands, that is, the *constellation of demands*. It is this level of DC-S analysis that characterizes most discussions of interpreting ethics (Dean & Pollard, 2006, 2009c, 2011; Dean et al., 2004). Even the DC-S control categories of preassignment, assignment, and postassignment controls are somewhat less relevant to ethical analyses since ethical discussions most frequently focus on what behaviors the interpreter engages in *during* an assignment.

These caveats notwithstanding, the concept of EIPI demands at the theoretical construct level stimulates students and practitioners to begin to anticipate demands (in preparing for work) and enables students, practitioners, and educators to share knowledge and discuss interpreting demands. Palmer (1998) alludes to this process as creating "knowers" out of amateurs, which is a far more effective educational design than many traditional methods. In the following section we provide thoughts on how an educator might use the theoretical construct to create knowers.

ENVIRONMENTAL DEMANDS

Environmental demands articulate the foundational elements of the practice setting and therefore present the broadest teaching opportunities. When teaching about setting-specific content (K–12, medical, mental health, legal, etc.), educators can directly teach or assign students to investigate the environmental demands—that is, the *where, who,* and *why* of an interpreting assignment. Environmental demands are the springboard from which demands in the three other categories (interpersonal, paralinguistic, and intrapersonal) can be hypothesized. The skill of predicting these other types of demands, which are based on recognized environmental demands, is the best way to prepare for actual interpreting assignments.

Environmental demands often are the easiest to identify. For example, consider eliciting the environmental demands of an emergency room (ER) based solely upon the students' own experiences as an ER patient or visitor. (Note that personal experience can also serve as a useful stimulus for experiential education.) To elicit a rich listing of environmental demands, the teacher simply has to pose questions based on the subcategories of the broader environmental demand category (Dean & Pollard, 2008a; Dean et al., 2004): the goal of the environment, the personnel and clientele who are present, the specialized terminology used in that setting, and the nature of the physical surroundings.

While the teacher may need to fill in certain knowledge gaps regarding ER settings or assign students to investigate such gaps themselves, the students will generate much useful content. In our teaching, we do not reveal the PowerPoint slides where our ER environmental demand list appears until the attendees finish generating their own list as a collective group. They never fail to generate at least 90% of the data we would otherwise provide as the perceived "experts" (a conclusion we deliberately point out after the exercise). Palmer (1998) and Feasey (2002) both suggest that the traditional expert/amateur mentality is less effective for learning. Let us further explore this ER example by demonstrating how exploration of the environmental demand subcategories can lead to important teaching opportunities.

Goal of the ER

The goal of the environment is frequently confused with consumers' communication objectives, which are actually interpersonal demands. The goal of the environment is broader; it is a function of and is established by the system in which the work is taking place. All of the parties who work in a given system are working to help achieve the goal of the environment. All of the parties who engage in the system, whether they are aware of it or not, yield to the goal of the environment. Moreover, as we have suggested elsewhere (Dean & Pollard, 2006, 2011), the proper ethical objective of an interpreter is to also work in service of, or at the very least yield to, the goal of the environment. The goal of an ER is to triage patients' medical needs, stabilize the patients, treat their medical needs only when it is expedient to do so, and otherwise discharge them to a more appropriate level of care. It sometimes surprises students and even practitioners that the goal of an ER is not to "help" patients in the broadest sense of that term. The ER is a system set up to address only certain kinds of problems—acute, urgent, life threatening, and so on, which may mean that patients who do not meet those criteria after an ER evaluation are told to go home, follow up with their primary care physician, and return to the ER only if their symptoms worsen.

Personnel in an ER

It is usually obvious that an ER environment includes doctors, nurses, and various technicians, but it also is important to note other types of workers who may be present in the ER since they, too, may present interpreting demands. Such personnel include janitorial staff, administrative staff, social workers, students of many types, ambulance personnel, emergency medical technicians, and possibly law enforcement agents or security officers.

Clientele in an ER

An ER will be serving many patients other than the deaf individual who is at the center of an experiential learning scenario. These other patients also compete for time, attention, and resources, which may well impact an interpreter's work. Additionally, family members and visitors are a likely source of demands.

Terminology in an ER

In the DC-S theoretical construct, the use of specialized terminology is categorized as an environmental demand. In the ER, there are many "points of contact" between workers and patients. It is helpful to break down and consider each of these to devise a more comprehensive list of specialized vocabulary terms that may be used. For example, vocabulary will be derived from conversations about health insurance (with the administrator at check-in), medicines (with the nurse in charge of triage), symptoms, diseases, anatomy and physiology (with the provider examining the patient's condition), and medical tests and procedures (by the clinician or technician who conducts these tests).

Physical Surroundings of an ER

This subcategory of environmental demands is likely the most familiar to anyone who has been in an ER. While exceptions to the rule certainly exist, most people report that an ER is chilly, brightly lit, and crowded with people and equipment. They note the variety of distracting smells and sounds, such as sterile or chemical smells, odors from bodily fluids like urine and vomit, and noises made by machinery, intercoms, pagers, or patients in distress, children crying, and so on.

While the environmental demand subcategory of terminology might present the most obvious learning opportunity for students, each of the aforementioned subcategories provides the teacher with an opportunity to explore the reasons that content included in those subcategories may well constitute interpreting demands. In summary, knowing the goal of the ER environment prepares interpreters to work within a system that (a) prioritizes patient care based on a patient's immediate medical condition; therefore, extended waiting periods are a common experience for patients and interpreters; (b) patients may undergo multiple types of tests if their medical condition has not been sufficiently determined; (c) patients may be discharged before they actually feel better. In ER settings, interpreters should be prepared to work with many different types of clinicians (not just doctors), each of whom have different responsibilities and communication objectives. Interpreters should also be prepared to deal with patients' family members and friends—who actually may be their deaf client rather than the patient. In addition, of course, interpreters need to be prepared for the myriad sights, smells, and sounds of the ER.

INTERPERSONAL AND PARALINGUISTIC DEMANDS

If environmental demands can be described as the *where*, *who*, and *why* of an interpreting assignment, interpersonal demands can be described as the *what* of the assignment (i.e., demands associated with people's interactions), and paralinguistic demands as the *how* of the assignment (i.e., the quality of the linguistic utterances of hearing or deaf consumers). In other words, interpersonal and paralinguistic demands encompass *what happened* or *what was said* and *how it was said.*

We typically link paralinguistic demands with interpersonal ones since paralinguistic demands rarely stand alone. They are usually evidenced within the context of interpersonal demands. In the earlier example of the patient with depression, it was noted that she smiled at the same time she said, "I just don't know what to do with me"—a comment that obviously conveyed painful emotion. The pitch of her voice also increased as she said this to the clinician. These are paralinguistic demands, albeit subtle ones, since they matter in interpretation, and they were manifest in the interpersonal context of the dialogue with the clinician. Paralinguistic demands may be more overt and less tied to interpersonal demands when they are more extreme, for example, when the expression of linguistic material is so compromised that it is unable even to be accessed interpersonally (e.g., when a person waking up from anesthesia is mumbling unintelligibly).

Our DC-S observation forms for medical and mental health interpreting settings are structured to stimulate consideration of interpersonal and paralinguistic demands in a variety of ways. First, learners are prompted to report data as directly and objectively as possible by completing a table with headings such as "what happened?" "what was said?" and "how was it said?" Specific questions intended to further elucidate interpersonal demands are also posed: "What is the reason for the visit?" and, "if known, what is the patient's history?" Additionally, some questions foster more subtle consideration of interpersonal demands: "What mood or emotions were expressed? What conflicts or miscommunications, if any, did you observe?"

Whereas a simple picture or scenario description can serve as an easy stimulus for generating environmental demands, a realistic consideration of interpersonal and paralinguistic demands usually requires a richer form of stimulus, such as in-vivo observation or videos. Educators are cautioned, however, that discussions that follow the identification of interpersonal and paralinguistic demands can too quickly turn to the topic of controls: "How should the interpreter respond?" or "what should the interpreter do?" We recommend delaying that aspect of the conversation until a thorough analysis of the full constellation of demands has taken place. Doing so will not only equip students and practitioners with important knowledge but, with repetition, also instill important values and cognitive skills that lead to a thorough rather than a superficial demand analysis. Effective ethical decision making must begin with a nuanced analysis of the EIPI demands of the work scenario (Cesna & Mosier, 2005; Cottone & Claus, 2000; Dean & Pollard, 2009b, 2011). The identification of consequences and potential resulting demands that we teach via DC-S dialogic work analysis is often predicated on the identification of less obvious demands (e.g., the clinician's thought world). Next we provide examples of how the interpersonal and paralinguistic categories can provide the necessary structure to highlight these demands.

Returning to the psychiatrist-patient dialogue in the earlier example, imagine that at the end of the segment a workshop attendee states, "The clinician seems very blasé about what the patient is saying—like he doesn't care what she is saying—and he even confirms that she *should* be hopeless!" While the verbatim interview dialogue reproduced earlier does not convey the interpersonal dynamics visible on camera, this is a common viewer response to the clinician's calm and objective demeanor, words, and tone of voice. Asking what an interpreter would do in response to this demand is premature since the comment is not yet articulated as a demand.

In this comment, the word "blasé" is referring to the words and the tone the clinician used. Language that is evaluative or judgmental ("blasé") goes beyond data reporting—which is the objective of demand identification—and crosses over into analysis and opinion. However, such evaluative comments should not be dismissed entirely since they are typically reflective of important interpreter reactions. These are addressed when we discuss *intrapersonal* demands. Evaluative or judgmental comments do not constitute properly articulated interpersonal demands.[3] If judgment language is used when the educator has direct access to the stimulus material (e.g., a video or a group observation), the educator can guide the students or practitioners to remain focused on pinpointing what happened, what was said, and so on in their search to identify interpersonal demands. However, if the educator did not directly observe the stimulus experience, and the data reporting includes evaluative or judgmental language, it may be harder for

---

3. For a detailed description of the standards that constitute a quality demand-control analysis, see the *DC-S Rubric and Rubric Guidelines*, available from the authors.

the learners to revisit and properly articulate the necessary material. Once learners have stored information as interpretations or judgments, they are less likely to accurately recall the original events that led to those reactions and opinions. It typically requires several trials before students and practitioners accurately identify and articulate interpersonal demands because it is not a skill that most have been taught. For example, after observing an ER interview, it took a student three tries to accurately articulate the interpersonal demand that she had initially framed using judgment language. She first stated, "The doctor was rude." When pressed for a depiction of what actually happened, which led her to this opinion, the student stated, "The doctor was ignoring the patient's questions," which is still not sufficient. Eventually she said, "The doctor delayed answering the patient's question while he asked the patient further questions about the patient's symptoms." That is a properly articulated interpersonal demand that led to a more productive discussion of potential control responses.

What the attendee in these examples is likely responding to *can*, with proper guidance, be framed effectively as demands. In the case of the mental health scenario that stimulates many viewers to use judgment language, these demands can be articulated as follows: (1) The clinician asks pointed questions about sensitive material (in lay conversations such questions would often be considered taboo); (2) his tone is neither apologetic nor tentative as he poses these questions; (3) his questions follow one after another without much verbal feedback to the patient's answers; (4) when he does respond, he rephrases or "reflects" back what he perceives the patient to be saying; he does not offer an opinion or support or attempt to counteract the patient's depressed perceptions. It is interesting to contrast these four distinctly stated demands with the two evaluative terms the attendees originally offered ("blasé" and "doesn't care").

While these interpersonal and paralinguistic demands are certainly worth noting, a discussion about controls that might be employed in response to these demands would still be premature. Students and practitioners must understand the clinician's communication objectives (another type of interpersonal demand), that is, the reason he is asking these questions and doing so in a particular manner. In fact, the clinician is exhibiting well-established techniques of psychiatric data collection and therapeutic intervention. For example, at the end of the dialogue segment, he is not *confirming* that the patient should be without hope. Rather, he is *affirming* that he understands what the patient is trying to reveal. In mental health settings, this common type of communication objective is referred to as "reflection" and/or "validation" (Pedersen, 2005).

This diagnostic interview example further allows the educator to generalize the interpersonal demand discussion to a broader examination of clinicians' communication objectives during mental health evaluations. Such objectives include gaining the patient's cooperation or "engagement," emergency assessment and intervention as necessary in light of risks to the patient's safety, obtaining sufficient data to make a differential diagnosis and recommend disposition (a decision regarding the level of care needed and initial treatment plan), and determining whether further information needs to be obtained before a differential diagnosis and disposition can be arrived at.

This same interview segment presents another important learning point that should be explored and then generalized; that is, attendees' common misjudgments about the appropriateness of the communication exchange more broadly. Many viewers perceive the clinician's interactions with the patient to be problematic or at least strange, especially when imagining that the patient is deaf. When interpreters perceive a communication style as not befitting the linguistic and cultural norms of ASL and Deaf[4] people (i.e., they see it as a demand), they are frequently primed to employ controls to compensate for this perceived mismatch. If that demand *is* perceived accurately, then linguistic or cultural mediation may indeed be appropriate. However, in this psychiatric interview example, the demands were not accurately perceived or stated, a clue virtually always revealed via judgment or evaluative language.

In this case, the interpreter articulated the demand as "the clinician seems very blasé" and assumes that a hypothetical deaf patient might then perceive the clinician as apathetic (which is not a foregone conclusion). If the demand is perceived this way, the interpreter might be inclined to add more emotional content or feedback cues when interpreting than the source

---

4. Per contemporary practice in the deafness field, the upper case "Deaf" is used in this chapter when referring broadly to the community of individuals (or the organizations they establish) who use sign language and otherwise manifest a sociocultural affiliation with the values, norms, and practices of the American Deaf community. The lower case "deaf" is used when making reference to individuals with severe to profound hearing loss without regard to their potential linguistic or sociocultural affiliation with the American Deaf community.

message contains. While in some situations this might be fine, if the interpreter made such decisions in this situation, the interpreter would be augmenting and perhaps even thwarting the clinician's therapeutic technique and objective. The lesson here is that interpreters should take great care in how they articulate demands so as to respond to them in their pure, interpersonal state without influence from the interpreters' own *intrapersonal* demands (Dean, 2009). When one considers how often interpreters work in settings with which they are not familiar, encountering "demands" that are not accurately perceived or stated is a common phenomenon. Students' and practitioners' use of evaluative or judgment language when attempting to articulate interpersonal demands is a "red flag" to educators indicating the need for assistance and redirection.

INTRAPERSONAL DEMANDS

Intrapersonal demands are demands that stem from the interpreter's emotional, psychological, physical, or cognitive state. Intrapersonal demands are likely to surface in response to any experiential learning stimulus material but tend to be more acutely experienced in response to in-vivo observations. Contrary to popular interpreting rhetoric, interpreters have *many* opinions and reactions to settings, people, and dynamics in their work. In-vivo observations are an excellent way to draw out overt, suppressed, or even unconscious intrapersonal responses so they can be dealt with effectively. Learning to acknowledge, recognize, and properly respond to intrapersonal demands is a career-long process for interpreters and, arguably, all practice professionals. We address the topic of intrapersonal demands more extensively in our publications on ethics (Dean, 2009; Dean & Pollard, 2006, 2011).

In the intrapersonal demand section of our observation forms, we ask students and practitioners to first list any and all of their physical, cognitive, emotional, and psychological reactions to the observed event. Then we ask them to return to their list and indicate which items constitute intrapersonal demands and which are simply intrapersonal experiences. Distinguishing between the two is an important step since not every fleeting thought, feeling, or emotion necessarily constitutes an intrapersonal demand. (Just as the green curtain in the CAT scan example is an environmental factor but not an environmental demand.) Again, to meet the definition of a "demand" the intrapersonal reaction in question must rise to a level of significance that impacts interpreting work.

Again in contrast to much interpreting rhetoric, when a student or a practitioner identifies an intrapersonal demand, it should not be dismissed with advice to "just deal with it" or the expectation that interpreters must (or even can) always remain neutral (Metzger, 1999). If interpreters are exposed to a bloody ER trauma and start to feel weak-kneed, "stuffing it" is not likely to address the problem, whereas sitting down, excusing themselves for a short time, and so on, may resolve the problem (and allow them to resume their work in an effective, not a compromised, manner). The very existence of the intrapersonal demand category in DC-S reflects our desire to validate the human consequences of being exposed to physically challenging and emotion-laden events, consistent with our use of the term "demand" generally to validate the many things that "matter" in interpreting work beyond linguistic utterances themselves. By elevating the significance of intrapersonal demands to a unique category, we are also encouraging interpreters to learn how to recognize and cope with them as distinct from interpersonal demands (which, as noted earlier, can be challenging for many interpreters). Skillfully and consistently accomplishing this distinction is how we define and operationalized *neutrality* in DC-S.

Striving to "be neutral" simply by valuing that state does not automatically yield the desired effect. Practitioners' "donning" neutrality as one might a don an overcoat often leads to the denial of important and influential intrapersonal responses. When this happens, interpreters are at great risk of projecting their own cognitive and emotional state onto the deaf and hearing individuals in the assignment, usually by misidentifying their perceptions as interpersonal demands. Using DC-S structure, educators can help students and practitioners appreciate the likelihood and the impact of intrapersonal demands and aid them in taking the potential ramifications of these seriously.

To illustrate, let us describe another common attendee response to the video featuring the patient with depression. Before much viewing time has passed, someone will state, "I feel really bad for her; she seems really desperate" or words to that effect. After affirming this as an intrapersonal demand (and a common one), we contrast it with empathy—which was noted earlier as a control. This allows us to draw the important distinction between the interpreter's intrapersonal demands and the interpreter's controls. Both originate from the interpreter, so they are often lumped together inappropriately. In this example, feeling bad for the patient would be a distraction and diminish the interpreter's available cognitive and emotional resources. In contrast, empathy (which is indeed different from "feeling bad" for someone) would serve as an investment in one's work and therefore be a likely source of energy. Often, making a proper distinction between intrapersonal demands and controls allows an interpreter to channel the compromising energy associated with intrapersonal demands into the positive energy associated with controls.

When intrapersonal demands remain unrecognized by the student or practitioner, they cannot be effectively addressed and will very likely impact consumers and the interaction. This occurs most often when the interpreter misperceives the unrecognized intrapersonal demand as an interpersonal one and then employs an inappropriate control. When an educator or mentor simply tells learners what the latter's intrapersonal demands are, that is, when an educator or mentor identifies learners' intrapersonal demands before the learners have done so on their own, the beneficial effect is much less. Indeed, McKeachie (1999) reminds us that self-reflection and awareness are important steps in self-regulation (p. 315). The DC-S structure and experiential learning opportunities can facilitate this process of discovery. In the earlier example, the attendee had a strong reaction to how the clinician interacted with the depressed patient (labeling the clinician blasé and indifferent). As we have noted, the use of evaluative language indicates that intrapersonal psychological or cognitive responses are at play.

Upon learning the more accurate explanation of the clinician's behavior and intentions (via a proper demand analysis, as illustrated earlier), most students and practitioners do not feel the same way as they originally did. In contrast, they either ask valid and appropriate questions about the clinician's comments, questions, and mind-set or determine for themselves the clinical relevance of his phrasing and tone. We attribute these more effective learning accomplishments (in comparison to those achieved with less structured forms of experiential learning) to the illuminating structure of DC-S.

Controls

One of the ways the concept of controls is used in our experiential learning activities is to directly examine with students and practitioners the new controls they have acquired as a result of their observational experiences and subsequent DC-S analyses. When controls are understood only as the interpreter's "response," then this conversation is rarely fruitful. Identifying and articulating demands, even when done well, will not automatically result in a repertoire of potential interpreter *actions*. However, when the definition of controls is properly broadened to include knowledge, respect, understanding, appreciation, and so on, students and practitioners are able to recognize and articulate considerable acquisition of controls via DC-S structured experiential learning.

Knowledge is an important control and one that is frequently gleaned from effective experiential learning practices. In the earlier examples, knowledge reframed an intrapersonal demand as a useful control (empathy). Knowledge of the "strange" communication techniques clinicians sometimes use allowed the interpreter to respond effectively, in particular, by not responding as if it were an interpersonal demand requiring her intervention (a Deaf-hearing culture conflict). Knowledge that depression can lead to suicidal thoughts and behavior prepares interpreters to work more effectively amid this common reality in mental health settings. Knowledge of the wide array of environmental demands in the ER prepares interpreters to recognize that they may end up interpreting for a police officer interviewing a patient who has been transported to the ER after a car accident.

Using the structure of DC-S in experiential learning to help students and practitioners understand that "this can happen" (anything from the mundane to the bizarre) goes a long way in increasing interpreters' work effectiveness because it directly contributes to their control resources. The observations they and their peers describe (via accurate and well-articulated demands) lead to new controls. The subsequent analyses of these experiences, including distinguishing between intra- and interpersonal demands and the value of doing so, lead to further controls. The process of career-long learning and intentional, reasoned awareness of one's observed or personal work experiences is reflective of interpreting as a practice profession.

CONCLUSION

Educators in and outside of the interpreting profession praise the value of experiential learning opportunities. While scholars agree that these educational processes improve students' learning of practice realities (Palmer,

1998; McKeachie, 1999; Fogarty, 1997; Frost 1996), Mercer (2000) and McKeachie (1999) warn educators to close the educational loop by overtly connecting students' experiences with relevant, practical applications to work. Additionally, McKeachie (1999) suggests that an effective practice schema will maximize the benefits of experiential learning. Once a schema is created to scaffold or cohesively organize the learning experiences, the process of articulating and analyzing the most salient aspects of the experiential data is a critical next step (Mercer, 2000). Palmer (1998) encourages educators to enhance this process by creating "knowers"—by activating students' existing knowledge and experience of a subject even if their knowledge is limited to just one experiential activity. Mercer (2000) reminds us that "interthinking" among group members allows for a level of understanding that cannot occur through self-reflection alone.

Here we have provided several examples of how the theoretical construct of DC-S (Dean & Pollard, 2011; Dean et al., 2004) can be employed to "close the educational loop" by making experiential learning opportunities overtly relevant to interpreting practice realities: "How will this impact your work (demands), and, in light of that, what will be needed from you as an interpreter (controls)?" By merely using the constructs of EIPI demands and controls, students are able to identify and activate information collected during an experiential learning event. From these reported data, educators can ensure the accurate articulation of interpreting demands, highlight practice relevancy, and guide student discussions about available and necessary controls. Additionally, the collection of multiple students' experiences and the analyses or interthinking that follows allow for exponentially greater and richer exposure to the pragmatics of interpreting practice.

REFERENCES

Bently-Sassaman, J. (2009). The experiential learning theory and interpreter education. *International Journal of Interpreter Education, 1,* 62–67. Conference of Interpreter Trainers.

Cesna, M., & Mosier, K. (2005). Using a prediction paradigm to compare levels of expertise and decision making among critical care nurses. In H. Montgomery, R. Lipshitz, & B. Brehmer (Eds.), *How professionals make decisions* (pp. 107–17). Mahwah, NJ: Erlbaum.

Cottone, R. R., & Claus, R. E. (2000). Ethical decision-making models: A review of the literature. *Journal of Counseling and Development, 78,* 275–83.

Dean, R. K. (2009). Challenges in interpreting addressed by demand-control schema analysis. In B. E. Cartwright (Ed.), *Encounters with reality: 1,001 interpreter scenarios* (2nd ed.) (pp. 307–17). Silver Spring, MD: RID Press.

Dean, R. K., Davis, J., Barnett, H., Graham, L. E., Hammond, L., & Hinchey, K. (2003, January). Training medically qualified interpreters: New approaches, new applications, promising results. *VIEWS, 20*(1), 10–12.

Dean, R. K., & Pollard, R. Q. (2001). Application of demand-control theory to sign language interpreting: Implications for stress and interpreter training. *Journal of Deaf Studies and Deaf Education, 6*(1), 1–14.

Dean, R. K., & Pollard, R. Q. (2004). A practice-profession model of ethical reasoning. *VIEWS, 21*(9) (October), 1, 28–29.

Dean, R. K., & Pollard, R. Q. (2005). Consumers and service effectiveness in interpreting work: A practice profession perspective. In M. Marschark, R. Peterson, & E. Winston (Eds.), *Interpreting and interpreter education: Directions for research and practice.* New York: Oxford University Press.

Dean, R. K., & Pollard, R. Q. (2006). From best practice to best practice process: Shifting ethical thinking and teaching. In E. M. Maroney (Ed.), *A new chapter in interpreter education: Accreditation, research, and technology.* Proceedings of the 16th National Convention of the Conference of Interpreter Trainers (CIT) (pp. 259–82). Monmouth, OR: CIT.

Dean, R. K., & Pollard, R. Q. (2008a). Evolution and current status of the DC-S body of work. In R. Q Pollard and R. K. Dean (Eds.), *Applications of demand-control schema in interpreter education* (pp. 1–6). Proceedings of the August 3, 2007, preconference meeting at the national convention of the Registry of Interpreters for the Deaf. Rochester, NY: University of Rochester.

Dean, R. K., & Pollard, R. Q. (2008b). "Just when I figured out the answers, someone changed the questions": Thoughts about the interview portion of the NIC. *VIEWS, 25*(8) (October), 21–22.

Dean, R. K., & Pollard, R. Q. (2009a). Deontological and teleological ethics. *Newsli: Magazine for the Association of Sign Language Interpreters for England, Wales, and Northern Ireland, 67* (January), 3–5.

Dean, R. K., & Pollard, R. Q. (2009b). Effectiveness of observation-supervision training in community mental health interpreting settings. *REDIT E-journal on the Didactics of Translation and Interpreting, 3,* 1–17.

Dean, R. K., & Pollard, R. Q. (2009c). "I don't think we're supposed to be talking about this": Case conferencing and supervision for interpreters. *VIEWS, 26* (Fall), 28–30.

Dean, R. K., & Pollard, R. Q. (2011). Context-based ethical reasoning in interpreting: A demand-control schema perspective. *Interpreter and Translator Trainer, 5*(1), 155–82.

Dean, R. K., Pollard, R. Q, Davis, J., Griffin, M., LaCava, C., Morrison, B., Parmir, J., Smith, A., Storme, S., & Suback, L. (2004). The demand-control schema: Effective curricular implementation. In E. M. Maroney (Ed.), *CIT: Still shining after 25 years: Proceedings of the 15th National Convention of the Conference of Interpreter Trainers* (pp. 145–61). Monmouth, OR: CIT.

Dean, R. K., Pollard, R. Q, & English, M. A. (2004). Observation-supervision in mental health interpreter training. In E. M. Maroney (Ed.), *CIT: Still shining after 25 years: Proceedings of the 15th National Convention of the Conference of Interpreter Trainers* (pp. 55–75). Monmouth, OR: CIT.

Dean, R. K., Pollard, R. Q, & Samar V. J. (2010). RID research grant underscores occupational health risks: VRS and K–12 settings most concerning. *VIEWS*, 27(1) (Winter), 41–43.

Feasey, D. (2002). *Good practice in supervision with psychotherapists and counselors: The relational approach.* London: WhurrFilms for the Humanities and Sciences (Producer). (1994). *Diagnosis according to the DSM-IV* [Motion picture]. (Distributed by Program Development Associates, 5620 Business Ave., Suite B, Cicero, NY 13039)

Fogarty, R. (1997). *Problem-based learning and other curriculum models for the multiple intelligences classroom.* Arlington Heights, IL: IRI/SkyLight Training and Publishing.

Frost, M. (1996). An analysis of the scope and value of problem-based learning in the education of health care professionals [Review]. *Journal of Advanced Nursing*, 24(5), 1047–53.

Kennedy, N. S., & Kennedy, D. (2010). Between chaos and entropy: Community of inquiry from a systems perspective. *Complicity: An International Journal of Complexity and Education*, 7(2), 1–15.

Kolb, D. A. (1984). *Experiential learning: Experience as the source of learning and development.* Englewood Cliffs, NJ: Prentice-Hall.

Mandelbaum, M. (1955). *The phenomenology of moral experience.* Glencoe, IL: Free Press.

McKeachie, W. J. (1999). *McKeachie's teaching tips: Strategies, research, and theory for college and university teachers.* Boston: Houghton Mifflin.

Mercer, N. (2000). *Words and minds: How we use language to think together.* London: Routledge.

Metzger, M. (1999). *Sign language interpreting: Deconstructing the myth of neutrality.* Washington, DC: Gallaudet University Press.

Monikowski, C., & Peterson, R. (2005). Service learning in interpreting education: Living and learning. In M. Marschark, R. Peterson, & E. Winston (Eds.), *Interpreting and interpreter education: Directions for research and practice.* New York: Oxford University Press.

Namy, C. (1977). Reflections on the training of simultaneous interpreters: A metalinguistic approach. In D. Gerver & H. W. Sinaiko (Eds.), *Language interpreting and communication* (pp. 25–33). New York: Plenum.

Niebuhr, H. R. (1963). *The responsible self: An essay in Christian moral philosophy.* Louisville: Westminster John Knox Press.

Palmer, P. J. (1998). *The courage to teach.* San Francisco: Jossey-Bass.

Pedersen, D. D. (2005). *Psych notes: Clinical pocket guide.* Philadelphia: Davis.

Pollard, R. Q, & Dean, R. K. (Eds.) (2008). *Applications of demand-control schema in interpreter education.* Proceedings of the August 3, 2007, preconference meeting at the national convention of the Registry of Interpreters for the Deaf. Rochester, NY: University of Rochester.

Turner, G. H. (2005). Toward real interpreting. In M. Marschark, R. Peterson, & E. Winston (Eds.), *Interpreting and interpreter education: Directions for research and practice* (pp. 29–56). New York: Oxford University Press.

Winston, E. A. (2005). Designing a curriculum for American Sign Language/ English interpreting educators. In M. Marschark, R. Peterson, & E. Winston (Eds.), *Interpreting and interpreter education: Directions for research and practice* (pp. 208–34). New York: Oxford University Press.

APPENDIX

Demand Control Schema (DCS) Example

Setting/Environment:				Date:
Goal of the Environment: (ALWAYS consider as concurrent demand)				
Environmental Demands Physical surroundings	**Pre-Assignment Controls**			**Assignment Controls**
Personnel/clientele Terminology	**Interpersonal Demands**	**Paralinguistic Demands**	**Intrapersonal Demands**	
Post-Assignment Controls				

Based on the Demand Control Schema Theory of Interpreting by R. Dean and R. Pollard, University of Rochester, New York. Graphic by L. Zinsky   rev. 8/10

KAREN BONTEMPO AND
KAREN MALCOLM

An Ounce of Prevention
Is Worth a Pound of Cure

Educating Interpreters about the Risk of
Vicarious Trauma in Healthcare Settings

INTERPRETERS WORKING in healthcare situations often must manage the
transfer of information under difficult circumstances. The content of the
message may be highly emotional or primarily negative, or one or more of
the parties in the interpreted encounter may be extremely vulnerable or in
a debilitated psychological or physical state. Such circumstances particularly
ring true in the healthcare context. In these cases, an interpreter's repeated
exposure to traumatic information and the traumatized states of others
can lead to a significant accumulation of occupational stress. For the well-
being of interpreters working in health care, employers, practitioners, and
educators in the field must develop an understanding of the potential for
the vicarious traumatization of healthcare interpreters.

VICARIOUS TRAUMA DEFINED

Stress is the state that people experience when they perceive that the demands being placed upon them exceed the internal or external supports
and coping resources they are able to mobilize. Stress is normal and even
healthy to an extent, and a certain amount of "facilitating stress" may in fact
enhance job performance. There is a difference, however, between what
might be described as typical job-related stress and the kind of occupational
stress in which the characteristics of the work environment or events related

to being in the workplace generate intense or cumulative levels of stress that lead to physical or psychological ill health. Some occupations are more likely than others to expose workers to hazardous work environments and circumstances (Cahill, 1996), and the outcome can cause workers to become vicariously traumatized as a result of these experiences.

Figley describes vicarious traumatization as "the natural behaviors and emotions that arise from knowing about a traumatizing event experienced by a significant other" (1995, p. xiv). Other terms that describe vicarious traumatization include *secondary traumatic stress, secondary traumatic stress disorder, traumatic countertransference, burnout, compassion stress, and compassion fatigue* (Moulden & Firestone, 2007; Salston & Figley, 2003). Although the definitions of these terms have subtle differences, this chapter uses the more common term, *vicarious trauma*, as coined by McCann and Pearlman (1990).

Symptoms suggesting vicarious trauma may include consistent headaches, sleepiness, feelings of dread prior to attending work assignments, intrusive thoughts, dreams, and flashbacks. Some people may experience numbness and exhaustion, while others experience hyperarousal, which manifests in behaviors such as hypervigilance, insomnia, or difficulty concentrating (Moulden & Firestone, 2007). Somatic complaints, stomach problems, irritability, loss of concentration, emotional withdrawal from family and friends, disassociation, and anxiety may also result (Cahill, 1996). Feelings of exhaustion can arise, and workers sometimes develop a cynical attitude as a coping strategy to distance themselves emotionally and mentally from the work (Bakker, Van Emmerik, & Van Riet, 2008). Vicarious traumatization is an acknowledged phenomenon in healthcare settings and among medical and allied healthcare personnel, and there is no reason to assume an interpreter would be immune to the same experience if working in the same environment.

As interpreters listen, comprehend, process, and reformulate the discourse of consumers as they talk about their trauma, they bear witness to their victimization (Harvey, 2001, 2003). Any traumatic experience told through an interpreter may test the interpreters' own beliefs about their safety or that of their children or other loved ones and may affect their willingness or ability to trust in others. However, the key issue is whether the transformation potentially produced by interpreting these traumatic experiences is of a cumulative and pervasive nature and how this affects the individual interpreter.

Much of the research on vicarious trauma has traditionally focused on people working in the front lines of caring and helping professions, people such as doctors, nurses, therapists, and crisis counselors. However, all workers who engage in empathic communication with trauma survivors are potentially vulnerable to cumulative changes in their own thinking, behavior, and emotions. More recent research on vicarious trauma includes a wider range of people who work with trauma survivors, including social workers, humanitarian workers, and the clergy. Research has recently started to document how and in what circumstances interpreters may be vicariously traumatized.

CHALLENGES OF HEALTHCARE SETTINGS FOR INTERPRETERS

Interpreting is an inherently stressful occupation (Kurz, 2003). Interpreters often lack the contextual information to make sense of an interaction; they have limited control over the workload and the pace of information delivery. Assignments that conflict with personal goals, values, or beliefs can cause intense stress, and the management of complex message transfer among parties can often be challenging. These factors are amplified in healthcare settings, where outcomes are often very serious and potentially life threatening. The individuals involved are frequently medically compromised and emotionally vulnerable and are likely to be experiencing high levels of physical and/or psychological distress.

Searching for a source-text equivalent in the target language can be very challenging for interpreters working in medical and mental health settings. Even a patient conversing with a healthcare provider in the *same* language may be confounded by the highly esoteric nature of the technical language used at times. Patients accessing a health service via an interpreter are dependent on the interpreter's capacity to comprehend and faithfully render such specialized jargon. This presents a degree of difficulty for the interpreter, particularly as signed languages historically have not had an opportunity to evolve within the domain of professional discourses due to the barriers to higher education and employment opportunities that have traditionally existed for Deaf people. This has resulted in lexical gaps for highly specific medical and mental health terminology in signed languages. Furthermore, interpreters are unlikely to have an intimate knowledge of healthcare jargon even in the spoken language of the interpreted encounter unless they have had a specialized education, and this lack of understanding potentially increases the risk of error in a high-stakes environment.

In addition to managing the language aspect and the pressures of transfer of meaning with fidelity in a healthcare setting, interpreters need to deal with environmental and interpersonal factors and their own intrapersonal demands (Dean & Pollard, 2001). Environmental factors might include working in a cramped doctors' office or waiting for several hours in a busy emergency room of a large hospital. Some sights, smells, and sounds may be unfamiliar and unpleasant. There may be occupational health and safety issues unique to the healthcare environment, such as the risk of exposure to communicable diseases in a hospital or threats to personal safety in a locked ward.

Interpersonal factors come into play when the interpreter engages with a wide range of personalities, some of whom may be traumatized or upset. Professionally detached healthcare practitioners may even come across as aloof or insensitive when exchanging information with distressed patients, creating cognitive dissonance for interpreters as they transfer messages between two parties who are exhibiting dramatically different affects.

On an intrapersonal level, interpreters may be dealing with assignments that conflict with personal goals, values, and beliefs. Individuals vary in their responses to stress, so what may be a traumatic interaction for one interpreter may not affect another. By the same token, what may not be traumatic to interpret one day may be problematic at another time if the interpreter is fatigued or overworked or has had a recent personal experience that is triggered by the content of the interpreted interaction.

Intense and traumatic interpreting experiences or the cumulative effect of such events may cause an interpreter to experience vicarious trauma. The first steps in managing the effects of such trauma are to recognize the potential for it to occur and to be mindful of ways to identify it. Given the potential for traumatic content to be conveyed in healthcare settings, interpreters should be properly prepared during interpreter education programs via training opportunities or through mentoring to help them understand the gravity of some of the challenging scenarios they may face in the healthcare context.

Interpreting traumatic content takes a toll. Interpreters may develop relationships with clients they work with, particularly if the medical care is of a prolonged nature. Interpreting for someone with terminal cancer from time of diagnosis through treatment efforts and during palliative care will be difficult. Such situations become particularly challenging in small Deaf communities in regional and remote areas, where the interpreting pool is limited. Interpreting during the medical evidence collection for a teen-age girl after a sexual assault or for the pediatric oncologist who must tell parents their child's brain tumor is highly aggressive or for the obstetrician who is advising an expectant mother of the loss in utero of a baby near full term are all realistic healthcare interpreting assignments that undoubtedly present significant challenges to the interpreter.

Given the potential for interpreters to experience vicarious trauma, it behooves the educators of interpreters to address the topic and prepare interpreters for the possibility of its occurrence. However, certain barriers impede both the understanding of vicarious trauma in the interpreting profession and the recognition of it by interpreter educators.

Dispelling the Myth of Neutrality

A significant barrier to developing an understanding of the impact of vicarious trauma on interpreters is the machine model metaphor for the role of the interpreter and the paradigm of thinking and behaviors this model precipitates. Many associations of spoken and signed language inter-preters around the world have adopted formal codes of ethics—guidelines for conduct and standards of behavior for professionals in the field. Such codes frequently include statements that implicitly—and at times quite explicitly—dehumanize interpreters and their role in the interaction. The intention of these types of statements is respect for the autonomy of con-sumers and the desire for interpreters to maintain impartiality and refrain from unduly influencing the outcome of interpreted events. In practice, however, such statements have led to the conceptualization of interpreters as machines or conduits who simply transfer meaning from one language and culture to another, with no impact on the communicated event and, consequently, with no impact on the interpreter as a person. The resulting misconception is that the impartiality is accompanied by a lack of reaction or feeling within the interpreter.

A number of studies in recent years have altered our understanding of the role that interpreters play and have fostered a growing acknowledgment in interpreting pedagogy and practice of the way in which an interpreter actively co-constructs meaning in interpreted interactions. Such studies have been instrumental in countering the traditional concept of interpreters as "machines." The seminal contributions of Wadensjö (1998), Metzger (1999), and Roy (2000) were the first to challenge the prevailing view of the interpreter as a conduit. Angelelli (2003) added to this body of work inasmuch as her findings reinforce the visibility of interpreters in interpreted events: "[I]nterpreters become visible when they do the following: explore answers, expand and summarize statements, broker comprehension and explain technical terms, bridge cultural gaps, express affect, and replace interlocutors" (2003, p. 24).

Angelelli also states that "another assumption is that the interpreter can temporarily block the self and all the behaviors that may result (automatically or voluntarily) as a consequence of being a social person who interacts with the other two parties" (2003, p. 3). The concept of "blocking the self" can be seen to relate to the machine model concept of interpreting and is evidently an untenable metaphor in reality. It is never possible to temporarily block the self despite the premise in interpreter education until recently that this is precisely what interpreter students needed to work toward achieving. Some interpreter educators may still hold students to this rhetoric despite the research and practice in the field.

A study by Gold Brunson and Lawrence (2002) of interpreters in mental health settings demonstrates that an interpreter's display of particular emotions influenced the participants in an interpreted interaction. Gold Brunson and Lawrence investigated the impact of interpreter and therapist mood and affective reactions on the therapeutic process. They established two mood conditions: despondent and neutral/slightly cheerful. They then created therapist/interpreter teams in which (i) both employed the same mood state; (ii) the therapist was despondent and the interpreter neutral/slightly cheerful; and (iii) the therapist was neutral/slightly cheerful and the interpreter despondent. Resulting responses from the Deaf participants in the study indicated less willingness to interact with the team in the future when both the therapist and interpreter were despondent and more willingness to interact when both were neutral/slightly cheerful. However, of particular interest is the reported increased willingness to interact when the therapist was despondent and the interpreter neutral/slightly cheerful and decreased willingness when the therapist was neutral/slightly cheerful and the interpreter despondent. This study provides evidence that the interpreter is not invisible to participants and that an interpreter's mood can impact interactions. It reasonably follows that the interpreter may also be affected by the moods and feelings of the other participants in an interaction.

Effective interpreting involves, in part, conveying the affect of a speaker. The ability to recognize and appropriately reflect affect requires empathy on the part of the interpreter in order to recognize others' emotions and feelings before being able to convey them. Given that in healthcare settings interpreters may encounter disclosures about abuse, violence, loss, pain, suffering, trauma, death, and grief, it is clear that interpreters are exposed to highly emotional content in this work context. In fact, they are not only exposed to it but are the means whereby these messages are expressed. The use of first person heightens this exposure: For example, rather than saying, "He grabbed her and pushed her down and then raped her," the interpreter says, "He grabbed me and pushed me down and raped me." The use of first-person voice in conveying such emotionally laden content potentially increases the interpreter's risk of experiencing vicarious trauma.

Recent findings by neuroscientists offer new insights for our understanding of empathy. Mirror neurons are a type of brain cell that responds equally when we perform an action and when we witness someone else performing the same activity (Winerman, 2005). Both producing and observing facial expressions activate the same regions of the brain, according to Iacoboni (2008), and neural activity takes place in the same region of the brain regardless of whether a person experiences pain or watches a loved one do so. In addition, Iacoboni reports that the same segment of the brain is activated whether participants smell something noxious or watch a video of someone smelling something noxious. Similarly, being lightly touched or watching someone be lightly touched also engages the same area of the brain. Iacoboni notes that we understand what others are feeling through mirroring. The existence of this involuntary and automatic neural mechanism further supports the argument that interpreters may be susceptible to triggers on an emotional or psychosomatic level from the content or ramifications of what they are interpreting.

All of this research points us away from conceptualizing the interpreter as a machine or conduit. The interpreter is not only a participant but is also empathically affected by the engagement of mirror neurons. The potential for emotional contagion leading to the manifestation of vicarious trauma is therefore a genuine risk for interpreters in the healthcare setting.

RESEARCH ON VICARIOUS TRAUMATIZATION OF INTERPRETERS

Not everyone who works with traumatic material develops vicarious trauma. Key to educating interpreters about the potential for vicarious trauma is understanding more about who may be most at risk and why. The literature provides a wide range of studies aimed at identifying the predictors of vicarious trauma in at-risk workers. Much of this body of scholarly work documents the experiences of frontline human service workers rather than those of interpreters. There are some exceptions, however.

Baistow (1999, cited in Pöchhacker, 2004) surveyed nearly 300 community interpreters in five European countries and found that more than half of the respondents reported "significant emotional stress arising from their work or the circumstances of their clients" (p. 173). Weigand (2000) indicates that posttraumatic stress disorder has been reported in interpreters associated with the hearings of the South African Truth and Reconciliation Commission. Westermeyer (1990) found that interpreters who share the same country of origin as the refugees for whom they interpret may be more vulnerable to psychiatric disorders. Røkenes (1992) found that 66% of the interpreter respondents in Norway "now and again" experienced emotional reactions to their work, rising to a level that made their work difficult, while Loutan, Farinelli, and Pampallona (1999) found that interpreters' feelings of distress and related symptoms increased in direct proportion to the number of sessions they had to interpret for victims of organized violence.

Adding credibility to the findings of these studies on interpreting and vicarious traumatization, Rousseau and Foxen (2010) argue that a clear link exists between empathy and the transmission of trauma. Given that interpreters effectively "coexperience" the information exchange in a traumatic interpreted event, an empathic response by the interpreter as a result of this transmission is natural and human. Harvey (2003) reports the following:

> [Interpreters are] in danger of empathically drowning . . . [T]ypically in this scenario, we become depleted of energy; we withdraw from family, friends, and colleagues, perhaps accentuated by the belief that no one could possibly understand our distress; in the case of interpreters, one may also withdraw because of misinterpreting the code of ethics as prohibiting the discussion of any thoughts and feelings concerning an anonymous Deaf consumer. We experience profound alterations of our identity, self-esteem, and worldview; our ability to manage strong feelings suffers; we are vulnerable to intrusive imagery and other post-traumatic stress symptomatology. In short, we are vicariously traumatized. (Harvey, 2003, p. 211)

Valero-Garcés (2005) makes reference to the work of Corsellis, noting that it may be possible to identify the specific features of interpreted situations that may present greater risk for interpreters. These include interpreting for clients with whom the interpreter feels a strong sense of identification or shares certain characteristics; interpreting in situations where violence, torture, tragedy, grief, or other highly negative or distressing content is discussed; interpreting for clients who are in a vulnerable or deteriorated physical or psychological state; and interpreting in emotionally difficult circumstances in which there is the impossibility of direct help on the part of the interpreter and a sense of helplessness is pervasive for the interpreter post assignment.

The interpreted event itself is not the only determinant in developing vicarious trauma. A great deal depends on the individuals' response and reaction to an event or series of traumatic exposures, and some people are naturally more resilient than others. In addition, the potential for vicarious trauma is mitigated to an extent by "compassion satisfaction"—the rewards that outweigh the negative psychological reactions to stressful work and the overall sense of enjoyment one draws from performing one's job. However, a compassionate nature also presents a potential hazard for interpreters if they overidentify with the people they interpret for and the situations they are in. Too much empathy places interpreters in a position of risk (Harvey, 2003). Interpreter educators should flag these research findings and discuss the role of empathy with interpreting students to prepare them for their work in the healthcare sector, thereby increasing their awareness of any personal susceptibilities.

PERSONALITY AND COPING

The impact of personality on coping is important and is well documented in relation to occupational stress, job strain, and traumatic reactions (Alarcon, Eschleman, & Bowling, 2009; Moulden & Firestone, 2007). People demonstrate dispositional tendencies in responding to trauma: For example, persons high in agreeableness or extraversion may be more skilled (and therefore more likely to be successful) in obtaining social support/peer support as a coping strategy. High levels of neuroticism and introversion, on the other hand, are predictive of the development of stress disorders (Gil & Capsi, 2006). Individuals who are likely to experience job burnout are highly empathic and idealistic in their beliefs about how they can help others (Salston & Figley, 2003). So, an employer who makes changes to job design, introduces workplace supports, and attempts to mitigate job stressors through various strategies and organizational interventions may still be faced with individuals who are more prone to vicarious trauma largely as a result of their personality and their limited range and efficacy of coping resources.

In regard to coping, neuroticism in particular seems to be a personality dimension of interest. A large-scale meta-analysis of research studies on personality and coping by Connor-Smith and Flachsbart (2007) found that traits of neuroticism, such as wishful thinking, withdrawal, and other negative emotion–based coping methods, predict poor coping strategies. Bozionelos (2004) reports that individuals who score high on neuroticism measures often have poor self-confidence, are more emotionally reactive, become anxious more rapidly, and are more vulnerable to stress. On the other hand, individuals who score low in neuroticism tend to be more emotionally stable and calm, display a more positive outlook on life, have better coping strategies, and are less reactive to stress. Neuroticism is closely linked to trait anxiety and can be described and measured on some personality tests as "negative affectivity"—an enduring tendency to experience negative mood and emotion (Watson & Clark, 1984).

A study by O'Brien, Terry, & Jimmieson (2008) reports that, when presented with high-demand tasks with low behavioral controls, people with high negative affectivity were more likely to use negative and often emotion-based coping strategies such as self-blame and later reported lower levels of task and job satisfaction. O'Brien et al. also report that people high in negative affectivity are particularly responsive to the amount of personal control they have in their work environment and can be very reactive to negative features of the environment. Negative affectivity is linked with disengagement as a coping strategy and less flexibility in coping in various situations (Lee-Baggley, Preece, & DeLongis, 2005) and is a potent predictor of high levels of occupational stress and strain (Mak & Mueller, 2000).

Bontempo and Napier (2011) investigated negative affectivity in Auslan (Australian Sign Language)/English interpreters in a study of factors that might be predictive of performance as an interpreter. The study, which examined 110 interpreters, consisted of a detailed self-report questionnaire identifying skills gaps, ratings of interpreter competence, and a series of personality measures. Among the personality inventories, participants completed the Positive and Negative Affect Schedule (PANAS) developed by Watson, Clark, and Tellegen (1988). This tool demonstrates high levels of internal consistency and stability and is widely considered a reliable, valid, and efficient means of measuring dimensions of positive and negative affectivity. It correlates highly with other tools that measure similar constructs (for example, the negative affectivity items on the PANAS correlate well with the Beck Depression Inventory). The 10-item version (for each—positive affectivity and negative affectivity) of the PANAS was administered in the survey.

Results indicate that negative affectivity is a significant predictor of interpreter competence: That is, respondents with high levels of negative affectivity reported lower levels of competence as an interpreter. The self-perceived competence rating was validated by a trend in accreditation level (interpreting qualification held): More competent and highly accredited interpreters showed lower levels of negative affectivity and vice versa.

Bontempo and Napier's findings are further reinforced by data reported by Bontempo (2010) in a separate study of interpreter disposition. Survey responses collected from 205 Auslan/English interpreter participants in Australia examined the "big five" of personality (openness to experience;

conscientiousness; extraversion; agreeableness; and neuroticism) using scales drawn from the IPIP (International Personality Item Pool), as well as the psychological constructs of perfectionism (IPIP scale) and self-esteem (measured by the Rosenberg self-esteem scale).

Self-esteem and conscientiousness proved to be significant predictors of self-perceived competence as an interpreter. Level of competence also correlated with level of accreditation; that is, higher levels of self-perceived competence were associated with higher levels of interpreter accreditation. Low self-esteem and high negative affectivity are closely related, reconfirming the strength of these particular personality variables as important inasmuch as they impact interpreter competence. In addition to affecting one's competence as a practitioner, fragile self-esteem and affective instability may also make less competent interpreters more susceptible to vicarious trauma, given the link between certain personality traits and coping.

Key to the effective management of traumatic exposure in an occupational context are the coping strategies one uses to deal with stressors. These may be classified as *engagement* or *active* coping (positive) strategies and *disengagement* or *avoidant* coping (negative) strategies. As well as the highlighted links between personality and coping, differences in age, experience, gender, and cognitive ability may also affect the way a person responds to a stressful work environment. The type and the severity of the stressor affect one's capacity for coping, and the impact of coping changes over time: Responses that are useful for an individual one day may not always be suitable the next. It is therefore important for individuals to have a range of coping strategies to draw upon when needed.

NEGATIVE COPING STRATEGIES

Unfortunately, negative coping strategies are often the first line of response when an individual experiences vicarious trauma. Overuse of alcohol and drugs and overwork as coping strategies are largely acceptable in the Western world. Isolating oneself, denial, and avoidance are other common coping strategies that ultimately leave the trauma unresolved. Additional negative coping strategies include trivializing the situation or inappropriately blaming oneself or others. Figure 1 depicts a range of possible negative coping strategies that may be adopted, intentionally or unintentionally,

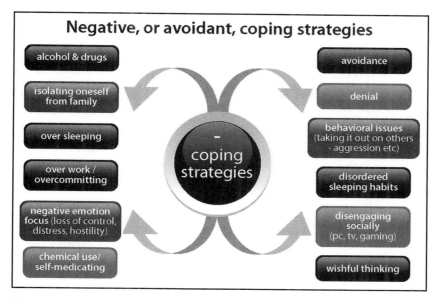

Figure 1. Negative coping strategies.

by an individual experiencing significant occupational stress or vicarious traumatization.

It is important to note that improving one's personal coping strategies from negative or avoidant methods to more positive coping mechanisms may not always effect significant change for individuals if an employer does not address the work environment and conditions that put workers at risk of traumatization. Changes made within workplaces, booking agencies, and interpreter education programs can more effectively scaffold and support individuals if undertaken in combination with interventions that aim to increase the range of positive personal coping skills of people in hazardous occupations (Cahill, 1996).

Positive Coping Strategies

Responding to traumatic material or circumstances by feeling bad and by experiencing negative emotions is a normal response for a healthy human being. Since this response is normal, it would benefit interpreter educators to prepare students for this normal emotional response and assist them in identifying positive, action-oriented coping strategies rather than defaulting to the negative strategies highlighted in Figure 1. Moulden and Firestone (2007) report that the strongest predictor of whether therapists experienced vicarious trauma is their use of negative or positive coping strategies. Some of the coping strategies operate at an individual level, some at an organizational level, and many can be raised for discussion in education programs for interpreters.

Figure 2 highlights a number of positive coping strategies that could be employed to reduce the impact of exposure to traumatic material in the course of interpreting work.

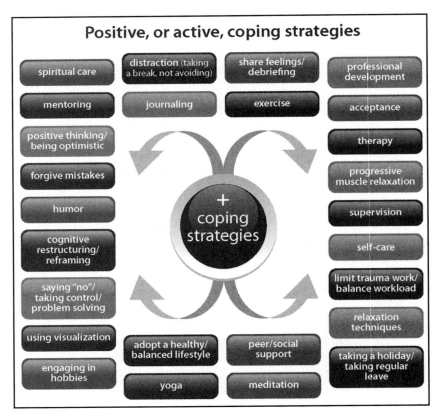

Figure 2. Positive coping strategies.

Many of the positive coping strategies outlined in Figure 2 could be teased out further. For example, the self-care component is very broad and could include a wide range of diversions ranging from recreational activities (watching a movie or attending a concert), spiritual practices (attending religious services, belonging to a spiritual group), physical activities (having monthly massages, doing some gardening), and so forth. Where appropriate, such pursuits might also allow the individual to connect/reconnect with people.

Nurturing oneself should be a priority rather than a luxury that is squeezed into a busy schedule. Understandably, it is hard for interpreters to take time out for themselves, especially if working on a piecemeal basis or as a freelance interpreter to earn a casual income. Nonetheless, it is a necessity to take the time to "check in" with oneself on a daily basis even if it is only for a short time. As Salston and Figley (2003) note, we need to "balance caring for others with caring for ourselves" (p. 173). Having hobbies, activities, interests, and a life outside of interpreting is important. Developing stress buffers and self-protection/self-healing strategies helps one to manage occupational stress and responses to trauma. Educators and employers should encourage students or employees to build a self-care plan that takes into account regulating and caring for the following:

1. Physical health (diet, sleep, and exercise are important)
2. Emotional health (being human and acknowledging normal human reactions to traumatic material)
3. Social needs (family and friends are critical)
4. Spiritual needs (a belief system about the world helps)
5. Financial needs (determining how much is needed vs. how much is wanted helps one say "no" to work if necessary) (Bontempo & van Loggerenberg, 2010)

Murphy's (1996) meta-analysis of stress management interventions in the workplace found that, as a single technique, meditation provided the most positive and consistent results in terms of an intervention. However, combining interventions (for example, muscle relaxation plus cognitive reframing) were far more effective at reducing occupational stress than applying any single technique alone.

As a general principle, specific interventions and coping strategies need to match the problem and the outcomes targeted for change, and strategies that are not found beneficial need to be changed. One's natural resilience can be scaffolded and enhanced by engaging in positive coping strategies. Optimism has proven important in the coping literature (Carver & Connor-Smith, 2010), and cognitive restructuring and figuring out ways to see challenging circumstances and difficult situations in a more positive light have also proven useful strategies adopted by traumatized workers (Schauben & Frazier, 1995).

Interpreting-Specific Coping Strategies

As well as the positive coping strategies outlined here, interpreters may be able to make use of job-specific strategies, such as drafting a discourse map to help prepare for an interpreting assignment that may be challenging or stressful (Napier, McKee, & Goswell, 2010). To help mentally prepare for potentially emotionally difficult material, the interpreter can think through some of the demands of the setting and interaction in advance of the job.

Journaling and reflecting on the assignment afterward might also prove helpful to the individual interpreter as a method of coping postassignment. Keeping a stress journal is another alternative—logging the situations that may generate stress or act as triggers and recording how the stressor was managed on that occasion. Some strategies that may also work and will maintain confidentiality include sending yourself an email describing your feelings about the traumatic interpreted event (i.e., an email that is never sent to anyone else) and drawing, scribbling, or jotting notes about any frustrations in a small personal notepad to offload the thoughts from the head to the page—the notes could then be burned, torn up, or shredded.

Some interpreters may practice visualization of some kind to separate oneself from the traumatic content of the day. An example may be visualizing the front door of one's home as a shower, where an imaginary row of water droplets falling from above as one walks through the door and into the home effectively cleanses the interpreter and washes away the dirty parts of the day.

Allowing time to transition between work and home can be helpful. This may mean using time in the car or on the train on the way home to "dump" the information of the day and to adjust to home life. Alternatively, the interpreter might allocate a certain period of time to ruminate about an assignment; when the time expires, the interpreter—by a self-agreement—cognitively moves on. An interpreter might engage in a ritual upon arriving home (such as changing clothes—out of the interpreting garb and into personal, at-home clothing—or switching handbags from the work bag to the personal bag before going out after work) or go for a jog. Such "transition" activities can serve as on/off switches for separating and compartmentalizing parts of the day and help psychologically shift the individual into different modes as needed.

Ensuring that interpreters do not take on more work than is healthy and spacing out challenging clients and assignments can be a useful coping strategy. Similarly, developing relationships with coworkers, mentors, educators, employers, and so on can be a very important coping mechanism. Attending professional development seminars and other training with colleagues cannot be underestimated—the better resourced workers are, the more effectively they can do their job. Becoming a member of the local professional interpreting association is also important in terms of developing support networks.

ORGANIZATIONAL STRATEGIES

Organizations can help their interpreting staff avoid vicarious trauma in a variety of ways and address it if they do become affected. These organization-based strategies should be raised with interpreting students so that they can advocate for their needs if working in an organization that has not adopted these practices. Good coping strategies on a personal level will not be sufficient protection for interpreters if organizations are remiss in managing deficiencies in their work practices and working conditions.

As a basic protective strategy, organizations should ensure that not just one individual is doing all of the trauma work. The primary predictor of experiencing vicarious trauma is one's *exposure to the trauma of others*. If employers ensure safe working conditions for employees, such as distributing workload in order to limit the traumatic exposure of any one worker, they can minimize the effects of vicarious trauma. The organization needs to be responsive to the needs of an employee who reports becoming too affected and ensure that the interpreter's workload changes. Organizations should offer training and professional development opportunities for interpreters specifically on dealing with emotionally challenging material. These activities could focus on areas such as stress reduction and developing resilience.

Novice interpreters coming into organizations could be allocated a "buddy" to act as a mentor of sorts during the initial period of service. New interpreters should be able to contact this buddy for support and advice and should be encouraged to do so in particular if and when they are exposed to traumatic material.

Debriefing is an organizational strategy that could be formalized for interpreters; however, it is also a support mechanism that can occur informally. Interpreters may access debriefing services via their employer, perhaps from their manager or a peer on staff in the organization, or more formally via external sources such as psychologists or counselors through the employee assistance program (EAP), if applicable. Informally, interpreters may debrief with their team interpreter, an interpreting colleague, a mentor, a knowledgeable friend, or simply someone who is a good listener within their network of social supports. Interpreting students should be advised that the code of ethics does not prevent the interpreter from speaking about deidentified challenging aspects of a traumatic assignment. Debriefing should be optional for interpreters—not compulsory—but certainly should be made available. The efficacy of compulsory and immediate critical incident debriefing has been questioned in recent years (van Emmerik et al. 2002; Gist and Devilly 2002), so, when possible, it should be left to interpreters as professionals to seek out debriefing if needed rather than forcing it upon them. Nonetheless, contact from a manager after an interpreter has been sent to a potentially traumatic setting would demonstrate support for the employee and open the door for debriefing, if desired.

EAPs are becoming increasingly commonplace in organizations. They are corporate counseling agencies that contract with an organization to provide psychological support services to the organization's employees and their immediate family members. In addition to counseling, EAPs often provide telephone advice and professional development courses for staff on topics such as stress management and conflict resolution. An EAP may be able to provide interpreting employees with training on vicarious trauma.

Clinical supervision is another way that organizations can assist employees working in challenging environments or with traumatic material. Supervision is clearly identified as a moderator of job burnout in the helping professions (Salston & Figley, 2003). Dean, Pollard, and English (2004) note the importance of supervision in the use of an observation-supervision model in preparing interpreters to work in mental health settings. They note that supervision is not intended to be a punitive process but rather a process of discussion among professionals with an aim to improving the effectiveness of their work. Moreover, they report that "seeking supervision on complex cases, ethical issues, etc., is a fundamental and common practice that all mental health professionals engage in" (p. 66). These discussions take place within a context of confidentiality and are always mindful of the purpose for discussion, which is the betterment of service. The use of supervision may afford interpreters an opportunity to address challenges in their interpreting work, some of which could potentially be the root cause of vicarious trauma.

Education and Training Perspective

It should be evident by now that education programs for interpreters need to address the issue of vicarious trauma with students. Students need to understand that interpreters are affected to varying degrees by what they interpret and that interpreters may vicariously experience traumatization as a result. Whether information is provided to students in the form of a lecture series, workshops, or a module of study during an interpreting program, it is important to learn about situations of risk and the importance of strategizing in advance about how to minimize traumatic stress in work settings.

Suggestions on integrating a trauma curriculum into a program of study are outlined in Gere, Dass-Brailsford, and Tsoi Hoshmand (2009), and although based on a counseling program of study, some of the guidelines they outline could prove useful when adapted for interpreter education program purposes. In addition, Cunningham (2004) provides a broad range of suggestions for teaching social workers about trauma, the premises of which could be easily adopted into interpreting pedagogy. Incorporating trait awareness into interpreter training and developing skills such as self-confidence, positive coping strategies, assertiveness, and resilience would also most certainly be useful, given the research evidence pointing to these aspects of personality as relevant for reducing stress and maintaining effective occupational performance. Teaching interpreting students and accredited practitioners to better manage anxiety may also be conducive to improving overall interpreting performance, further to the findings of Bontempo and Napier (2011).

Educators may be able to address traumatic content and discuss the impact on the interpreter by conducting role plays based on stimulus pieces, such as scenarios written to generate fear, anxiety, or sadness in the interpreting student. Suitable role-play material that interpreting students may find emotionally challenging may be found in training materials for frontline human service workers, such as social workers, and many online training resources are aimed at increasing knowledge and skills around the issue of vicarious trauma.[1] Learning opportunities via role plays based on realistic scenarios written around a threat or crisis need to be carefully managed, however, as strong emotional reactions to traumatic content in course material can in itself provoke vicarious trauma in some circumstances. For this reason, establishing ground rules and boundaries in the classroom is critical before setting up role-play experiences for students. Despite the need to effectively manage the learning environment, the contained and controlled classroom space is certainly a better place for initial exposure to such concepts and emotional reactions and for discussing coping strategies.

Examples of safeguards include obtaining input and guidelines from the students themselves regarding the material they are willing to explore and any topics they consider too challenging to address in class. Helping students understand that negative reactions to challenging material are normal is important in early discussions. It may be useful to provide a list in advance of dates on which certain content will be covered in class so that students are forewarned and can prepare themselves or, in some circumstances, even opt not to attend a particular class for personal reasons. These approaches to safeguarding students' interests may also help to nurture a trusting relationship between students and teacher, strengthening the students' perception of support networks available to them upon graduation from an interpreter education program.

As a less intimidating alternative to role plays or perhaps as a complementary activity, vignettes of traumatic interpreting assignments and of case studies of crisis situations presented to students provide opportunities for collaborative, problem-based learning through discussion in the classroom. Realistic vignettes can provide rich and authentic opportunities for students to engage with emotionally charged material with instructor

---

1. Refer to http://www.proqol.org/Links.html.

support and guidance. Journal writing that reflects on the vignettes and case studies can also be encouraged, as sometimes students are willing to write and share with the teacher what they are not eager to reveal in a class setting. This can be powerful for students also in recognizing their own responses to stressful scenarios and perhaps to traumatic realities in their own lives by helping them consider how they plan to manage such personal material in a professional setting.

Interpreter education programs should permit opportunity for discussion in class on how to distinguish professional relationships from friendships in the Deaf community, and explore with students how they might create appropriate boundaries and clearly delineate aspects of their professional identity as interpreters from their personal identity as friends or relatives of Deaf community members. Students with their own personal experiences of oppression, victimization, or abuse may need specific referrals to professional counselors to deal with these experiences to minimize the impact of their own emotional baggage on the way they interact with the Deaf community, their interpreting peers, and the hearing people they may come across in the course of their work.

In the learning environment, the peer group is of great importance. If students learn to trust one another in the classroom, they are more likely to feel connected to their peers and to more readily trust other interpreters once they graduate. Having a supportive peer network is a significant positive coping strategy, so educators who take the time to build cooperative classrooms that function collaboratively rather than competitively will create long-term benefits for students. Similarly, entering into a constructive mentoring relationship can provide a novice interpreter and a more experienced one with a support network in which the parties are concerned for each other's personal well-being and professional growth, so students should be encouraged to seek out positive mentoring relationships upon graduation.

Formal learning about grief, loss, suicide, depression, neglect, mental health, abuse, and other emotionally difficult topics, when integrated into interpreter education programs, would help mitigate to an extent the powerful impact of these topics in a real crisis. Information is power, and effective coping in a traumatic situation will be enhanced by having a range of problem-solving strategies, practical information about what to expect, and tangible support networks.

According to website information, the Deaf Studies and Interpreting program at Ohio University, which confers an AAS degree, includes a module in interpreting in critical and traumatic situations. The course outline indicates that it addresses "sexual abuse of Deaf children, including causes, incident rate, interviewing techniques, investigation problems, and involvement of law enforcement agencies, schools, hospitals, DARE, and crime prevention programs. Also discusses deaf people in disaster situations, emergency response centers, first responders, and problems of victimization of deaf in research projects."[2] This kind of formal preparation and information may greatly assist novice interpreters, upon graduation, in dealing with emotionally challenging situations of this nature. Yet, this program appears to be unique—an online search of a range of programs failed to turn up any others that made reference in such detail to a module on trauma interpreting.

The findings of Bontempo and Napier (2011) and Bontempo (2010) regarding the impact of negative affectivity and low self-esteem on interpreter competence and the link between these personality traits and vulnerability to stress and ineffective coping suggest that introducing positive coping strategies and resilience building into interpreter education course curricula would be useful. Teaching interpreting students and accredited practitioners to know themselves and to better understand their own disposition and their default coping styles may be constructive as well.

CONCLUSION

In the process of providing interpreting services to traumatized individuals, interpreters are exposed to material that may affect their own emotions, belief system, and worldview. It is normal for a human being to empathically engage with another person, particularly over traumatic material, and such engagement can be quite transformative in nature—in positive ways that may help the interpreter grow and learn from the experience or in ways that can be highly negative and debilitating to the interpreter. Key to the management of the experience is how these individuals recognize,

---

2. http://www.catalogs.ohio.edu/preview_program.php?catoid=19&poid=4315&returnto=973.

accept, and cope with their "humanness" and the potential for vicarious trauma. Unquestionably, the signed language interpreter is not immune to the effects of trauma exposure. All workers in healthcare settings deal with the impact of traumatic realities on a daily basis and develop a range of personal strategies to cope with the nature of their work. They have education and training systems that acknowledge the potential impact of trauma. They belong to organizational bodies that recognize the risk to workers, and they adapt work environments and implement interventions to mitigate the effects of severe occupational stress and critical incidents in the workplace. It is time for the interpreting profession to recognize the vulnerability of interpreters when working in traumatic settings or with emotionally challenging material and to respond appropriately.

Developing and applying good personal coping mechanisms and accessing effective organizational systems of support can ameliorate difficult working conditions for the interpreter, thereby reducing the risk of vicarious trauma. Interpreter educators can introduce teaching tools that make traumatic realities accessible in a safe learning environment. Authentic, controlled activities in the classroom will help students develop coping skills and strategies for dealing with occupational stress and cumulative trauma experiences, better equipping them for future interpreting work in healthcare settings as a result.

While wholesale change throughout the profession—in education programs, within interpreting organizations, and among practitioners—may be difficult to bring about at least in the short term, any incremental efforts to effect change and to acknowledge interpreters' human reactions to traumatic material will eventually take hold. Such interventions and preparations are the obligation of everyone involved in the field in order to protect signed language interpreters from the hazards of the work. Prevention is far better than a cure in the healthcare context; the adage also holds true for the vicarious traumatization of signed language interpreters.

Acknowledgments

We are grateful to Dr. Valerie van Loggerenberg, a psychologist in private practice in Western Australia who is familiar with the work of interpreters, for contributing several ideas on positive coping strategies for this chapter.

REFERENCES

Alarcon, G., Eschleman, K. J., and Bowling, N. A. (2009). Relationships between personality variables and burnout: A meta-analysis. *Work and Stress, 23*(3): 244–63.

Angelelli, C. (2003). The visible co-participant: The interpreter's role in doctor-patient encounters. In M. Metzger, S. Collins, V. Dively, and R. Shaw (Eds.), *From topic boundaries to omission: New research on interpretation* (pp. 3–26). Washington, DC: Gallaudet University Press.

Bakker, A. B., Van Emmerik, H., & Van Riet, P. (2008). How job demands, resources, and burnout predict objective performance: A constructive replication. *Anxiety, Stress, and Coping, 21*(3): 308–24.

Bontempo, Karen. (2010). *The art of connecting: Exploring the role of personality in interpreter education and practice.* Paper presented at the Conference of Interpreter Trainers, San Antonio, TX, October 27–30.

Bontempo, K., & Napier, J. (2011). Evaluating emotional stability as a predictor of interpreter competence and aptitude for interpreting. In M. Shlesinger & F. Pöchhacker (Eds.), *Aptitude for Interpreting: Special Issue of Interpreting, 13*(1), 85–105.

Bontempo, K., & van Loggerenberg, V. (2010). *Managing occupational stress: Coping strategies for interpreters.* Paper presented at the SDP Online Conference, February 3–6.

Bozionelos, N. (2004). The relationship between disposition and career success: A British study. *Journal of Occupational and Organisational Psychology, 77*, 403–20.

Cahill, J. (1996). Psychosocial aspects of interventions in occupational safety and health. *American Journal of Industrial Medicine, 29*, 308–13.

Carver, C. S., & Connor-Smith, J. (2010). Personality and coping. *Annual Review of Psychology, 61*, 679–704.

Connor-Smith, J. K., & Flachsbart, C. (2007). Relations between personality and coping: A meta-analysis. *Journal of Personality and Social Psychology, 93*, 1080–1107.

Cunningham, M. (2004). Teaching social workers about trauma: Reducing the risks of vicarious traumatization in the classroom. *Journal of Social Work Education, 40*(2), 305.

Dean, R. K., & Pollard, R. Q. (2001). Application of demand-control theory to sign language interpreting: Implications for stress and interpreter training. *Journal of Deaf Studies and Deaf Education, 6*(1), 1–14.

Dean, R. K., Pollard, R. Q., & English, M. (2004). Observation and supervision in mental health interpreter training. In E. Maroney (Ed.), *CIT: Still shining after 25 years: Proceedings of the 15th National Conference* (pp. 55–75). Washington, DC: Conference of Interpreter Trainers.

Figley, C. R. (1995). *Compassion fatigue: Coping with secondary traumatic stress disorder in those who treat the traumatized.* New York: Brunner/Mazel.

Gere, S. H., Dass-Brailsford, P., & Tsoi Hoshmand, L. (2009). Issues in integrating trauma curriculum into a graduate counselling psychology program. *Asian Journal of Counselling, 16*(1), 67–88.

Gil, S., & Capsi, Y. (2006). Personality traits, coping style, and perceived threat as predictors of post-traumatic stress disorder after exposure to a terrorist attack: A prospective study. *Psychosomatic Medicine, 68*(6), 904–909.

Gist, R., & Devilly, G. J. (2002). Post-trauma debriefing: The road too frequently travelled. *Lancet, 360*, 741–42.

Gold Brunson, J., & Lawrence, P. S. (2002). Impact of sign language interpreter and therapist moods on deaf recipient mood. *Professional Psychology: Research and Practice, 33*(6): 576–80.

Harvey, M. (2001). Vicarious emotional trauma of interpreters: A clinical psychologist's perspective. *Journal of Interpretation*, 85–98.

Harvey, M. (2003). Shielding yourself from the perils of empathy: The case of sign language interpreters. *Journal of Deaf Studies and Deaf Education, 8*, 207–13.

Iacoboni, M. (2008). *Mirroring people: The new science of how we connect with others.* New York: Farrar, Strauss, Giroux.

Kurz, I. (2003). Physiological stress during simultaneous interpreting: A comparison of experts and novices. *Interpreters' Newsletter 12*, 51–67. Edizioni Università di Trieste (EUT).

Lee-Baggley, D., Preece, M., & DeLongis, A. (2005). Coping with interpersonal stress: Role of big five traits. *Journal of Personality, 73*(5), 1141–80.

Loutan, L., Farinelli, T., & Pampallona, S. (1999). Medical interpreters have feelings, too. *Sozial- und Präventivmedizin, 44*, 280–82.

Mak, A. S., & Mueller, J. (2000). Job security, coping resources, and personality dispositions in occupational strain. *Work and Stress, 14*, 312–28.

McCann, I. L., & Pearlman, L. A. (1990). Vicarious traumatization: A framework for understanding the psychological effects of working with victims. *Journal of Traumatic Stress, 3*(1), 131–49.

Metzger, M. (1999). *Sign language interpreting: Deconstructing the myth of neutrality.* Washington, DC: Gallaudet University Press.

Moulden, H. M., & Firestone, P. (2007). Vicarious traumatization: The impact on therapists who work with sexual offenders. *Trauma, Violence, and Abuse, 8*(1), 67–83.

Murphy, L. R. (1996). Stress management in work settings: A critical review of the health effects. *American Journal of Health Promotion, 11*(2), 112–35.

Napier, J., McKee, R., & Goswell, D. (2010). *Sign language interpreting: Theory and practice in Australia and New Zealand* (2nd ed.). Sydney: Federation Press.

O'Brien, A., Terry, D., & Jimmieson, N. L. (2008). Negative affectivity and responses to work stressors: An experimental study. *Anxiety, Stress, and Coping, 21*(1), 55–83.

Pöchhacker, F. (2004). *Introducing interpreting studies.* London: Routledge.

Røkenes, O. H. (1992). When the therapist needs an interpreter—what does the interpreter need? The role and the reactions of the interpreter in interpreting in psychological treatment. *Linjer, 2*(2), 3–7.

Rousseau, C., & Foxen, P. (2010). "Look me in the eye": Empathy and the transmission of trauma in the refugee determination process. *Transcultural Psychiatry, 47*(1), 70–92.

Roy, C. (2000). *Interpreting as a discourse process.* New York: Oxford University Press.

Salston, M., & Figley, C. R. (2003). Secondary traumatic stress effects of working with survivors of criminal victimization. *Journal of Traumatic Stress, 16*(2), 167–74.

Schauben, L. J., & Frazier, P. A. (1995). Vicarious trauma: The effects on female counselors of working with sexual violence survivors. *Psychology of Women Quarterly, 19,* 49–64.

Valero-Garcés, C. (2005) Emotional and psychological effects on interpreters in public services—A critical factor to bear in mind. Translation Journal 9 (3). Retrieved from http://accurapid.com/journal/33ips.htm. Accessed September 12, 2010.

Van Emmerik, A. A. P., Kamphuis, J. H., Hulsbosch, A. M., & Emmelkamp, P. M. G. (2002). Single-session debriefing after psychological trauma: A meta-analysis. *Lancet, 360,* 766–71.

Wadensjö, C. (1998). *Interpreting as interaction.* New York: Addison Wesley Longman.

Watson, D., & Clark, L. A. (1984). Negative affectivity: The disposition to experience aversive emotional states. *Psychological Bulletin, 96,* 465–90.

Watson, D., Clark, L. A., & Tellegen, A. (1988). Development and validation of brief measures of positive and negative affect: The PANAS scales. *Journal of Personality and Social Psychology, 54*(6), 1063–70.

Weigand, C. (2000). Role of the interpreter in the healing of a nation: An emotional view. In R. Roberts, S. E. Carr, A. Dufour, & D. Abraham, (Eds.), *The critical link 2: Interpreters in the community.* Amsterdam: John Benjamins.

Westermeyer, J. (1990). Working with an interpreter in psychiatric assessment and treatment. *Journal of Nervous and Mental Disease, 178,* 745–49.

Winerman, L. (2005). The mind's mirror. *Monitor, 36*(9), 48.

DOUG BOWEN-BAILEY

Just What the Doctor Ordered?

Online Possibilities for Healthcare Interpreting Education

INTERPRETING IN healthcare settings is a multifaceted task requiring significant knowledge and skills. For educators, the challenge is to determine how to most effectively help interpreters acquire and develop the requisite competencies. While the field is responding to the challenge in many ways, the Internet is a significant tool for consideration. This chapter focuses on the potential role of online education and several principles for making that role effective.

Before considering online education, however, it is important to explain why it is needed and how it might be used. Given that we are looking at online education in the context of healthcare interpreting, consider the following analogy as an entry point to this issue.

Imagine a new patient coming in to meet with a general practitioner. After the nurse brings the patient to a room and asks some initial questions, the physician enters and asks a series of questions: "What brought you here today? What are your concerns? Where are you having difficulties?" These initial questions lead to further directions of inquiry, including a variety of tests and assessments. On the basis of this information, the physician makes a diagnosis and offers the patient some options for treatment.

This should be a familiar scene—a standard example of how doctors practice their craft, but I would like you to replace your image of the patient with the profession of sign language interpreters and the needs of the Deaf community. To some degree, this "appointment" happened between 2005 and 2010, during which time the National Consortium of Interpreter Education Centers (NCIEC) played the role of the general practitioner.

131

The NCIEC conducted a needs assessment with input from interpreters, as well as deaf, deaf-blind, and hard of hearing consumers, in order to determine what ails the interpreting community and the impact it has on consumers of interpreting services.

One of the "tests" was a needs assessment of deaf consumers of interpreting services. This two-phase process included an electronic survey and a series of interviews and focus groups. A significant finding was that quality interpreting in health care was the second highest priority for deaf consumers and the most difficult setting in which to obtain quality services (Cokely & Winston, 2009, p. 13).

For the interpreting profession, this finding has significant implications. If our goal is to meet the needs of the communities we serve, then a focus on interpreting in healthcare settings is obviously needed. For interpreter educators, the task is then to figure out how to treat this ailment. Just what should the doctor order?

Responding to the Diagnosis: Identifying the Demands of Interpreting and the Needs of Interpreters

Interpreting in healthcare settings is a multifaceted task requiring a wide variety of competencies. Through the development of a draft document on the required domains and competencies, the NCIEC has documented the many skills interpreters need in order to effectively function in these settings (NCIEC, 2008). For educators, the task then becomes how to help interpreters acquire and develop the requisite competencies. The development of the Internet, particularly with broadband connections, has made possible options for online education in this area.

To address the needs expressed by Deaf consumers, it is not realistic to expect all interpreter education programs across the country to focus on the specific demands of healthcare interpreting. In another context, interpreter educators have begun to raise questions about how it is possible to "infuse" focus on many specializations in a curriculum without having to worry about the dilution of the actual education (Peterson, 2010). The interpreter education program at St. Catherine University (formerly the College of St. Catherine) has the distinction of being one of only a few to offer a specialization in healthcare interpreting. Yet, one program located in a specific geographic location cannot be expected to meet the needs of a nation. Moreover, since its beginning focus on the healthcare setting, even the St. Catherine program has expanded its emphasis to prepare interpreters for work in a variety of settings.

In the face of these realities for interpreter education programs, online education presents the possibility of creating educational programs that can be delivered to interpreters interested in healthcare specialization regardless of their geographic location. In addition, the Internet enables online modules to be included as options within both interpreter education programs and continuing education programs for working interpreters who seek specialized skills for working in health care.

TREATMENT OPTIONS: A FRAMEWORK FOR EFFECTIVE ONLINE HEALTHCARE INTERPRETING EDUCATION

Because the Internet and digital video are relatively new and the changes in the technology are so rapid, there has been a great deal of experimentation with online approaches to healthcare interpreting education. In many respects, the profession is at the point of clinical trials—trying to determine what actually works. A variety of options exist, including webinars, lectures, full online courses with instructors, and independent study projects.

Evaluating all of these approaches is beyond the scope of this chapter. Rather, I here offer a perspective on the overall educational context in which online education is developing and present some principles for a framework in which to create effective educational options that truly respond to the needs identified in healthcare settings.

Online Education for Healthcare Specialization in the Age of CEUs

Any treatment option must recognize the context in which an ailment exists. It is also important for interpreter educators to consider the current context of interpreter education and professional development, particularly for interpreters who are already working in the field. While many factors affect the development of online education, this chapter focuses on two.

The first dynamic is the increasing recognition of the merits of specialization. Witter-Merithew and Nicodemus (2010) "argue for a proactive and intentional development of specialization areas within the interpreting profession" (p. 136). Specializations occur as any profession develops and are driven by a variety of factors, including legislative trends, market developments, consumers' needs and demographics, and practitioners' interests (p. 137–38). In relation to healthcare settings, these identified factors are quite relevant and supportive of the development of a specialization in health care.

Another dynamic for consideration is the way in which the need to earn continuing education units (CEUs) affects interpreters' professional development choices. The advent of RID's Certificate Maintenance Program (CMP) ushered in an important shift in the field of interpreting. In order to maintain certification, interpreters now must document their continuing education, thus promoting currency in our field and ongoing professional development. As the first unanimous vote in RID's history (Affiliate Chapter Relations Committee, 2006), it was a united statement of the priority of continuing education as a means of maintaining the vitality of our work.

The irony in the development of the CMP is that many interpreters now find themselves in the position of "needing CEUs" at the end of their cycle. With a deadline looming, the quest for professional development often becomes subordinated to the quest for CEUs. Online education offers an effective way to reach interpreters by avoiding the need for travel and allowing for flexible scheduling, yet it can also lead to interpreters' taking a series of disconnected workshops that do not really engage them in professional growth or contribute to the development of the skills necessary to take their practice to the next level. (Of course, this can also be true of more traditional workshops, not just online offerings.)

The following principles provide the start of a framework for addressing the needs of the community through online education while taking into account the context in which interpreters are seeking CEUs.

Principle #1: Keep the Big Picture in Mind

In "Intentional Development of Interpreter Specialization" Witter-Merithew and Nicodemus (2010) reference Kasher in asserting that "the functional and specialty-distinctive competencies of any specialty are acquired in an organized and integrated program" (Kasher, 2005). In developing online resources for healthcare interpreting education, it is important to have a comprehensive approach to addressing what is required. Angelelli (2006, 25) suggests that "healthcare interpreting education (HIE) involves the development of skills in at least six different areas: cognitive processing, interpersonal, linguistics, professional, setting-specific, and sociocultural." Malcolm (2008), in a concept map created for the NCIEC, outlined eight domains to be addressed with separate comprehensive modules:

- Orientation/Overview of Mental Health/Medical Interpreting
- Conditions and Treatments
- Language Use in Mental Health/Medical Settings
- Ethics and Boundaries
- Interpreting Skills
- Interpersonal Skills
- Self-Care and Self-Awareness
- Professional and Research Skills

While Angelelli and Malcolm propose slightly different categories, the important point is that online resources need to be organized and integrated into a larger whole in which students can see how the learning activities contribute to building the skills required for working in healthcare settings.

Whether as a designer of courses or a participant in them, it is important to look for a larger framework into which a particular learning opportunity fits. Workshops or courses should fit together to form a coherent whole. At this point, the field has not moved to the point of having a truly integrated program that covers all facets that would lead to a specialization in healthcare interpreting. The Rochester Institute of Technology has developed a Certificate in Healthcare Interpreting program began in the summer of 2011. The program, which includes a prerequisite online course on medical terminology, consists of four courses: Human Body Systems for the Professional Interpreter I & II and Healthcare Interpreting Practical I & II. These four courses take place offline, yet they are a significant step forward in providing an integrated program in healthcare interpreting.

In terms of online education, González and Gany (2010) report on a project to develop competency for Spanish-English spoken-language interpreters through the Center for Immigrant Health at New York University.

This project, delivered online with a combination of synchronous and asynchronous elements, provides a model of how interpreter education can be delivered in an online setting. It includes a series of 10 didactic modules and 10 lab or practice modules. Such a comprehensive approach may provide an effective model for ASL-English interpreters to follow.

Principle #2: Design Online Education to Build Higher Order Skills

Specialization within our professions requires changes within the interpreting profession. Witter-Merithew and Nicodemus (2010) suggest that, in the long run, specialized competencies "are built upon and integrated with the foundational competencies of generalist practitioners and are acquired through graduate level certificate or degree programs" (p. 89).

However, we do not yet have graduate programs specializing in healthcare interpreting. While that may be the direction in which we are heading, in the age of CEUs, when a preponderance of online education focuses on working interpreters, it is important to keep in mind some educational principles to make sure that the "treatment" is actually directed toward "curing what ails us." Given that the NCIEC needs assessment identified access to qualified interpreters in healthcare settings as a deficit, we must make sure that online educational offerings lead to the practical skills required for effective interpreting.

One framework that is useful in considering an effective design for online offerings is Bloom's taxonomy. Bloom's description of the skills in the cognitive domain is likely the best known of these (Bloom, 1956). This taxonomy suggests that students move through a series of cognitive skills in order to master a subject. The steps are as follows: knowledge → comprehension → application → analysis → synthesis → evaluation. In the 1990s, Lorin Anderson (Anderson & Krathwohl, 2001), a student of Bloom's, led a group of cognitive psychologists in revising the taxonomy. The labels shifted from nouns to verbs, and the top two levels were flipped, resulting in the following levels: remembering → understanding → applying → analyzing → evaluating → creating.

More significantly, the revised taxonomy includes both the cognitive-processing dimension as shown in Figure 1 and a knowledge dimension that recognizes the different levels of knowledge about any given topic.

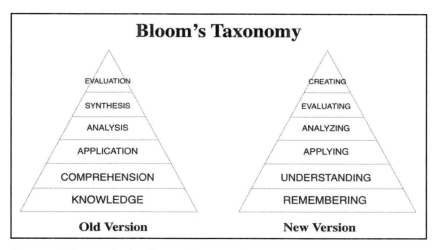

Figure 1. The standard and revised version of Bloom's taxonomy of the cognitive domain.

Table 1. A Revision of Bloom's Taxonomy of Educational Objectives

A Revision of Bloom's Taxonomy of Educational Objectives		Cognitive Processing Dimension					
		Remembering	Understanding	Applying	Analyzing	Evaluating	Creating
Knowledge Dimension	Factual Knowledge *(What - details)*						
	Conceptual Knowledge *(What - big picture)*						
	Procedural Knowledge *(How)*						
	Metacognitive Knowledge *(Why)*						

The result is Table 1,[1] where each box represents a different educational objective that educators should consider in promoting a student's mastery of a given subject. In general, moving downward and to the right on the chart represents a movement toward more complex, higher-order skills.

In healthcare interpreting education, it is vital that online education move beyond simply remembering and understanding. Instead, we need

---

1. Table 1 is adapted from Anderson and Krathwohl (2001, p. 28). I added the questions of "What, How, and Why" in the "knowledge" dimension to further illustrate the dimensions. For more on this, please see the original authors' explanation.

to foster the higher-order skills of applying, analyzing, evaluating, and creating, in addition to moving along the knowledge dimension beyond facts and concepts and into understanding how things work, the context in which they operate, and then articulating the reasons behind the choices practitioners make. Developing educational opportunities that foster these higher-order skills is a more challenging task, but it is indeed what our profession needs.

For online education, a paradox appears in remembering the field's response to the creation of RID's Certificate Maintenance Program and the temptation to focus on earning the requisite number of CEUs though not always with regard to the type of professional development being offered. Realistically, it is easier to create and evaluate online educational experiences that focus on the lower-order skills of knowledge and comprehension (i.e., dealing only with facts and concepts). It is often easier for participants as well. Put in your time. Watch a lecture. Read an article. Answer a few questions, and you have your CEUs.

Put yourself in the position of a resource creator who is thinking about developing an online course and then consider the list of verbs in Table 2, which are associated with the revised taxonomy created by Anderson, Krathwohl and their collaborators (2001, pp. 67–68). It is far more straightforward to determine whether someone can identify or classify something

Table 2. Revised Taxonomy Levels and Associated Verbs

Level of Cognitive Processing	Associated Verbs/Actions:
Remembering	recognize, identify, recall, retrieve
Understanding	clarify, paraphrase, represent, translate, illustrate, classify, summarize, generalize, predict, compare, contrast, match
Applying	execute, carry out, implement, use
Analyzing	differentiate, organize, deconstruct, outline, structure, discriminate, focus, select, distinguish
Evaluating	check, monitor, test, coordinate, critique, judge
Creating	generate, hypothesize, plan, produce, construct, design

(using multiple-choice, true/false, or matching questions) than it is to find out how effectively they can execute, discriminate, critique, or construct during an activity. Given that a strong focus is on the quantity of CEUs (as well as affordability), what path seems the most prudent?

Whatever its prudence, focusing on the lower-level skills only scratches the surface of what online education can offer. More important, it does not help interpreters develop the higher-order skills required in healthcare settings. In order to do that, it is useful to look at theories of how people learn and how this knowledge can provide a framework to attain the higher-order competencies required for interpreting in healthcare settings.

Constructivist Framework for Online Education

Constructivism, as an educational paradigm, asserts that learning is a process in which the learner must be actively involved in creating skills and knowledge rather than simply acquiring this knowledge (Learning Theories Knowledgebase, 2010a). It rejects the "banking" model of education, in which learners come with empty heads to repositories of knowledge such as schools to get their fill (Freire, 1970).

One of the foundations for constructivism is the social development theory of L. S. Vygotsky. A constructivist framework, which uses Vygotsky's ideas, offers a format for engaging students in material that moves them along the continuum of Bloom's taxonomy toward the skills required to address the identified needs.

Vygotsky (1978, 1986) believed that students learn through social interaction and that they first work with the tools of human culture to communicate their needs. Then, by working with others who are more knowledgeable, they move to the position of beginning to internalize these tools in a way that leads to higher-order skills.

In this process, Vygotsky introduced the concept of a zone of proximal development (ZPD), which he defines as "the distance between the actual developmental level as determined by independent problem solving and the level of potential development as determined through problem solving under adult guidance or in collaboration with more capable peers" (Vygotsky 1978, p. 86). In other words, if tasks are seen on a continuum of challenge, the ZPD is the area in which a learner can experience success, given appropriate support (see Figure 2).

Cannot Do Tasks	Zone of Proximal Development		Can Do Tasks Independently
Too difficult even with support	Need more support	Need less support	Have internalized skills

Figure 2. Initial Zone of Proximal Development.

In designing online education for healthcare interpreting, the goal is to provide both learning tasks that fall within a learner's ZPD and the appropriate supports to move the learner along the continuum and develop the number and complexity of skills that they internalize. This support, sometimes described as "scaffolding," needs to be at the appropriate level based on the learner's current skill level. If the activity is successful, a learner's ZPD should shift as shown in Figure 3.

Based on Vygotsky's concepts, the learning dynamic can be distilled into the following steps:

• Work with object
• Work with more knowledgeable other (MKO)
• Work with self

I will explain these steps in the context of an online workshop, "Body Language: Talking about Anatomy in ASL," which was designed as an independent study that can be done individually or in small groups (Bowen-Bailey, 2010). The workshop is designed to help interpreters enhance their language use in medical settings, particularly their use of space and classifiers. In an attempt to foster the higher-order skills required for interpreting, the workshop uses the preceding steps to provide a framework for participants.

Work with Object

This first step requires learners to engage with an object or a challenge without significant support. In the workshop, participants read informa-

Cannot Do Tasks	Zone of Proximal Development		Can Do Tasks Independently
Too difficult even with support	Need more support	Need less support	Have internalized skills

Figure 3. ZPD after working with appropriate supports

tion related to anatomical topics or medical conditions using written English, diagrams, and videos. For example, the first topic is "blood pressure." Participants use the provided web resources to build their own understanding of the topic and then create a video of themselves explaining this topic in ASL.

This assignment provides a baseline that lets the participants see what their linguistic capability was prior to moving through the process. In other words, it helps establish what skills they have already integrated and can do independently. It also shows learners which parts of the topic provide specific challenges. This information helps focus their attention in the next step.

Work with More Knowledgeable Other

This step, also known as "Work with Resource," is an opportunity for learners to enter into their own ZPD and work with some resource person who has a greater level of skill in a certain are. For "Body Language," the primary MKO is Nigel Howard, a Deaf interpreter and educator who frequently presents on anatomy and interpreting in medical settings. For each topic, participants can view a sample explanation in ASL by Nigel. They are encouraged to also follow Nigel's example to be more engaged with his description (see Figure 4).

Figure 4. Nigel Howard from the online workshop, "Body Language"

Other resources are also provided. Most of the topics have links to videos at www.DeafMD.org, a website with ASL translations of material from the Centers for Disease Control and Prevention and the National Institutes of Health. Additionally, as creator of the workshop, I also provide ASL explanations. As a nonnative signer, I include videos I have created for several reasons. First, I find that in workshops it is important not to ask participants to attempt any task that I am not willing to do myself. Second, providing multiple examples of how to do something requires participants to use the higher-order skills of analyzing and evaluating. In looking at the two samples, participants can determine what is similar and what is different and, most important, consider why certain choices are more effective. Finally, providing multiple ASL explanations allows a greater range in the type and level of support for the learner so there is more opportunity to provide the appropriate scaffolding to move a learner along. In my experience, some interpreters may see a native signer explain something and think that it is outside of their ability to replicate. Seeing a nonnative signer do something not quite as proficiently may seem more within their reach. It is still vital for them to see the native signer so that a native-level standard is held out as a goal, yet the variety may provide more rungs on the ladder of skill development.

It is important to note that, for an online workshop that is designed to work without a facilitator, it is harder to provide adjustments to optimize learning. This adds to the need for a variety of resources in this step. Additionally, it requires that significant consideration be given to entry-level requirements so that participants will join with ZPDs that are within the range of what can be accommodated within a given workshop or course.

One approach to ensuring that a workshop is within a participant's ZPD is to encourage participants to take online courses in a small group as a cohort. For the first offering of "Body Language," which took place in March 2011, participants were able to take the workshop as individuals. However, if they took it as part of a group, they were able both to earn more CEUs and to pay less money to take the workshop. Having a cohort provides an opportunity for discussion that can help customize the learning. Participants can ask questions and learn from their colleagues' postings and examples. Essentially, the presence of a cohort provides more resources to play the role of the "other" as Vygotsky envisioned.

It is important for a cohort to have an established relationship. As part of a beta testing of "Body Language," three interpreters were offered an opportunity to try out the workshop. However, because there was no pre-established relationship among them, there was no sense of a cohort, and they progressed through the workshop at very different paces and essentially independently. This led to the decision to provide incentives for people to create their own groups. At the time of writing, "Body Language" is still in its first offering so it is too early to tell how successful this approach will prove to be.

Work with Self

After getting the support of the MKO, learners then need to internalize the skill and be able to incorporate it on their own. In terms of the workshop, "Body Language," the participants are asked to re-create an ASL explanation of the topic. Using whatever seemed most relevant to them from Nigel's explanation or from the other resources, they video themselves again and attempt to integrate these new skills into their work. Those who are part of a cohort can then post their work in a discussion forum and take part in ongoing discussions with their peers.

This step asks participants to internalize new skills and hopefully shift their ZPD slightly so that they are able to do more activities independently. Of course, this doesn't happen immediately. Rather, progress requires repeating the process in a variety of settings and with different topics. Each time learners go through the three steps, they move forward on the continuum of learning but in a spiral fashion rather than linearly (Figure 5).

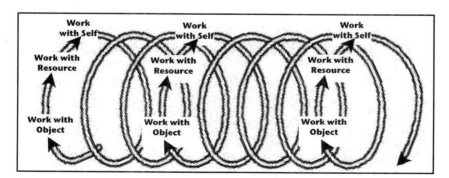

Figure 5. A spiral of learning based on Vygotsky's framework.

So, it is important to provide an opportunity for many cycles of this process to occur so that progress from the first time "Work with Object" can be compared with the final step, "Work with Self."

In "Body Language," participants have the chance to work with 12 different topics. At the time of this writing, it is too early to provide evidence that this spiral effect does indeed take place. However, the fundamental educational theory undergirding the design holds much promise.

More Models Promoting Higher-Order Learning

In my experience, this three-step process based on Vygotsky's concepts of ZPD and MKO provides a framework that can engage learners in ways that develop higher-order skills. However, it is certainly not the only model available. Bentley-Sassaman (2009) describes Kolb's experiential learning theory and its application to interpreter education. Problem-based learning (Barrows & Tamblyn, 1980) can also provide an engaging dynamic for education related to medical settings. The important thing is that online education for healthcare interpreting needs to be created with a structure that fosters participants' development of higher-order skills.

Conclusion

In the future, the Internet will undoubtedly play a significant role in the education of interpreters who work in healthcare settings. Numerous factors will influence the success of these efforts. Movements toward the establishment of interpreting in health care as a specialization may lead to a graduate program that delivers a comprehensive program all or in part online.

Currently, many of the online educational opportunities related to interpreting in health care are single workshops or courses rather than part of a comprehensive approach. Additionally, these opportunities are targeted at working interpreters who are maintaining their certifications through RID's CMP. Given this dynamic, it is vital for creators of online educational opportunities to consider how a single workshop or course can fit into the larger schema of what is required of a healthcare interpreter. Furthermore, the course must be designed with a learning dynamic that encourages interpreters to work toward the higher-order skills required for effective interpreting.

Is online education just what the doctor ordered? That question is yet to be answered, but by considering the principles outlined in this chapter, we will surely agree that our "treatments" have a better chance for successful outcomes for interpreters and the communities and healthcare practitioners that they serve.

REFERENCES

Affiliate Chapter Relations Committee, Registry of Interpreters for the Deaf, Inc. (2006). RID history: The bridge to the future. In *Affiliate chapter handbook* (3rd ed.). Retrieved November 10, 2010, from http://www.rid.org/UserFiles /File/pdfs/Affiliate_Chapter_Handbook_pdfs/ACHB_SECTION_1.pdf

Anderson, L. W., & Krathwohl, D. R. (Eds.). (2001). *A taxonomy for learning, teaching, and assessing: A revision of Bloom's taxonomy of educational objectives* (complete ed.). New York: Longman.

Angelelli, C. (2006). Designing curriculum for healthcare interpreting education: A principles approach. In C. Roy (Ed.), *New approaches to interpreter education.* Washington, DC: Gallaudet University Press.

Barrows, H. S., & Tamblyn, R. M. (1980). *Problem-based learning: An approach to medical education.* New York: Springer.

Bentley-Sassaman, J. (2009). The experiential learning theory and interpreter education. In J. Napier (Ed.), *International Journal of Interpreter Education*, vol. 1. Conference of Interpreter Trainers. Retrieved from http://www.cit-asl.org /Journal/2009_Vol1/BentleySassaman.html. Full article retrieved November 10, 2010, from http://cit-asl.org/IJIE/2009_Vol1/BentleySassaman.html

Bloom B. S. (1956). *Taxonomy of educational objectives, handbook I: The cognitive domain.* New York: David McKay.

Bowen-Bailey, D. (2010). *Body language: Talking about anatomy in ASL.* Retrieved November 29, 2010, from http://www.medicalinterpreting.org/moodle/course /view.php?id=7

Clark, D. R. (1999). Bloom's taxonomy of learning domains. Retrieved November 10, 2010, from http://www.nwlink.com/~donclark/hrd/bloom.html

Cokely, D., & Winston, B. (2008). Phase I deaf consumer needs assessment: Final report. NCIEC. Retrieved November 14, 2010, from http://www.nciec.org /resource/docs/FinalPhaseIDCReport.pdf

Cokely, D., & Winston, B. (2009). Phase II deaf consumer needs assessment: Final report. NCIEC. Retrieved November 14, 2010, from http://www.nciec.org /resource/docs/FinalPhaseIIDCReport.pdf

Freire, P. (1970). *Pedagogy of the oppressed.* New York: Continuum.

Galloway, C. M. (2001). Vygotsky's constructionism. In M. Orey (Ed.), *Emerging perspectives on learning, teaching, and technology.* Retrieved October 24, 2010, from http://projects.coe.uga.edu/epltt/

González, J., & Gany, F. (2010). VITAL: Virtual Interpreter Training and Learning. In J. Napier (Ed.), *International Journal of Interpreter Education*, vol. 2. Conference of Interpreter Trainers. Retrieved November 10, 2010, from http://www.cit-asl.org/IJIE/2010_Vol2/Gonzales-full.html

Kasher, A. (2005). Professional ethics and collective professional autonomy: A conceptual analysis. *Journal of European Ethics Network, 11*(1), 67–98.

Learning Theories Knowledgebase. (2010a, November). Constructivism at Learning -Theories.com. Retrieved November 12, 2010, from http://www.learning -theories.com/constructivism.html

Learning Theories Knowledgebase. (2010b, November). Experiential learning (Kolb) at Learning-Theories.com. Retrieved November 12, 2010, from http://www.learning-theories.com/experiential-learning-kolb.html

Learning Theories Knowledgebase. (2010c, November). Social development theory (Vygotsky) at Learning-Theories.com. Retrieved November 12, 2010, from http://www.learning-theories.com/vygotskys-social-learning-theory.html

Malcolm, K. (2008.) Concept map for mental health/medical interpreting education. NCIEC: Unpublished paper. Retrieved March 15, 2011, from http://healthcareinterpreting.org/new/educators/curriculum-ideas/concept-map.html

NCIEC. (2008). Draft domains and competencies for ASL/English medical interpreters. Retrieved June 30, 2011, from http://healthcareinterpreting.org/new /educators/domains-competencies/164-draft-domains-and-competencies-for -medical-interpreters.html

Overbaugh, R. C., & Schultz, L. (n.d.). "Bloom's Taxonomy." Retrieved March 3, 2011, from http://www.odu.edu/educ/roverbau/Bloom/blooms_taxonomy.htm

Peterson, R. (2010). Curriculum infusion/curriculum dilution. In *CIT News, 30*(4). Retrieved October 20, 2010, from http://cit-asl.org/newsletter/Oct10/dilution .html

RIT/NTID. Certificate in healthcare interpreting: Program overview. Retrieved February 9, 2011, from http://www.ntid.rit.edu/aslie/heathcare_interpreting.php

Vygotsky, L. (1978). *Mind in society.* Cambridge, MA: Harvard University Press.

Vygotsky, L. (1986). *Thought and language.* Cambridge, MA: MIT Press.

Witter-Merithew, A., & Nicodemus, B. (2010). Intentional development of interpreter specialization: Assumptions and principles for interpreter educators. In J. Napier (Ed.), *International Journal of Interpreter Education*, vol. 2. Conference of Interpreter Trainers. http://www.cit-asl.org/Journal/2010_Vol2/Witter -Merithew-abstract.html Full article retrieved November 1, 2010, from http://www.cit-asl.org/IJIE/2010_Vol2/Witter-Merithew-full.html

CHRISTOPHER MORELAND
AND TODD AGAN

Educating Interpreters as Medical Specialists with Deaf Health Professionals

SIGNED LANGUAGE interpreters have long worked to bridge the communication distance between the deaf patient and the hearing healthcare provider. In recent years, however, deaf people have gradually assumed the role of the provider, as physicians and nurses, for example. In close parallel to the advent of deaf healthcare professionals (DHPs) has come a demand for interpreters who not only have experience in the realm of medicine but also specialize in working with medical professionals. Nevertheless, formal training for interpreters as medical specialists is sparse, with virtually none for those who work with deaf healthcare professionals. Hauser, Finch, and Hauser (2008) have labeled those interpreters who work specifically with deaf professionals as *designated interpreters.* In this chapter, interpreters who work predominantly with DHPs are identified as *designated healthcare interpreters* (DHIs).

Multiple factors have stimulated the development of DHPs; two of the most powerful forces have been national legislation and technological advances. In the United States, the Rehabilitation Act of 1973 (US DOJ, 1973) and the Americans with Disabilities Act of 1990 (US DOJ, 1990) have empowered deaf students, trainees, and employees to obtain accommodations during professional education and employment. The creation of telephone devices and electronic auditory and visual stethoscopes has allowed for the modification of technologies that were traditionally obstacles for those with difficulty hearing.[1] Given the strongly interpersonal nature

147

of health care, however, interpreters remain irreplaceable for face-to-face communication when a DHP requires the use of signed language.

No current data reliably indicate how many DHPs work in the United States.[2] The exact prevalence of DHPs who use signed communication or work with interpreters in at least one venue is equally unclear. At the time of this writing, we have worked as a DHP (CM) and DHI (TA) team for nearly a decade at hospitals and clinics at three academic medical centers. In addition, several of our colleagues are also DHP-DHI teams in healthcare specialties ranging from obstetrics/gynecology to dermatology. In the absence of quantitative data, we draw primarily from our own and our colleagues' experiences to describe common obstacles and possible solutions faced by DHP-DHI teams.

This chapter divides the challenges that confront DHP-DHI teams into four broad categories: financial, linguistic, environmental, and social. Although these categories are not mutually exclusive and do not fully represent the complexity of medical interpreting, they cut across the healthcare disciplines and specialties of DHPs.[3] Furthermore, we describe potential elements of formal education programs for interpreters who are interested in becoming DHIs. While some interpreter education programs (IEPs) in the United States provide training specifically in the medical field, to our knowledge, none of them are targeted to provide education for future DHIs. We hope that these recommendations will contribute to the creation of such specialized programs.

Personal experience will indubitably color this chapter. For the purpose of transparency, we explain our current occupations. Christopher Moreland (CM) is a deaf internal medicine faculty physician who practices hospital medicine at an academic medical center, where he teaches medical students and residents (physicians in training). He communicates through spoken and signed English, as well as American Sign Language. Todd Agan (TA), an interpreter certified by the Registry of Interpreters for the Deaf with nearly two decades of experience, is a DHI at a teaching hospital and has worked extensively with numerous other DHPs. He is also an interpreter mentor and educator and teaches medical interpreting to students and working interpreters at the local, regional, and national levels. Both CM and TA routinely participate in the education of interpreting students, community interpreters interested in the healthcare field, and deaf healthcare students.

Demands Faced by Designated Healthcare Interpreters

Financial

The financial impact of providing interpretation services for DHPs who use signed language is often the first challenge that potential employers consider. Although this is not a demand the interpreters themselves face, the financial impact of a DHI position remains a consideration for interpreters who strive to negotiate for an adequately funded position. While the cost cannot be ignored, the financial burden borne by the hiring individual or organization can often be minimized by creating staff interpreter positions. When compared to contracting with agencies for interpreting services, hiring interpreters into a staff position may represent a potential means of significant savings to the medical institution even when a standard benefits package is included.

Another proposed benefit to both the DHP-DHI team and the hiring medical institution and which also supports the creation of a staff interpreter position is patient safety. A staff interpreter usually develops greater familiarity not only with the workings of the organization but also with details about the DHP's patients. When not distracted by esoteric details regarding the mechanics of patient care, the DHI can focus on providing a richer and more accurate interpretation of the interactions among healthcare team members and patients. Furthermore, a staff interpreter is more likely to have access to correct and complete patient-related information. This information is as essential to accurate interpretation by the DHI as the medical history is to the correct diagnosis by the DHP.

Despite the importance of the DHI's holding a staff interpreter position, creating such a position and developing a job description may prove to be an obstacle. Significant time and compromise may be required to craft a job description that meets the specific needs of the hiring institution. A well-written job description may increase the DHI's perceived value to the organization by emphasizing certain components, including specifying the DHI's primary role with the DHP (rather than as a generalist medical interpreter who happens to work with a DHP). As part of the healthcare team, the staff DHI should be recognized as an allied health professional with a specific skill set. Beyond interpreting, a comprehensive job description may permit some DHIs to pursue teaching, research, or administrative duties as the DHP-DHI teams' desires and schedules permit.

Linguistic

Linguistic demands are inherent in the interpretation process as each interpreter simultaneously manages at least two languages. Thus, the generalist interpreter who strives to become an effective DHI must already possess proficiency in both languages. However, certain challenges are specific to the language spoken by medical professionals. In medical jargon, the terms themselves and the contextualized social register in which they are used can seem overwhelming.

The Terms

Many terms may appear unusual to the inexperienced eye and ear: tachycardia, erythema, myocardial infarction, and (one of our favorites) dysdiadochokinesia. Some words have simple definitions ("erythema" means "redness"), while others are complex concepts ("dysdiadochokinesia" suggests a difficulty in performing rapidly alternating movements, such as rotating the wrists to flip the hands from side to side). To add to the interpreter's workload, single terms may have different implications for different healthcare specialists. How then to manage this cacophony of jargon?

Various tactics can be employed, none of which is inherently better than any other: using single signs (whether from ASL or English-based sign systems), breaking a word into its root components, or coding a term. Earhart and Hauser, who worked together as a DHP-DHI team in the field of obstetrics and gynecology, describe the development of a sign for tachycardia: "[T]he term tachycardia means rapid heartbeat. The designated interpreter can simply sign the standard sign for *heartbeat* with a fast pace to indicate a rapid heartbeat."[3] This team seized upon the concept of a heartbeat and modified the ASL sign's timing accordingly to match the full meaning of "tachycardia." Another approach utilizes the word roots "tachy-" and "cardia," which respectively translate into "fast" and "heart." A DHI can then sign FAST+HEART, conveying the same concept.

Other terms, which may be expressed by actual signs, may also be communicated using the written coding system seen in many patients' medical records. Physicians have developed standard spoken and written abbreviations that are used in verbal communications with colleagues, on paper charts, and in computerized records. The term "myocardial infarction," more widely known as "heart attack," is often written and spoken as "MI." Some DHIs might sign HEART-ATTACK; others might fingerspell M-I even when the full phrase is spoken (which may be considered a form of coding rather than interpreting). Clearly, a variety of approaches can prove successful for communicating the most technical medical language.

To complicate matters further, the meanings of medical terms do not necessarily carry across medical specialties. In internal medicine, for instance, TRANSFUSION (the replacement of blood components) is often signed as directed to the inner midarm, where an intravenous (IV) needle might be placed to transfuse blood. However, when signed in this fashion during an obstetrics discussion, one DHP requested that the sign be directed toward the abdomen, where a fetus would receive a transfusion. Thus, even a single word or concept might be signed differently among DHPs, necessitating that sign development be targeted to each team's context and needs.

The Register

DHIs must consider not only the language of medicine but also the register in which it is used; in other words, they must ask themselves what is appropriate language use in the current social environment? Resident physicians will speak differently with one another than with their supervising physicians or patients. Unusual or improper choices of language during interpretation can impact the way the hearing person perceives the DHI and even the DHP, particularly if the DHI is interpreting into spoken English. To use the aforementioned example of the term "myocardial infarction," a physician might say "heart attack" when discussing a heart condition with a patient. However, using this lay phrase with a colleague might inadvertently and incorrectly suggest that the DHP is less skilled in the DHP's field of practice. Such problems may be magnified when speaking by telephone (a situation very common in health care). The DHP can often minimize the potential for this problem by describing to the DHI beforehand the nature of the phone call (e.g., whether it is to a patient or a nurse) and any crucial concepts that will be communicated (e.g., the nefariously difficult name of a medication to be prescribed and therefore enunciated). In turn, the DHI can and should ask questions about an imminent discussion. Both techniques, of course, are used in interpreting in general.

Environmental

One of the great difficulties of interpreting as a newly hired designated interpreter is the need to adapt to a healthcare environment not designed for either a DHP or a DHI. Among other considerations, the DHP must contend with the auditory traditions of stethoscopes and phone usage. Here, the discussion is limited to potential environmental challenges for the DHI. These are presented here in two broad categories: the physical milieu and the healthcare system.

The Physical Milieu

When first entering a hospital room, interpreters may be overwhelmed by the white sheets and curtain, the patient scarcely robed in a gown with tubes running to and from a nearby IV pole, and other disquieting sights, sounds, and smells. This scenario is suffused with a sense of sterility; some interpreters may be hesitant to engage this situation for fear of displacing or contaminating some crucial element. Much of this discomfort stems from a lack of knowledge about what is or is not appropriate in the healthcare environment. Nevertheless, these physical and structural conflicts may be managed with careful consideration and forethought.

Out of necessity, interpreters often maneuver themselves into the best possible sightline with deaf consumers, while simultaneously maximizing their own ability to hear what is being spoken. In a teaching hospital, the healthcare team may consist of the attending (supervising) physician, three or more resident physicians, three or more medical students, and others such as pharmacy students. Add to the mix two interpreters, and there is a large group of people entering and exiting patient rooms, discussing the care of each patient while avoiding entanglement in IV tubing or equipment carts. To be able to mutually maximize sightlines and auditory gain without risking patient safety requires that DHIs become familiar with the environment and the safety protocols within each institution. For example, in the operating room or during certain procedures, specific surfaces are considered sterile fields; these areas are not to be approached by those who are not properly gowned and gloved (including the DHI). Furthermore, if the DHP is wearing a sterile gown during a procedure, it may seem impossible for the DHI to get the DHP's attention by touch (e.g., a shoulder tap) unless the DHI is aware that the back of the shoulder is generally not considered sterile. Additionally, certain patients may harbor resistant bacteria (such as the increasingly prevalent MRSA [methicillin-resistant *Staphylococcus aureus*]) and should not be touched without proper gowning. To this end, DHIs can remain aware of which patients require such contact precautions by following the DHP's lead and watching for signs outside each room indicating such precautions. These are only a few of the coping mechanisms developed by DHP-DHI teams in response to the physical challenges of interpreting in the healthcare setting.

The medical milieu is remarkable not only structurally but also acoustically. In addition to what is spoken by those present, DHIs must remain aware of other auditory cues. Machine alarms may be incessant and intrusive in the intensive care unit. A hubbub of activity will create a noisy background in the emergency department. It is imperative that the DHI be able to focus on the discussion among the healthcare team and the patient being interviewed. If a patient exhibits slurred speech (something not always visible), this may be a critical clinical indicator of an underlying condition such as alcohol intoxication or a stroke. While most generalist interpreters might not know about or feel comfortable conveying elements such as slurred speech, the DHI can provide such crucial information so that the DHP can immediately expedite diagnosis and treatment of the appropriate medical condition, treatment that might be otherwise delayed. Occasionally, an overhead announcement will declare a "code blue" or other emergency, requiring that the DHP and DHI race to another location to support a rapidly decompensating patient. Just down the hall, another healthcare team may mention information relevant to the DHP's patient, something the DHI can be aware of only if familiar with the DHP's patients. (In other words, while at work, the DHI is never off duty.) By working together to decide which information is timely and relevant, the DHP-DHI team can optimize the communication of surrounding auditory cues without creating alert fatigue by interpreting every sound.

Other physical experiences can assault the senses of DHIs and DHPs: Invasive procedures may produce sprays of blood, or festering wounds may leak odorous pus. Many people are unable to tolerate even the sound of vomiting without becoming nauseated themselves. The least tolerable experience for many people may be the sight of other human beings (and their families) who are in pain or dying. Barnum and Gill (personal communication, November 2008) have listed four "Ss" (sights, smells, sounds, and suffering) as factors that potential medical interpreters must consider. Such unpleasant experiences should not preclude interpreters from the noble goal of contributing to health care. Rather, DHIs should remain aware of their particular sensitivities and anticipate or accommodate to situations that may particularly affect them.

Taking into account the typically long hours of DHPs (particularly those in training), along with the slew of auditory cues, physical hazards, and other sensory input, it is hardly surprising that the DHIs may experience physical and psychological fatigue. For instance, DHIs may be so focused on the task at hand that they fail to notice their exhaustion. It is critical that the DHI team develop preventive self-care skills and management techniques for when fatigue occurs at inopportune times, such as in the middle of a shift. We have successfully negotiated a break at such times; for example, the DHP might be able to delay seeing the next patient for 10 minutes, focusing instead on paperwork while the DHI rests.

The Healthcare System

Healthcare professionals in every clinic, hospital, and administrative office must interface with other healthcare organizations to ensure the timely and appropriate transitions of patient care from one provider to the next. Familiarity with the names and even the locations of outpatient and in-patient facilities in the surrounding areas is requisite for understanding a patient's medical background and follow-up opportunities. The healthcare team must recognize whether hospitals and clinics in a certain city are part of a larger healthcare institution or are autonomous organizations. Helping patients obtain health insurance if they qualify is tantamount to ensuring continuity of care. By studying the administrative structure of the DHP's division or department and healthcare organization and by appreciating the outlying healthcare organizations through which the DHP's patients move, the DHI may be able to provide more accurate interpretation of discussions among healthcare team members and patients.

On a larger scale, the impact of health-related legislation is substantial and may likewise arise during a DHPs' discussions with colleagues. For example, the Health Information Portability and Accountability Act of

1996 (HIPAA) and the Patient Protection and Affordable Care Act of 2010 (PPACA, informally referred to as the healthcare reform law) are examples of national legislation under the U.S. Department of Health and Human Services, impacting virtually every healthcare provider in the nation. A DHI's basic understanding of these legislative principles also contributes significantly toward improved interpretation of such specific information.

Social

Working in health care requires extensive collaboration with a variety of other members of the healthcare team. This, in turn, may necessitate the use of tact and negotiation to address interpersonal conflicts that may arise.

Many interpreters with years or decades of experience may consider themselves professionals on par with attending physicians. While both the interpreter and the physician have dedicated their lives to intensive training in their respective fields, healthcare professionals may not perceive comprehensive interpreting experience as conferring equivalent status within the medical field. Furthermore, the DHI who behaves authoritatively may reflect poorly on the DHP trainee; many hearing colleagues will see the interpreter as the DHP's representative and will interpret any behavior as originating with the DHP. As an illustration, consider that, in teaching hospitals, large healthcare teams visit each patient daily (often called "rounds" or "rounding"). In such groups, by the traditional medical hierarchy from attending to resident to medical student, third-year medical students may be relegated to the back of the group, where they may not be able to hear pertinent discussion about the patient. Most interpreters would step to the center of the group, near the attending, to hear as much information as possible. The DHP and DHI, however, must balance the benefit of increased access with the risk of appearing too forward or even arrogant. To minimize such conflicts, the DHP-DHI team should discuss potential tactics for positioning in advance. Such discussions will increase the DHP's and the DHI's understanding of one another's preferences, concerns, and limitations while allowing them to negotiate toward the mutual goal of optimal medical education and patient care.

In addition, DHP-DHI teams often involve more than one interpreter, which is appropriate given the potentially intense interpreting requirements of the healthcare environment and therefore the risk of repetitive injury to a single interpreter. As a result, team interactions evolve to include DHP-DHI, DHI-DHI, and whole-group dynamics. With this increased complexity of interpersonal relationships comes an increasing possibility of miscommunication. When working with multiple DHIs, frequent meetings (ranging from weekly to monthly) with the DHP and the full team of DHIs to discuss scheduling and recent problems encourage many concerns to be discussed promptly and even preventively. Each team member feels heard. Such meetings are often opportunities for feedback from DHP to DHI and DHI to DHP, as well as from DHI to DHI. For example, the DHP can teach the interpreters appropriate concepts behind certain medical terms. In return, the DHIs can clarify for the DHP what a reasonable interpreting schedule is and when to bring in a team interpreter. Such open communication may strengthen the team as a whole and increase job satisfaction for all parties.

These same communication skills also help the DHP-DHI team establish clear expectations and define its roles with other medical colleagues. A nurse once admonished one of us (TA) for giving an order she thought inappropriate; TA responded by clarifying that he had simply voiced a verbal order. In contrast, during an emergency (a "code blue") in a crowded patient room, a nurse asked TA to leave the room, believing he was nonessential personnel; CM responded by stating, "He's with me," which rapidly defused the situation and refocused all three participants on the patient at hand. Both situations worked effectively, yet the team used different tactics in each. There are no teachable rules dictating what to do in each situation. Nevertheless, DHP-DHI teams must communicate frequently and carefully to ensure that each party is able to function effectively both within the team and within the larger healthcare environment.

The aforementioned examples also illustrate the need to develop positive relationships with non-deaf colleagues, not only for the DHP but also for the DHI. Some hearing healthcare providers, not realizing that the DHI is interpreting, may strike up a conversation with the DHI. In one such situation, one of us (CM) lightheartedly responded, "He's good but not so good that he can chat and interpret at the same time." While educating colleagues, this approach also avoids potential offense by not rejecting outright another person's attempt to relate with a member of the interpreting team. Many DHIs, when not interpreting, will actively develop collegial relationships with faculty and staff members in order to cement further their roles as part of the healthcare team.

As a healthcare professional working side by side with a DHP, a DHI will likely be involved in particularly stressful situations; end-of-life discussions provide a powerful illustration. We have worked through many such discussions with patients (and families) who are nearing their end. Regardless of whether the patient and family are logical, prepared, or outright distraught, such conversations take their toll on every person present. Likewise, medical emergencies require immediate action with very little time to discuss decisions and outcomes. These situations may involve watching a patient die rapidly and unexpectedly. The DHI must possess the emotional maturity to work through such stressors, potentially by reviewing situations with an interpreter colleague outside of the team. Some interpreters have branded these emotional responses as vicarious trauma experienced through the deaf person; they seem better described as direct emotional trauma, equal in force and import to that experienced by any other healthcare professional.

Such emotional and physical situations can act as the ultimate test, the final point at which all of the DHP's and the DHIs' vocabulary and social knowledge, skills, team dynamics, coping mechanisms, and mutually developed tactics coalesce into fluid actions, each moving toward the same goal as every healthcare provider in the room: the care of the patient.

RECOMMENDATIONS FOR A DHI CURRICULUM

The demand is small yet expanding for specifically trained interpreters who function effectively as specialized interpreters with deaf professionals. As increasing numbers of deaf students matriculate through medical education, the need for DHIs is growing: interpreters whose education, skills, and knowledge extend beyond that which has historically been considered adequate for signed language interpreters.

The role of interpreting for a DHP is rich and complex. The DHI may need to interpret in an academic environment that is similar to graduate school. A DHI may work in either a clinic or a hospital, an academic medical center, or a private institution. One may venture into a world where patients are fortunate enough to carry health insurance or may be medically, socially, or financially impoverished. Professional posture must parallel the DHP's medical skill level, whether a neophyte trainee or a licensed, supervising physician. Thus, the DHI must be consummately adaptable in such a diverse environment.

Medical education itself is also highly dynamic. While medical students traditionally begin their education with didactics, they initiate their clinical exposure by observing physicians interacting with patients in order to better understand the doctoring process itself. Thus far, however, the interpreter education process generally emphasizes abstract discussion and interpreting practice and provides minimal opportunities to observe professional interpreters in their daily practice. Medical interpreter training has only recently begun to take a lesson from the medical education system: It is imperative that interpreting students understand not only the work that a DHI must do but also the context in which the DHI must do it.

Despite the particular requirements of any specialized interpreting, a curriculum for designated interpreters should start with the foundations of interpreting. Those pursuing education as a DHI should first be adequately trained as a generalist interpreter. We recommend that all DHIs graduate from an accredited interpreter education program that teaches the necessary foundations to become a successful interpreter in any field.

Two Approaches to DHI Education

A successful DHI training program might borrow from the observation-supervision approach guided by the demand-control schema as described by Dean et al. (2003). Those establishing curricular topics should also strongly consider the medical interpreting domains and competencies as developed at the Collaborative for Advancement of Teaching Interpreting Excellence (CATIE Center, 2008). Just as physicians or teachers pursue specialized education, interpreters who aspire to work in the healthcare field should look to these guidelines to help elucidate the context in which they will be practicing. The historical approach of teaching interpreters basic interpreting skills and then expecting them to interface seamlessly with specialized settings and unusual protocols should no longer be seen as adequate preparation. To create proficient service providers, interpreter educators must reexamine the way they prepare interpreters to fill the emerging role of the DHI; mastering the role of a traditional interpreter is insufficient to function successfully as a DHI.

As in law or medicine, interpreting is a practice profession (Dean & Pollard, 2004). Dean and colleagues (2003) wrote that "academic preparation and skills development precede a career in human service." In line with this philosophy, they piloted a program for interpreting students that mirrored the training of medical students. Interpreters shadowed physicians to better understand the *demands* of interpreting in a medical setting (the factors to which an interpreter must in some way respond) and the *controls* an interpreter needs (skill sets, resources, and funds of knowledge) to successfully maneuver through such settings. In these assignments, students shadowed hearing physicians as they interacted with hearing patients. Absent the additional responsibility of interpreting, interpreters were better able to analyze the linguistic and nonlinguistic demands inherent in the medical setting:

> Through their shadowing assignments with physicians, students are being exposed to basic medical knowledge, varied medical settings, and typical doctor-patient interactions/conversations through direct observation, in contrast to the superficial, non-contextualized learning that takes place through traditional classroom or workshop instruction methods. (Dean & Pollard, 2003)

As with the preceding approach, modern DHI instruction must include reflective learning and discussion. After an observation opportunity, students should be expected to research and discuss interesting observations. Not only does such self-reflection encourage greater understanding of the material on a personal level, but it also fosters the ability to find relevant resources in a self-directed fashion; these are crucial skills for any professional.

Beginning with a field observation experience (an observation-supervision period), apprentice interpreters who are training to become DHIs should be placed in academic medical settings alongside healthcare students from medicine, nursing, pharmacy, and other healthcare fields. A well-designed program would include rotations in both hospital and outpatient clinical rounds with various physician specialties (e.g., internal medicine, general surgery, psychiatry) and should include private, public, and charity settings. Academic medical centers would be the preferred avenue of access as these programs are already accustomed to working with student observers in a myriad of healthcare education programs. Furthermore, students should be required to attend didactic lectures that span informal teaching sessions to Grand Rounds (a large forum usually for medical case discussions). To maximize these experiences, interpreting students should pair with seasoned healthcare interpreting mentors who would regularly debrief and discuss observations. This broad exposure would allow interpreting students to develop further their own schema for the range of environments encountered in the medical milieu.

The logical starting point for trainees in any profession is to establish a foundation, a common language upon which to structure the practical application of their newly acquired funds of knowledge. An observation-supervision mentor who has been meeting regularly with a student to discuss the student's progress should ultimately become an internship mentor. The student would then shadow the supervisor as the supervisor works alongside DHPs. As time permits during assignments, the trainee and supervisor should discuss choices and circumstances on the job and consider meeting outside of interpreting assignments for more extensive discussion. As training progresses, the apprentice DHI should begin to provide some of the interpreting services under the mentor's guidance. These mentoring moments would supplement the didactic learning sessions in which the DHI apprentice participates and would contribute toward the ultimate goal: The DHI student becomes able to provide services independently and unsupervised, thus transforming into a successful DHI.

Further Elements of a Successful DHI Curriculum

A DHI program should consider didactic sessions that provide background information applicable to healthcare settings. Potential topics include (but are not necessarily limited to) the following:

• Introduction to medical concepts such as anatomy, physiology, pharmacology, and microbiology/infectious diseases (including their relevance to isolation precautions to prevent disease transmission by healthcare professionals)
• The language of medicine: Greek and Latin word roots and how interpreters can apply them to decoding and retaining medical terminology
• The process of providing health care: how and why physicians perform

medical interviews and physical examinations and how they synthesize the resulting data to develop diagnoses and treatment plans

- The language of medical discussions: how healthcare trainees and professionals discuss their work at events like Grand Rounds (didactic sessions in which patient cases or clinical topics are discussed in depth) and morning report (where educators guide trainees through clinical problem solving)
- The medical education system: the processes by which nurses, pharmacists, physicians, and other healthcare professionals are trained, licensed, and accredited at state and national levels; the academic structure of medical education (such as the roles of attending physicians, resident physicians, and medical students)
- The healthcare insurance structure: how hospitals and clinics operate; the various forms of insurance at county, state, and national levels; how academic medical centers relate to their partner healthcare institutions
- The healthcare institutional structure: an overview of the outpatient and inpatient settings, including emergency departments, and their roles in providing health care; how patients transition from one healthcare environment to another (e.g., from hospital discharge to clinic follow-up) and how they flow through each environment (e.g., from check-in at the clinic's front desk to making the next appointment); self-reflection on how each DHI's noninterpreting skills can contribute to one's work within the healthcare system (e.g., educating colleagues about interpreters or proposing job descriptions)
- The legal aspects of health care: the history behind current local, state, and national policies that regulate multiple aspects of healthcare (such as HIPAA and PPACA) and how they impact medical interpreters; legal documentation encountered in health care (including consent for admission and billing, consents for procedures and operations, advance directives, living wills, healthcare proxy designations, and goals of care discussions)
- Self-care: the need and rationale for healthcare professionals' regular disease surveillance (e.g., annual skin tests for tuberculosis) and immunizations (e.g., for influenza or hepatitis B), as well as the public health impact of such self-care
- The ethics of medicine: appropriate access to patient healthcare information, the question of neutrality as an interpreter, and end-of-life issues

CONCLUSION

Despite the foregoing discussion and recommendations, more data need to be collected and rigorously analyzed to address many questions about DHP-DHI teams. It remains unclear how many DHPs in the United States are currently in training or practicing and what their specialties, communication preferences, and requirements for accommodations are (including interpretation services). In parallel, further data are needed on the numbers of experienced DHIs and their specialties. More exploration into the common issues faced by DHPs and DHIs in a variety of locations and fields of practice is essential. How these knowledgeable DHP-DHI teams negotiate terminology, sign development, and team dynamics can guide the successful education of the next generation of healthcare providers and interpreters.

The next wave of deaf professionals is rapidly ascending through the educational ranks, preparing to assume roles as healthcare providers. With them come new and powerful opportunities for those interpreters who would work alongside DHPs. The interpreting community must therefore prepare to meet the challenges inherent in the burgeoning subspecialization of medical interpreting. The DHI faces the task of mastering not only basic interpreting skills but also the highly focused competencies and unusual demands of the medical world. With the DHI role still in its infancy, there is as yet no comprehensive, evidence-based, standardized curriculum to develop the skills necessary for this expert work. An arsenal of tools is available within previously described observation-supervision approaches and in the domains and competencies of medical interpreting. Nevertheless, no training program can instill in its developing DHIs a knowledge base broad enough to interpret for every healthcare professional in every situation. By fostering the evolution of flexible team communication skills, DHIs can ultimately decide the details of specific assignments through ongoing discussions and negotiations with DHPs and other DHIs.

Well-developed DHI training programs can cultivate the growth of strong alliances among designated healthcare interpreters, deaf healthcare professionals, and hearing healthcare colleagues. From face-to-face medical encounters to health system administration efforts, the patients served by proficient and well-supported DHP-DHI teams will reap the benefits.

Notes

1. To our knowledge, the most comprehensive reviews of visual and auditory stethoscopes can be found at the website for the Association of Medical Professionals with Hearing Losses (AMPHL). Retrieved October 13, 2010, from http://amphl.org/stethoscopes.php.

2. While DHPs are proliferating in other countries as well, we focus on those in the United States due to variations in educational, legal, and health systems.

3. For an excellent discussion of DHP-DHI experiences, see Angela Earhart and Angela B. Hauser, "On the other side of the curtain," in Peter C. Hauser, Karen L. Finch, and Angela B. Hauser (Eds.), *Deaf professionals and designated interpreters* (pp. 143–64). Washington, DC: Gallaudet University Press, 2008.

References

Barnum, M., & Gill, L. (2003, April). Interpreting in medical settings. Presented in Portland, OR.

CATIE Center, College of St. Catherine. (2008.) *ASL/English medical interpreter: Domains and competencies.* Retrieved October 13, 2010, from http://healthcareinterpreting.org/PDF/DomainsCompetencies10-09-08.pdf.

Dean, R. K., Davis, J., Dostal-Barnett, H., Graham, L. E., Hammond, L., & Hinchey, K. (2003, January). Training medically qualified interpreters: New approaches, new applications, promising results. *RID Views 20*(1), 10–12.

Dean, R., & Pollard, R. (2004, October). A practice profession model of ethical reasoning. *RID Views 21*(9), 28–29.

Hauser, P. C., Finch, K. L., & Hauser, A. B. (Eds.). (2008). *Deaf professionals and designated interpreters.* Washington, DC: Gallaudet University Press.

U.S. Department of Health and Human Services. Health Insurance Portability and Accountability Act of 1996, 42 U.S.C.§ 201 *et seq.* Retrieved October 13, 2010, from http://www.hhs.gov/ocr/privacy/hipaa/administrative/statute/index.html.

U.S. Department of Health and Human Services. Patient Protection and Affordable Care Act of 2010 (P.L. 111–148), 29 U.S.C. § 207 *et seq.* Retrieved October 13, 2010, from http://docs.house.gov/energycommerce/ppacacon.pdf.

U.S. Department of Justice. Americans with Disabilities Act of 1990, 42 U.S.C. §12101 *et seq.* Retrieved October 4, 2010, from http://www.ada.gov.

U.S. Department of Justice. Rehabilitation Act of 1973, Section 504, 29 U.S.C. §794 *et seq.* Retrieved October 4, 2010, from http://www.justice.gov.

TERI HEDDING AND
GARY KAUFMAN

Health Literacy and Deafness

Implications for Interpreter Education

HEALTH LITERACY is a fast-growing, nationwide concern among health-care professionals. In 2004, The Institute of Medicine in Washington, DC, reported that 90 million people in the United States have trouble understanding and using health information (Nielsen-Bohlman, Panzer, & Kindig, 2004). Furthermore, Deaf adults were found to have lower health literacy than their hearing counterparts as evidenced in several studies (National Council on Disability, 2009). Additionally, billions of dollars have been poured into research, policy making, and education to promote higher standards of health literacy, yet very little attention has been paid to the issue of health literacy in the Deaf population. The following scenarios illustrate some of the many situations that we have witnessed in our 20 years of combined experience:

A Deaf patient was happy when the doctor told him the test results showed he was HIV positive.

Another Deaf patient, who is diabetic, received a package of insulin; however, she put it away in her closet as she did not understand the purpose of the medicine.

One Deaf patient thought she was pregnant when she was actually going through menopause.

A Deaf patient—without an interpreter—signed the consent forms for an amputation without understanding the plan to remove her leg.

Deaf children without effective communication skills and transfer of information about health issues grow into adults who have significant gaps

164

in their knowledge of health, healthy living, and the patient's role within the healthcare system (Sinai Health System and Advocate Health Care, 2004). This lack of health literacy, in combination with interpreters who lack appropriate training (both in healthcare settings and in interpreting for patients with low health literacy), leads to ineffective health care among Deaf individuals.

This chapter examines health literacy among Deaf adults with the goal of preparing interpreters to work effectively with Deaf patients in medical settings. Ineffective health literacy as an adult can be traced to knowledge acquisition as a child: Incidental information is transferred from adult to child in family discussions of health and wellness, direct experiences with healthcare providers, and observation of one's caregivers navigating the healthcare system. If communication breakdown mitigates the information shared in these encounters, the result will be diminished health literacy. Professional factors also contribute greatly to this knowledge deficit, including a lack of training in cultural competence regarding the care of Deaf patients, medical perceptions of deafness as a disease, and widely held assumptions among healthcare professionals about the effectiveness of health literacy among members of the Deaf community. Finally, we consider the "interpreter factor" and provide some recommendations for educating interpreters to improve their medical interpreting skills.

HEALTH LITERACY DEFINITIONS

It is imperative for interpreters to understand the concept of "health literacy" to appreciate the challenges and barriers Deaf people encounter when seeking health care. Healthy People 2010, a health program run by the U.S. Department of Health and Services, defined "health literacy" as the "degree to which individuals have the capacity to obtain, process, and understand basic health information and services needed to make appropriate health decisions" (National Network of Libraries of Medicine, 2010).

Health literacy involves more than the ability to read and write. It requires a complex group of reading, listening, analytical, decision-making skills and the ability to apply these skills to health situations (National Network of Libraries of Medicine, 2010). *Medline Plus* (U.S. National Library of Medicine/National Institutes of Health, 2010) states that a person who has effective health literacy is able to do the following:

• Fill out complex forms
• Locate providers and services
• Understand consent forms
• Share health history with the doctor
• Follow the doctor's instructions
• Read the prescription instructions
• Maintain a healthy lifestyle
• Manage chronic diseases, and so on (U.S. National Library, 2010)

Studies have shown that people who are able accomplish these tasks will have better health outcomes (Berkman et al., 2004).

HEALTH DISPARITIES

One of the primary goals of Healthy People 2010 was to promote a healthy life for Americans and eliminate *health disparities* among them (National Network of Libraries of Medicine, 2010). Although information is limited, recent studies show that people with disabilities, including Deaf people, experience significant healthcare disparities as compared to the general population (National Council on Disability, 2009).

Social epidemiologist Paula Braveman defines "health disparities" as "group differences in health that are unnecessary, preventable, and unjust" (Braveman, 2006). In other words, minority groups such as elderly persons, immigrants, and low-income individuals receive poorer quality services or treatments for their health conditions as compared to the general population. For instance, a recent study in Chicago reports that health status indicators show that disparities between blacks and whites have widened significantly over time (Orsi, Margellos-Anast, & Whitman, 2010).

Deaf Population

The 2008 National Center for Health Statistics reports that Deaf adults are three times more likely to describe their health as fair to poor than their hearing counterparts (National Council on Disability, 2009). Further, the National Council on Disability has found that high blood pressure and diabetes are more prevalent among Deaf adults than among adults with normal hearing levels, especially when comparing those under age 65 (National Council on Disability, 2009). As both of these diseases are partly preventable with healthy lifestyles, these statistics suggest that Deaf people are not receiving or acting on the message provided by their healthcare professionals. Even though the Deaf patients had poorer health status, their healthcare utilization was low given their associated health problems (Barnett & Franks, 2002). Thus, it is highly likely that the main contributors to poor health status among Deaf adults are communication barriers in the healthcare system and low health literacy. We elaborate upon this later in the chapter as it has implications for educating interpreters to work in healthcare settings.

As stated earlier, a person must have basic literacy skills in order to attain health literacy, and many Deaf people struggle with the English language. Although the average reading skills of a Deaf high school graduate have been estimated to be at the fourth-grade level (Holt, 1993), some of the Deaf patients we have encountered at Sinai Health System's Deaf Access Program in Chicago, Illinois, had reading levels that were considerably below the fourth grade. This is confirmed by Dew's report (1999), which concluded that approximately 20% of Deaf students leave school with a reading level at or below the second grade. Finally, Pollard and Barnett's (2009) study is instrumental in linking poor reading skills among Deaf people with poor health outcomes. It also shows that those with poor reading skills are, not surprisingly, the most likely to have low health literacy and be at greater risk for health disparities than those with strong health literacy skills (Pollard & Barnett, 2009).

One component of health literacy is health knowledge. Past research on Deaf people's health knowledge is limited; however, several studies show similar results, indicating that Deaf people's knowledge of health in general is low (Kleinig & Mohay, 1990; Ries, 1994; Barnett & Franks, 2002; Davenport, 1977; McEwen & Anton-Culver, 1988; Steinberg et al., 2002; Pollard & Barnett, 2009). One of the first studies was conducted in New Orleans in 1978, when researchers found that more than half of the Deaf participants were unfamiliar with the medical terms "pediatrician," "nausea," and "allergic." This study also found that more than half of the

Deaf participants could not explain what action to take if they felt chest pain (Lass et al., 1978).

These results were supported by a comprehensive study done in Chicago in 2004, which surveyed 203 Deaf participants in two separate healthcare systems with programs specifically designed for the Deaf community:

40% of participants could *not* identify any of the *seven* most common warning signs of a heart attack. (Comparative studies of hearing persons found 90% of hearing responders identified chest pain as a symptom of a heart attack.) (p. 23)

62% could not identify any of the seven most common warning signs of a stroke. (p. 23)

Only 38% recognized the word "cholesterol." (p. 34)

In women subjects, only 48%, less than half of subjects defined the term "pap smear" correctly. (p. 34)

Nearly 60% thought that donating or receiving blood would place them at an *increased* risk of contracting the HIV virus. (p. 32)

56% did not identify having anal sex without a condom as increasing the risk of contracting the HIV virus. (Sinai, 2004, p. 32)

It is important to note that Deaf participants in this study demonstrated less health knowledge than their hearing counterparts regardless of education levels (Sinai, 2004). Steinberg et al.'s (2002) study, which included 31% of Deaf subjects with bachelor's degrees, and Pollard & Barnett's (2009) study, which included 80.8% of subjects with a college degree, also show that Deaf participants have less health knowledge regardless of their education levels.

We emphasize that many Deaf individuals demonstrate health knowledge similar to that of hearing persons. Typically, these patients are well educated and had effective communication with their families while growing up.

Incidental Learning

Incidental learning occurs when someone learns things indirectly—without formal training or education (Mealman, 1993). For a Deaf child, unless the communication environment is *totally* accessible (i.e., continuous use of visual communication *among* family members), opportunities to acquire knowledge through incidental learning are lost. Hauser et al. (2010) report that 95% of Deaf children are born into hearing families, whose members typically do not become fluent or even competent in ASL. As Deaf children have limited access to other types of information via television and radio, these combined insults to knowledge acquisition generate what Dr. Robert Pollard (1998, as cited in Pollard & Barnett, 2009, pp. 182–85) has referred to as "global fund-of-information deficit." It is imperative for interpreters to be aware of this deficit and to understand its impact on interpreting in healthcare settings. It may be appropriate for interpreters to engage in cultural mediation and to interpret implied information.

Deaf children often learn things through trial and error or after the fact. Additionally, Deaf children in hearing families typically experience "dinner table syndrome" (Hauser et al., 2010), whereby the children are left out of the family's conversations. Occasionally, parents or siblings fill a Deaf child in as to why the rest of the family is laughing or arguing but typically provide only a summary statement that is devoid of details.

Related to health care, parents may discuss how "Aunt Bessie" had a stroke. A hearing child may ask what a stroke is. The parents then give an informative response. In this case, the family exchange stimulates conversation between the parent and hearing child, which in turn develops the child's knowledge base. The hearing child learns the meaning of the word "stroke" and its symptoms. The hearing child is also given an opportunity to ask questions. However, this may be simplified and interpreted to the Deaf child only as "Aunt Bessie is sick," or the word "stroke" may be spelled out without defining it, as the parents lack the appropriate sign language vocabulary to convey the information. The Deaf child thus gets vague and telegraphic data and has no opportunity to ask questions or develop an adequate knowledge base. Additionally, it has long been known that memory is closely linked to emotion (i.e., our memories store emotional experiences better than neutral ones) (Holland & Kensinger, 2010). If, due to their limited knowledge of ASL, the families cannot impart their communications with the intensity of the associated emotion, connections are lost, and the message is unlikely to be stored for the child's future reference.

Deaf children who grow up with this information deficit can experience significant gaps in their health knowledge, subsequent healthy lifestyle choices, and their role within the healthcare system. This is supported by Mann, Zhou, McKee, and McDermott (2007, cited in Hauser, O'Hearn, McKee, Steider, & Thew, 2010) who state that "The lack of access and reduction in incidental learning opportunities may have a negative impact on Deaf individuals' physical health."

HEALTHCARE NAVIGATION

Navigation through the healthcare system can be a challenge for anyone. Communication barriers experienced by Deaf adults dramatically complicate this already difficult process. In our own experience, to navigate the healthcare system successfully, individuals must be exposed to the process early so that they can learn appropriate behaviors and reasonable patient expectations. This education starts as children accompany their parents to the doctor and also occurs through incidental learning. Deaf children without effective communication skills lose out on this process and enter adulthood without the necessary skills to navigate the healthcare system.

The health visit itself is full of educational experiences for children. We have observed that, whether going with a parent to the parent's medical appointment or going to their own appointment, hearing children are privy to the parent/doctor dialogue and acquire relevant information that they store for future use. Through this process, a child learns to copy the model of the parent as a patient, develop sets of expectations with regard to doctor visits, and optimally learn to become an effective healthcare consumer.

For illustrative purposes, we have divided the process into the appointments, registration, waiting room, nurse/triage, and doctor's dialogue/ physical exam.

Appointments

Before the doctor visit actually occurs, a patient or caregiver must contact the medical office, explain the nature and urgency of the problem, negotiate an appointment time, and develop a plan for transportation and child care. The hearing child will overhear much of this interaction. For instance, 6-year-old Tom overheard his mom making an appointment for his baby sister, who has an ear infection then calling his dad to to use the family car.

By the end of this encounter, Tom has begun to acquire the skills he will need when he makes his own appointments as an adult. A Deaf child may miss the correlation between making the phone call and the appointment and the importance of making plans for transportation or dependent care. The Deaf child, by contrast, may see his mom's taking him to the doctor's office as similar to a trip to the grocery store.

Registration

When one arrives at a medical clinic, one is expected to sign in, present one's ID and insurance information, pay a copayment, and wait patiently to be called by a nurse. Hearing children will naturally learn these skills with years of exposure. Deaf children, without auditory access to this information and unable to see what is happening over the counter, will absorb only a fraction of this exchange.

Waiting Room

Another important task modeled is the "waiting room" behavior. Hearing children witness the conversation between the parent and the receptionist, who instructs them to sit patiently in the waiting room until the nurse calls their name. Deaf children miss this. They also miss the ongoing updates from the staff, who explain the delays that can occur in a busy practice. In this situation, we recommend that interpreters intentionally provide environmental information and ongoing relevant conversation about the delays. This gives the Deaf child access to this information and an understanding of why the wait is longer than expected.

Triage

After the reception tasks are completed, patients must be triaged. Here patients have their vitals taken, relate their chief complaint, and wait patiently for the doctor. Again, hearing children, who learn via incidental knowledge acquisition, just seem to "get" this part. By contrast, Deaf children are often anxious about having a pointed probe accelerating toward their mouth, a blood pressure cuff tightening around their arm, and having their wrist restrained by the nurse who is taking their pulse. To Deaf children, things are being done to their body for no apparent reason. If they protest, the parent often admonishes them, further increasing their anxiety. Later, when the chief complaint is told to the nurse, Deaf children are typically unaware of this exchange. They therefore miss opportunities to acquire knowledge via incidental learning, which will impact both their current and future experiences when interacting with the healthcare system. It is a common mistake for new interpreters to try to engage the children in conversation without interpreting the complaint that the parent reports to the nurse. Deaf children must be involved in this interaction so they will learn the typical triage procedure; thus, this interaction should be interpreted.

Doctor's Dialogue and the Physical Exam

After the triage is completed, the patient sees the doctor. The tasks here include obtaining the patient's medical history; undergoing an exam; discussing the diagnosis, tests, treatment plans, and warning signs; and explaining the expected follow-up. For illustrative purposes we divide this into a parent's doctor visit and the child's own health visit.

A Parent's Visit to the Doctor's Office Accompanied by a Child

If the doctor's visit is for the parent, the hearing child has an opportunity to overhear the parent's ailments and the family's medical history being retold. As mentioned earlier, most hearing adults learn their family's medical history by overhearing family conversations. However, a significant amount of information is also acquired when the parents answer questions posed by their doctors (DiPietro, Knight, & Sams, 1981). For example, a hearing child might hear the parent talking about "Grandpa Jack," who is taking medication for high blood pressure and needs to "limit his salt intake," or about the horrible decline of "Aunt Fannie" before finally succumbing to colon cancer.

Contrast this with a Deaf child at the parent's appointment; the dialogue, considered private, is intentionally *not* shared with the child. The child, who is merely accompanying the parent, does not learn this vital family health information. Thus, without this passive knowledge acquisition or, alternatively, a direct intentional relay of information from parent to child, the child will not acquire this information. As we discuss later, upon reaching adulthood, this child will not be able to provide a meaningful family medical history.

The Child's Own Doctor Visit Accompanied by a Parent

When a child visits the doctor, the parents typically provide the bulk of information. Here, the hearing child passively acquires this *personal* information from the dialogue. From an early age (4 or 5 years), pediatricians start speaking directly to the child. The child may be asked about any hospitalizations in the past. The child, who was too young to recall, states that there were none. The parent then interrupts and explains to the doctor that the child had pneumonia at 7 months of age or a hernia at the age of 1 year. Thus, the child learns this personal historical information and gets to practice telling it in a nurturing environment. In this same visit, the parents relate the family's medical history to the doctor. This reinforces what was overheard during a parental visit to the doctor or at home and further codifies the information in the child's brain. Finally, the parents typically ask the doctor about the child's diagnosis and treatment. This information is therefore available to the hearing child to store for use later in life.

Deaf children, however, are often excluded from communication between their hearing parents and family doctors (Barnett, 2002). Typically, an interpreter is not provided for the child's appointment, and the parents assume the responsibility of communication with the doctor. The parent relays the history, completely unaware that the child is missing out on learning this vital information. As we discuss shortly, when, as adults, these Deaf individuals are asked for their medical history, they will be unable to provide meaningful answers.

For a Deaf child to acquire these critical building blocks for dealing successfully with the healthcare system when they grow up, hearing parents should request an interpreter for each doctor visit. Again, it is important for the interpreter, on a medical assignment with a Deaf child, to interpret all relevant data in the entire visit, including the registration process, the environmental cues in the waiting room, the triage, and finally the doctor's dialogue and exam. We also recommend interpreting even if the child does not seem to be paying attention. Just as hearing children surprise adults by recalling information relayed while the child was occupied, Deaf children can also scan "visual bites" and acquire needed information for later use and discussion.

Experiences of Deaf Adults without Effective Communication as Children

As demonstrated earlier, hearing children passively acquire—through incidental learning—the tools of healthcare navigation and the appropriate behaviors of being a patient. They witness the complex interaction needed to make appointments, complete the registration and triage tasks, succinctly relay their chief complaint, and ask appropriate questions of their doctors. With time and repetitive reinforcement, the child internalizes the basics without formal instruction. Again, if the child does not understand something, a dialogue with the parents typically ensues to clarify the matter.

A Deaf child, by contrast, requires visual cues and experiences in order to learn to navigate the healthcare system. Without effective modeling, the deaf child has no paradigm to copy and thus does not develop the skills needed for successful healthcare utilization. In this section we analyze the breakdowns that typically result when healthcare navigation skills have not been adequately developed in the adult Deaf patient. We follow a patient from setting up an appointment to after-visit consultant care and make recommendations for the interpreter where appropriate.

Without the knowledge that appointments need to be scheduled, the Deaf child, as an independent adult, is likely to show up at a doctor's office and expect to see the doctor. If an appointment is obtained, without access to parental planning for transportation and emphasis on punctuality, the Deaf adult is likely to arrive late as transportation was not appropriately planned. If, as a child, a Deaf person was not made aware of insurance transactions, copayments, and referral polices, the adult Deaf person is likely to struggle with these concepts. The net result is typically confusion and anger when asked for copayments or referrals.

Without access to the common announcement that the physician is behind schedule and the historical knowledge that this is typical of doctors, the Deaf adult is likely to become frustrated when the doctor runs late, question the need for appointments, and get angry at the doctor for being inconsiderate of the Deaf adult's time. We have witnessed many patients pacing the halls and being belligerent with the staff while waiting for their appointments. In this situation, it is common for Deaf patients to vent their frustration or anger to the interpreters about the delays. While the interpreters can show empathy for this annoyance, they must not encourage the patient's anger or take sides. Deaf patients should be empowered to speak about their irritation with the staff directly, using the interpreter solely as a conduit for communication. Eventually, with education, Deaf people learn the importance of calling in advance to make appointments and also come to recognize that situations that delay the physician commonly arise.

Deaf adults who are naïve about health care are likely to become frustrated upon having to repeat their story to the nurse, students or residents if applicable, and the physician. They may become irritated with the perceived lack of communication between nurses and doctors regarding the history the nurse had recently taken.

When the patient finally meets the physician, three overarching processes affect the success of the visit unrelated to the patient's knowledge of typical healthcare practices and the patient's medical history: feeling intimidated by the doctor, the "Deaf nod," and discordance between the doctor's and the patient's goals.

A common issue to all patients is a feeling of intimidation in the doctor's presence. The doctor, with many years of education and a completely foreign medical language, can seem aloof and distant. When the patient is Deaf, this distance can seem even greater. Furthermore, many Deaf individuals are sensitive about appearing unintelligent. This is evidenced in several studies in which Deaf patients reported they felt that the doctors viewed them as having mental retardation (Iezzoni et al., 2004; Barnett, 1999; McEwen & Anton-Culver, 1988). Hence, Deaf patients are often unwilling to fully engage in the dialogue for fear of misperceptions by the physician.

A related issue is the "Deaf nod." Here, Deaf patients may nod agreeably rather than question the doctor or admit they do not understand. This phenomenon is widely recognized among interpreters and other professionals who work with Deaf clients. Doctors tend to misinterpret this head nodding as agreement when it may actually function like "uh-huh" from a hearing patient (Ralston, Zazove, & Gorenflow, 1996). Or it may mean the patient is intimidated by the doctor and pretends to understand by nodding. This response to a doctor can be dangerous. Medication miscommunication can lead to underdosing, resulting in ineffective treatment, or overdosing, causing side effects and possibly fatal results. While the medical staff may pick up only the head nodding and miss the messages being conveyed through body language, interpreters can be *instrumental* in avoiding disaster by interpreting the body language to properly indicate the deaf patient's full message. It is essential that Deaf patients are educated to advocate for themselves and to ask questions for clarification so that their healthcare needs are addressed effectively. Interpreters can actively empower Deaf patients by encouraging them to become an active partner in their own health care.

Finally, discord may arise if the doctor's and the patient's goals differ. Current healthcare models require doctors to see an average of three to four patients per hour. However, many Deaf patients do not realize that doctors have constraints on their time. While the physician's goal is to take an accurate and thorough history as efficiently as possible, the patient's goal is to provide all of the information the patient thinks the doctor will need and in sufficient detail to emphasize the gravity of the ailment.

In our experiences, patients often present their medical history as they would tell it to a friend. They start the story long before the pertinent facts occurred, add many details for emphasis, and end with their perspective of the problem. For example, a Deaf patient requesting medication for a skin rash on his back might say the following:

> I had a rash on my legs and tried the doctor's medication, but it didn't go away. So, I was reading in a magazine, and it said to use lip balm, which I did. It went away. That was five years ago. My cousin also had a rash on her arm, but she is allergic to strawberries. I told her not to eat them, but she is stubborn.

In this example, the patient is unaware of what information is relevant to the doctor. The doctor, already behind schedule because of the extra time needed for interpretation, typically responds by prematurely ending the interview, leading to missed opportunities for appropriate diagnosis and treatment. To complicate matters further, when the history and physical are done, little time is left to explain the diagnosis, disease process, medications, and side effects to the patient. In several studies, Deaf adults complained that doctors did not understand them, that they misunderstand the doctors' instructions, and that they did not understand their diseases or treatments (Steinberg et al., 2006a, 2006b; Hochman, 2000; Woodroffe, et al., 1998; Zazove et al., 1993; McEwen & Anton-Culver, 1998; Schein & Delk, 1980; Lass, Franklin, Bertrand, & Baker, 1978; Davenport, 1977).

As we have seen, when taking a history, doctors can find it challenging to extract an accurate story. When obtaining medical, family, and medication histories, doctors may also struggle to extract meaningful data.

As mentioned earlier, during their pediatric visits, many Deaf children do not have access to information about their illnesses or even their general condition. Consider this example: A physician asks a patient about any previous hospitalizations, and the patient replies, "I think I was sick as a kid." Later, when the medical record arrives, the patient is told, "You were hospitalized for almost 1 month for asthma at age 4. You almost died." In our experience, the shock experienced by both patient and doctor is very common with Deaf individuals. The family history presents equal obstacles to the personal history, again arising from lack of communication. When a patient is asked about the family's medical history, the patient may respond, "Mother died because she was sick," but be unaware of the precise fatal illness. Furthermore, if a patient recalled her father's dying of a "heart stop" (heart attack), the patient would likely be unaware of the father's preexisting conditions, such as high cholesterol, diabetes, or high blood pressure. These details impact doctors' decisions for intervention. If doctors are unaware of early heart disease or cancer that has genetic links, appropriate early screening will not be scheduled and may result in dire consequences for the Deaf patient. It is important for parents to share their family medical history with their Deaf child.

Finally, communication breakdowns sometimes occur in medication histories. When the doctor asks Deaf patients who are naïve about health care what medication they are taking, they are often unaware of the names of these medicines. Instead, they reply, "I take a "blue pill" and a "little white pill." They believe the doctor can quickly discern from the thousands of available medications the name and dosage of the medication based on size and color. By this time in the interview, doctors can become very frustrated with a Deaf patient who does not know even "the basics," further jeopardizing the success of the visit

When the history and examination are complete, the doctor makes an assessment and presents a treatment plan. Here, the uninformed Deaf patient is likely to bring several misconceptions to the visit, leading to further confusion. We focus on the misconceptions of disease processes and their associated treatment, misconceptions of the doctor's role, and misconceptions about medications.

When some Deaf patients feel something out of the ordinary, their stomach rumbling, for example, they are likely to interpret this as a sign of something serious. Numerous attempts by the physician to reassure them are often unfruitful as the patient believes there *must* be something wrong. Conversely, some Deaf patients may misguidedly believe that if nothing hurts or *appears* abnormal, they cannot be ill. This makes it difficult for the doctor to treat a chronic disease without associated physical symptoms such as high cholesterol and high blood pressure. Screening exams, such as a colonoscopy, pap test, and mammography, are also challenging as these tests can provoke anxiety in an otherwise "normal-appearing" patient.

Another related misconception is an expectation of one-time treatment for every ailment. Children typically present to the doctor with infections that resolve over time or with a short course of medication. As adults with chronic diseases such as diabetes or thyroid problems, many Deaf patients are shocked to find out they have to continue taking medication for the rest of their lives.

Another misconception many Deaf patients have concerns the doctor's role. They believe that one doctor should be able to treat all aliments. A primary-care doctor at Mount Sinai Hospital who signs often receives this complaint: "You are a doctor. Why are you sending me to another doctor for my heart?" The doctor must explain the complexities of the human body and the extra knowledge and training that specialists receive to become an expert on one area of the human body. Patients often go but then wonder why they need primary care if they are seeing a specialist.

When health-naïve patients visit the specialist, they are likely to arrive without the referral and present multiple problems unrelated to the referral. The situation is typified in the scenario of a Deaf patient who was sent to a cardiologist for chest pain and was having stomach pain that day. The patient wanted the doctor to examine and treat her stomach, completely disregarding the chest pain. The doctor had no choice but to refer the patient to a gastroenterologist for stomach evaluation. When the patient returned to the primary-care doctor, the doctor had to figure out the miscommunication, call the cardiologist, explain the situation, and reschedule the patient. To alleviate this problem, we recommend such patients work with a case manager and an interpreter to ensure the patient has a solid understanding of the problem and the importance of obtaining a referral to a specialist for treatment.

Finally, we present another set of obstacles related to medications. As noted earlier, many Deaf patients rely on visual recognition of medications: "I take a round blue pill and a green and yellow capsule." This emphasis on visual identity of a medication causes further confusion when different manufacturers of the same medication are used. Despite being the identical prescription, many Deaf patients believe that two medications with different appearances are completely different drugs. Further, it is not uncommon for patients to complain that they had a reaction to one medicine but that the second medicine "worked just fine," only to find out that both medications comprised of the same ingredients. Associated with this is the misconception that strength in milligrams is comparative *between* medications. For example, some patients might believe that 600 mg of Ibuprofen would be more effective at controlling pain than 6 mg of morphine. An interpreter working in a medical setting should be prepared to interpret how two medicines can be *the same* even though they look different and that strength of dosage cannot be compared across medications.

PROFESSIONAL BARRIERS TO DOCTORS' PROPER CARE OF DEAF PATIENTS

The National Council on Disability (2009) finds that Deaf people often have poor communication with doctors, which likely leads to poor health care. This may impede the transfer of information that can help diagnose new health conditions and prolong or leave chronic problems untreated. We firmly believe this can be remedied by providing skilled interpreters.

Lack of Training on Deafness

Medical training programs rarely address the issues of caring for a Deaf patient. If any education is provided, the emphasis is on the pathology of hearing loss rather than effective communication. Medicine is focused on "curing" or restoring function. Deafness is considered a medical "problem" that is no different from a broken arm. The sound bite of information presented therefore tends to focus on cochlear implants, inappropriately considered as a cure to restore one's hearing. Deaf culture and the Deaf community are never discussed or represented in medical training. In fact, Iezzoni et al. (2004) interviewed Deaf individuals who reported that they felt that doctors did not see them as a linguistic minority but instead as having a pathologic condition. Without proper training or an understanding of deafness, doctors often underestimate the intelligence of Deaf patients and give reassurances or oversimplify their explanations (Davenport, 1977).

Furthermore, many healthcare providers assume Deaf adults can write and read English fluently. Most people in the general public do not understand that American Sign Language (ASL) is the first language and the preferred communication mode for "many" Deaf adults; that it has its own grammatical rules independent of English (Iezzoni et al., 2004); and that English is actually a second language for the majority of Deaf individuals. This leads to doctors' false assumptions when writing notes with a Deaf patient; they believe that the patient's "broken English" indicates the patient is not intelligent or has a cognitive disorder (National Council on Disability, 2009). Conversely, doctors may appear impatient and feel irritated writing notes back and forth with Deaf patients because of increasing time pressures already felt in an environment of patient capitation and decreased reimbursement. When in a rush to write notes, sometimes a doctor may use abbreviations that are unfamiliar to many patients, such as saying "4× a day," "prn" for "as needed," or "w/meals." Deaf persons whom Steinberg et al. (2006a) interviewed reported that it was difficult to communicate via note writing because of the "big words" the doctors used or that it was difficult to read the doctors' handwriting. Additionally, patient education handouts were found to be poorly understood by Deaf persons if their reading level did not exceed a sixth-grade level (Meader & Zazove, 2005).

Use of Interpreters

Ebert & Heckerling (1995) have reported that, although doctors understood the benefits of using an interpreter, the cost of hiring one prevented more than a minority of them from doing so when caring for Deaf patients. Similarly, many Deaf people reported that doctors refused to provide an interpreter or that Deaf patients were expected to provide their own interpreters. Deaf individuals have told us that they prefer to go to an emergency room instead of an outpatient clinic because they have learned that the former are more likely to comply with the Americans With Disabilities Act (ADA) and provide qualified interpreters. Other Deaf patients capitulate and bring family members or friends to "interpret" for them. However, they often considered the family members inadequate as interpreters and still felt excluded from the conversation (Steinberg et al., 2006a). Doctors unknowingly contribute to this practice as they often overestimate the sign language skills of family members or friends who are not certified or trained in medical interpreting.

INTERPRETER BARRIERS TO HEALTH CARE FOR DEAF PATIENTS

By the time Deaf individuals reach adulthood, several factors, as mentioned earlier, prevent them from navigating the healthcare system effectively. It is also important to acknowledge that interpreting in medical settings poses its own barriers to successful navigation of the healthcare system.

There is a severe dearth of certified interpreters who are qualified to interpret in medical settings. According to the Registry of Interpreters for the Deaf (RID), the United States has 8,774 certified interpreters (Butts, email, September 21, 2010). We can assume these interpreters possess a wide variety of skill levels. Even if we also assume that all of the 8,774 certified interpreters are qualified to work in medical settings, this number is still too small to meet the nationwide demands for medical interpreting needs. As a result, many Deaf patients receive medical services without an interpreter solely because of the limited supply. When interpreters are hired to work in a medical setting, it is imperative they be cognizant of their skills since their interpreting can help or hinder the Deaf patients' understanding of doctor visits. In fact, the interpreters in several focus groups stated that interpreters need to have a strong background in medical terminology, knowledge, and understanding of medical procedures and treatments to be effective in a healthcare setting (Taylor, 2007). Not surprisingly, Deaf people also reported that they prefer to work with interpreters who are experienced in medical interpreting (Steinberg et al., 2006a).

Generally speaking, interpreter training programs do not include a medical component in the curriculum. Ironically, unlike physicians, who are expected to learn thousands of medical words in 7-plus years of postcollege training, interpreters are expected to know how to interpret medical words without even a basic medical terminology class. Further on numerous occasions we have witnessed interpreters receiving the brunt of anger or frustration from a physician or patient when the communication is suboptimal.

Research related to the standards in medical interpreting for the Deaf is limited. In 2007 RID updated a standard practice paper on its website, which provides a framework for healthcare professionals regarding the use of interpreters in medical settings. If interpreters want to improve their medical interpreting skills, opportunities to participate in continuing education that focuses on medical interpreting are very limited. In fact, the very first national symposium on healthcare interpreting occurred at CATIE Center at St. Catherine University in St. Paul, Minnesota, only in 2010.

Aside from limited opportunities to acquire medical interpreting skills, challenges also arise because of differences between English and American Sign Language (ASL). As ASL employs classifiers to represent many medical concepts, interpreters must know what specific conditions, procedures, and treatments look like in order to use the appropriate classifiers and accurately interpret the message spoken by the medical staff.

When interpreters are not fully informed, they tend to fingerspell or make up signs for unfamiliar terms because they do not know an accurate ASL interpretation. The patient then receives an incomplete or even erroneous message. Examples of this are waving a C handshape to represent cholesterol or colonoscopy or signing the ASL sign for the animal "cat" and then fingerspelling s-c-a-n. To accurately interpret a colonoscopy, a skilled interpreter would use classifiers to represent the scope inserted into the rectum and viewing the intestines and colon.

Even if interpreters do understand the terminology, they may be not skilled users of classifiers and may be uncomfortable using their bodies as classifiers. This can be especially tricky when crossing genders. A female interpreter demonstrating urinating into a cup to a male patient is likely to find this interpretation awkward.

In the medical world most patients are familiar with typical medical questions such as "What brings you here today?" or "Do you have any medical problems?" or "On a scale of 1 to 10, what is your pain level?" Interpreters commonly struggle with the ASL translation of these questions. For example, if a doctor asks a patient, "Do you have any medical allergies?" it is common for a novice interpreter to sign the traditional signs ALLERGY HAVE? Deaf patients often misunderstand this question and associate "allergy" with cats, trees, or dust. Since the question was not interpreted properly, the patient may provide inaccurate information to the medical team. Another possible pitfall is an incomplete interpretation. Using the previous example, the interpreter may *appropriately* sign ALLERGY YOU HAVE CONNECTED WITH MEDICINE? AIRWAY CLOSING? RASH? ITCHING? However, the interpreter may have not considered facial swelling and redness. Patients may respond in the negative because the reaction they experienced was not presented. To overcome this problem, interpreters should ask the staff for the specific reactions that are of concern.

Another common example is translating the word "positive" in ASL as it relates to HIV infection. The novice interpreter will sign PLUS for the word "positive," leading to a miscommunication and a false sense of health by the Deaf patient. With knowledge, medical interpreters learn to translate "HIV positive" as H-I-V YOU HAVE.

In addition to insufficient medical training and knowledge, many interpreters also experience the "white coat" syndrome. They feel intimidated by healthcare professionals and do not feel sufficiently confident to ask for clarification of medical terminology unknown to the interpreter. Even if the interpreter overcomes these natural barriers, some doctors may have a difficult time explaining in layperson's terms.

Another challenge relates to the Deaf person's proficiency in ASL. It can be trying for even a seasoned interpreter to convey basic information to Deaf patients with minimal signed-language skills. An additional degree of difficulty arises when instructions involve complicated processes such as preparation for a colonoscopy. The preparation is a multistep process that spans 36 hours and uses confusing references such as clear liquids (yet permits coffee and juice as long as they are not red or purple). Time concepts can also be challenging because they require demonstrations to convey meanings. This extra skill set requires the medical interpreter to be comfortable in moving from the traditional "invisible" interpreter's role to being an active participant in the communication process between the doctor and Deaf patients. That is, interpreters must feel empowered to take control of the interpreting process. This includes asking the doctor to slow down; requesting a visual description of procedures, diagnoses, treatment plans; and asking for visual aids. At Sinai, after frequent requests for visual aids, one gastroenterologist obtained a medical drawing of the GI tract, complete with drawing of polyps and cancerous lesions, and kept it handy to show his Deaf patients the area that would be scoped.

Nowadays, with more and more hospitals providing free access to Wi-Fi, interpreters should take advantage of the many visual aids available on the Internet. Medical drawings, diagnostics, medication photographs, and manufacturers' logos are all available in popular search engines such as Yahoo or Google. Interpreters should also ask for books and brochures that are often readily available and an excellent visual resource for Deaf patients to use as a reference and to refresh their memory at home.

Finally, interpreters often find themselves in an awkward position when a doctor explains a plan to the *interpreter* and then leaves, expecting the interpreter to relay the information without the doctor being present. This can be dangerous as there is no medical authority to ask when questions arise, and interpreters, even if they believe they know the correct answer, must not generate answers to medical questions. They should therefore come to the assignment prepared to handle these situations.

OPTIMAL SERVICES

Several health delivery models have been tailored for Deaf patients in several cities, such as Baltimore, Chicago, and Rochester, where doctors are competent in ASL and staff interpreters are provided on site. The "health delivery model for Deaf patients" usually means that the hospital employs doctors, social workers, staff interpreters, and/or deaf individuals in managerial positions, all of whom are focused on the delivery of appropriate health care to Deaf patients. This model also usually involves in-service training in deafness and sign language lessons to general staff to provide enhanced communication and to make the environment "Deaf friendly." This kind of environment usually succeeds in drawing an increased number of Deaf patients for their routine and acute medical care. Studies have shown that Deaf patients who utilize these tailored services have successful health experiences, including a high level of satisfaction with communication with their doctors, improved preventive care outcomes, enhanced health maintenance and treatment compliance, and obtaining regular physical exams (Steinberg et al., 2006a; Barnett & Franks, 2002; MacKinney et al., 1995). If healthcare professionals are trained to take the time to fully explain, make use of visual aids, and hire medical interpreters, it is possible for Deaf individuals to realize positive healthcare outcomes.

In the optimal setting, providers are made aware that they should present health information in ASL through live interpreters or video formats and present the information using simple language and utilizing numerous pictures and printed materials (Meader & Zazove, 2005; Steinberg et al., 2002). Patients are encouraged to advocate for their right to an interpreter. When a Deaf patient has significant gaps in knowledge, explanations are repeated, and, if communication is still suboptimal, a Certified Deaf Interpreter (CDI) is employed. To work effectively with this population, interpreters actively engage with individuals who have unique communication needs, thereby developing their skills. To achieve this level of excellence, interpreters are strongly encouraged to utilize interpreter resources, such as a deaf mentor, in order to hone their interpreting skills. Interpreters must be honest in their self-assessment and recognize their limitations in order not to jeopardize a patient's health care by *ineffective interpretation between the patient and the doctor*. To this end we recommend attendance at local hospital health fairs where interpreters are provided. This both increases interactions with the Deaf community and expands an interpreter's medical knowledge. These events are often well attended and become social events based on health education; they are excellent opportunities to have informal interactions with this population.

RECOMMENDATIONS FOR INTERPRETER EDUCATORS AND INTERPRETER TRAINING PROGRAMS

With appropriate guidance and training, novice interpreter can interpret effectively in some medical situations with Deaf patients. Some recommendations for interpreters or interpreter training programs to consider are the following:

1. Collaborate with medical schools/programs (if available) located at the same institutions where the interpreting education programs are

housed. This will provide opportunities for interpreters to learn medical terms, diseases, testing, and procedures.

2. Add medical language competency to the traditional interpreting education programs. This will enable interpreters to practice their medical interpreting in a safe environment.

3. Require students to translate the everyday medical questions. For example, instead of signing ANY MEDICAL PROBLEMS YOU HAVE? the interpreter should be encouraged to think of other choices, such as HEART PROBLEMS, DIABETES? HIGH BLOOD PRESSURE? YOU FINISH EXPERIENCE— BEFORE? NOW? Interpreters should be guided to employ their creativity and medical knowledge and to use classifiers effectively.

4. Encourage interpreting students to enroll in medical terminology courses within the interpreter training program if offered.

5. Offer training in anatomy (e.g., cardiovascular system, reproductive system, digestive system, respiratory system). This provides both the terminology and visual images that they can later call upon in the field.

6. Arrange hospital tours so that interpreting students can become familiar with the different departments, machines, testing, procedures, and instruments. Again, this will allow a safe environment for them to learn about the "medical world."

7. Offer mentoring opportunities at hospitals or clinics.

8. Develop guides for mentors.

9. Observe interactions between doctors and hearing patients and then observe similar interactions between doctors and Deaf patients to compare the communication dynamics.

10. Provide hands-on interpreting opportunities for interpreting students under the supervision of a medically trained interpreter with permission from Deaf patients.

11. Encourage the interpreters to recognize their skills and limitations and decline an assignment if they are ill qualified.

12. Guide the students in determining when and how to use a CDI in medical settings.

13. Develop strategies with the students to convince an employer that a CDI with its associated cost is necessary for satisfactory communication.

14. Work to develop students' confidence so they feel empowered to ask questions of doctors to obtain clarification.

15. Work with the Deaf community to standardize ways of signing medical terminology in ASL.

16. Encourage interpreting students to create a "tool kit" that includes calendars and props to explain medical instructions such as pre-op directions and discharge planning.

17. Evaluate senior students and provide guidance as to which medical settings the student is qualified to interpret in.

18. Remind the students that the Internet provides valuable animated medical illustrations that an interpreter can use to learn about medical procedures.

In conclusion, health literacy remains an important component of delivering effective health care to the American public. The Deaf community, as a linguistic and cultural minority, is disproportionately affected by gaps in health literacy compared to the greater population. This lack of health literacy, in combination with interpreters who lack sufficient training, leads to ineffective health care for Deaf individuals, which, in turn, correlates with poor health status and health outcomes. We believe that by providing linguistic access to health information early in childhood and by using competent medical interpreters, the Deaf community can reach the national health objectives of Healthy People 2020.

REFERENCES

Barnett, S. (1999). Clinical and cultural issues in caring for deaf people. *Family Medicine, 31*(1), 17–22.

Barnett, S. (2002). Cross-cultural communication with patients who use American Sign Language. *Family Medicine 34*(5), 376–82.

Barnett, S., & Franks, P. (2002). Health care utilization and adults who are deaf: Relationship with age at onset of deafness. *Health Services Research, 37*(1), 103–18.

Berkman, N. D., Dewalt, D. A., Pignone, M. P., Sheridan, S. L., Lohr, K. N., Lux, I., Sutton, S. F., Swinson, T., & Bonito, A. J. (2004). *Literacy and health outcomes* (Summary, Evidence Report/Technology Assessment no. 87). Rockville, MD: Agency for Healthcare Research and Quality.

Braveman, P. (2006). Health disparities and health equity: Concepts and measurement. *Annual Review of Public Health 17,* 167–94.

Davenport, S. L. (1977). Improving communication with the deaf patient. *Journal of Family Practice, 4*(6), 1065–68.

Dew, D. (Ed.) (1999). *Serving individuals who are low-functioning deaf: Report of the*

Twenty-Fifth Institute on Rehabilitation Issues. Washington DC: George Washington University.

DiPietro, L. J., Knight, C. H., & Sams, J. S. (1981). Health care delivery for deaf patients: The provider's role. *American Annals of the Deaf 126*(2), 106–12.

Ebert, D. A., & Heckerling, P. S. (1995). Communication with deaf patients: Knowledge, beliefs, and practices of physicians. *Journal of the American Medical Association 273*(3), 227–29.

Hauser, P. C., O'Hearn, A., McKee, M., Steider, A., & Thew, D. (2010). Deaf epistemology: Deafhood and deafness. *American Annals of the Deaf, 154*(5), 486–92.

Hochman, F. (2000). Healthcare of the Deaf: Toward a new understanding. *Journal of the American Board of Family Medicine, 13*(1), 81–83.

Holland, A. C., & Kensinger, E. A. (2010). Emotion and autobiographical memory. *Physics of Life Review, 7*(1), 85–131.

Holt, J. (1993). Stanford Achievement Test, eighth ed.: Reading comprehension subgroup results. *American Annals of the Deaf, 138*, 172–75.

Iezzoni, L. I., O'Day, B. L., Killeen, M., & Harker, H. (2004). Communicating about health care: Observations from persons who are deaf or hard of hearing. *Annals of Internal Medicine, 140*(5), 356–62.

Kleinig, D., & Mohay, H. (1990). A comparison of the health knowledge of hearing impaired and hearing high school students. *American Annals of the Deaf, 135*(3), 246–51.

Lass, L. G., Franklin, R. R., Bertrand, W. E., & Baker, J. (1978). Health knowledge, attitudes, and practices of the deaf population in Greater Orleans: A pilot study. *American Annals of the Deaf, 123*, 960–67.

MacKinney, T. G., Walters, D., Bird, G. L., & Nattinger, A. B. (1995). Improvements in preventative care and communication for deaf patients: Results of a novel primary health care program. *Journal of General Internal Medicine, 10*(3), 133–37.

Mann, J. R., Zhou, L., McKee, M., & McDermott, S. (2007). Children with hearing loss and increased risk of injury. *Annals of Family Medicine, 5*(6), 528–33.

McEwen, E., & Anton-Culver, H. (1988). The medical communication of deaf patients. *Journal of Family Practice, 26*, 289–91.

Meader, H. E., & Zazove, P. (2005). Health care interaction with Deaf culture. *Journal of the American Board of Family Medicine, 18*(3), 218–22.

Mealman, C. A. (1993, October 13–15). Incidental learning by adults in a nontraditional degree program: A case study presented at the Midwest Research-to-Practice Conference in Adult, Continuing, and Community Education. Retrieved from http://nlu.nl.edu/academics/cas/ace/facultypapers/CraigMealman_Incidental.cfm.

National Council on Disability. (2009, September). *The current state of health care for people with disabilities*. Washington, DC: Author.

National Network of Libraries of Medicine. Retrieved September 29, 2010, from http://nnlm.gov/outreach/consumer/hlthlit.html.

Nielsen-Bohlman, L., Panzer, A. M., & Kindig, D. A. (2004). *Health literacy: A prescription to end confusion*. Washington, DC: National Academies.

Orsi, J., Margellos-Anast, H., & Whitman, S. (2010). Black-white health disparities in the United States and Chicago: A 15-year progress analysis. *American Journal of Public Health, 100*(2), 349–56.

Pollard, R. Q. (1998). Psychopathology. In M. Marschark and D. Clark (Eds.), *Psychological perspectives on deafness*, vol. 2 (pp. 171–97). Mahwah, NJ: Erlbaum.

Pollard, R. Q., Jr., & Barnett, S. (2009). Health-related vocabulary knowledge among deaf adults. *Rehabilitation Psychology, 54*(2), 182–85.

Ralston, E., Zazove, P., & Gorenflo, D. W. (1996). Physicians' attitudes and beliefs about deaf patients. *Journal of the American Board of Family Practice, 9*(3), 167–73.

Registry of Interpreters for the Deaf (RID). (2007). *Interpreting in health care settings*. Retrieved September 29, 2010, from Registry of Interpreters for the Deaf website: http://www.rid.org/UserFiles/File/pdfs/Standard_Practice_Papers/Drafts_June_2006/Health_Care_Settings_SPP.pdf.

Ries, P. W. (1994). Prevalence and characteristics of persons with hearing trouble: United States, 1990–1991. *Vital and Health Statistics, 10*(188).

Schein, J. D., & Delk, M. T. (1980). Survey of healthcare for deaf people. *Deaf American, 32*(5–6), 27.

Sinai Health System and Advocate Health Care. (2004, February). *Improving Access to health and mental health for Chicago's Deaf community: A survey of deaf adults*. Chicago: Author.

Steinberg, A. G., Barnett, S., Meader, H., Wiggins, E. A., & Zazove, P. (2006a). Health care system accessibility: Experiences and perceptions of deaf people. *Journal of General Internal Medicine 21*(3), 260–66.

Steinberg, A. G., Wiggins, E. A., Barmada, C. H., & Sullivan, V. J. (2002). Deaf women: Experiences and perceptions of healthcare system access. *Journal of Women's Health, 11*(8), 729–41.

Taylor, M. M. (2007, December). *Interpreting in medical settings: Synthesis of effective practices focus group discussion: A report commissioned by the College of St. Catherine, CATIE Center, and the NCIEC*. (Draft). Edmonton, Alberta, Canada. U.S. National Library of Medicine/National Institutes of Health. *Medline Plus*. Retrieved September 29, 2010, from http://www.nlm.nih.gov/medlineplus/healthliteracy.html.

Woodroffe, T., Gorenflo, D. W., Meador, H. E., & Zazove, P. (1998). Knowledge and attitudes about AIDS among deaf and hard of hearing persons. *AIDS Care, 10*, 377–86.

Zazove, P., Niemann, L. C., Gorenflo, D. W., Carmack, C., Mehr, D., Coyne, J. C., & Antonucci, T. (1993). The health status and health care utilization of deaf and hard of hearing persons. *Archives of Family Medicine, 2*, 745–52.

PAMELA MORGAN AND
ROBERT ADAM

Deaf Interpreters in Mental Health Settings

Some Reflections on and Thoughts about Deaf Interpreter Education

THIS CHAPTER is a collaboration between a Deaf interpreter of almost 20 years' experience working as both a Deaf interpreter and a counselor for Deaf people in the mental health field (Pamela Morgan) and a Deaf interpreter researcher (Robert Adam). We examine this experience, highlighting some of the current research, and consider some of it within a number of theoretical frameworks, particularly those related to information needed by those who are teaching Deaf interpreters to work in healthcare settings. We conclude with recommendations for best practices for Deaf interpreters, particularly those who work in healthcare settings.

WHAT IS A DEAF INTERPRETER?

At the outset it is useful to examine the different descriptions of the term "Deaf interpreter." To date the role of a Deaf interpreter (Boudreault, 2005) has not been particularly clear. Is it to relay information, interpret between two languages, or change one form of signing into another (par-

We would like to thank Dr. Christopher Stone for his suggestions for and feedback on earlier drafts of this chapter and Liz Scott Gibson for her thoughts on interpreting in mental health and child-protection settings.

The support of the Economic and Social Research Council (ESRC) is gratefully acknowledged. Robert Adam was supported by ESRC Deafness Cognition and Language Research Centre (DCAL) Grant RES-620-28-0002.

ticularly with respect to Deaf-Blind interpreting or working with people with atypical language skills, including those who are very late learners of sign language, those who have a cognitive or learning disability, or those who have not acquired a full sign language at all)? It is often seen as an emerging profession and thus has newer qualifications (where they exist) than those for hearing interpreters (Signature,[1] 2010; Bienvenu & Colonomos, 1992). If qualifications do exist, they are often based on hearing interpreters' qualifications rather than being specifically tailored to Deaf interpreters. What is not discussed as much, however, is the fact that this work has its historical roots in the Deaf community (Adam, Carty, & Stone, 2011). Deaf people have for centuries performed interpreting and/ or translation tasks for other Deaf people within the Deaf community. The earliest record of a Deaf person performing a translation activity was published in 1684 and concerned a Deaf man, Matthew Pratt, who wrote down the signed answers given by his wife, Sarah, in response to questions from hearing church elders (Carty, Macready, & Sayers, 2009).

Adam et al. (2011) discuss the terminology used in the literature by a variety of Deaf and hearing researchers and practitioners to describe Deaf people who perform interpreting or translation tasks. Bienvenu and Colonomos (1992) discuss "relay interpreters" (as well as "reverse interpreters" in relation to a certificate from the Registry of Interpreters for the Deaf in the United States). Boudreault (2005), on the other hand, discusses Deaf bilingual people who were "Deaf interpreters" and worked between two languages but notes that they were sometimes used as "language facilitators" or as a "mirroring interpreter" (one who "mirrors" another interpreter, often a hearing interpreter, to enable the Deaf audience to see a clear interpretation in sign language). Forestal (2005) refers to a time when Deaf interpreters were called "intermediary interpreters," with the hearing interpreter remaining the lead interpreter in any given situation, although intermediaries have a specific legal role in the UK (O'Rourke & Flynn, 2010), where they are trained to work in the justice system. Napier, McKee, and Goswell (2006, 144) also use the term "relay interpreting" and define the role as being an "intermediary communicator between a hearing interpreter and a deaf client, a deaf presenter and a

---

1. http://www.signature.org.uk/news.php?news_id=131.

DeafBlind client, or a hearing interpreter and a DeafBlind client." From this we are to understand that a relay interpreter is needed when clients do the following:

Use their own signs or homesigns
Use a foreign sign language
Are Deaf-Blind or have limited vision
Use signs particular to a region, ethnic, or age group that are not known
    to the hearing interpreter
Are in a mental state that makes ordinary interpreted conversation difficult
    (Napier et al., 2006)

Note that all of these situations may arise in healthcare settings.

Adam et al. (2011) refer to the older tradition of "ghostwriters," who were Deaf people who acted as language brokers by performing translation tasks for other Deaf people. Language brokering has been defined by Hall and Robinson (1999) as follows:

> an activity in an event during which it mediates between two different language speakers or writers/readers, and in which it is actively involved in converting meanings in one language into meanings in another. Such an activity is not simply a neutral, formal, linguistic, dictionary exercise in the ability to translate one set of words into another. (3)

The term *ghostwriters*, on the other hand, was hitherto informally used within a particular Deaf community context, was relatively unknown by hearing members of the community, and did not define a formal professional category.

As mentioned earlier, the definitions of Deaf interpreters focus on different aspects or reflect different perspectives: Some definitions, such as that by Napier et al. (2006), explain some of the tasks that an interpreter might be expected to do, while others, such as those by Forestal (2005) and Boudreault (2005), describe what can be considered a profession in itself. Adam et al. (2011) describe what has historically taken place within the Deaf community and its role in "apprenticing" future Deaf interpreters. On the other hand, the National Consortium of Interpreter Education Centers (NCIEC) has developed a working document on a set of competencies for

Deaf interpreters,[2] which says that "Deaf interpreters[3] work across the full gamut of community interpreting venues, but most commonly in social services, medical appointments, business meetings, VR/workplace, legal and mental health settings where setting-specific knowledge skill sets are required."

This chapter focuses specifically on the work of Deaf interpreters in medical and mental health settings and makes suggestions for developing a community-based model of Deaf interpreting. This can inform the development of Deaf interpreter training programs and the understanding of hearing professionals who may need to work with these highly skilled individuals in such settings.

WHY HAVE DEAF INTERPRETERS?

Some of the things Deaf people working as interpreters often face are reservations, misgivings, and occasional cynicism from the hearing professionals or even hearing sign language/spoken language interpreters as to the need for a Deaf interpreter. Drennan and Swartz refer to the "low status of interpreters in the institutional context" (1999, 170). These reservations appear to be a manifestation of this: Interpreters have a low status, and Deaf interpreters an even lower one.

Arranging a sign language interpreter is sometimes seen as enough of a challenge for some service providers without having to consider clients with complex needs, who may also require Deaf interpreters to work alongside their hearing interpreter colleagues. Even though this arrangement provides optimum access, organizing both a Deaf interpreter and a hearing interpreter is sometimes seen as an unnecessary extra. It has been the experience of some Deaf interpreters that this affects the professional status of the Deaf interpreter in certain situations; the value of the Deaf interpreter is sometimes put into question, not least because the hearing professionals have not fully understood this function.

---

2. http://diinstitute.org/wp-content/uploads/2011/06/DC_Final_Final.pdf.
3. Of interest also is the ASL sign for Deaf Interpreter: fingerspelled D+I, as distinct from INTERPRETER, which may refer more to hearing interpreters.

Napier et al. (2006) outline a number of the more practical reasons that Deaf interpreters are sometimes a desirable component of the interpreting process, but there has been little analysis, historically or otherwise, as to why Deaf interpreters are used. Adam et al. (2011), however, find that Deaf people are more comfortable with a Deaf person performing interpreting or translation tasks. They utilize the notion of "habitus" (Bourdieu, 1986) to explore this feeling of reassurance: Deaf people from a similar habitus or background were more comfortable about asking other Deaf people for assistance and were not embarrassed about their English literacy skills. Most often the members of a minority community have other members of the community interpret for them (Edwards, Temple, & Alexander, 2005) and feel more comfortable with this arrangement. As Boudreault (2005) notes, some of these Deaf interpreters, though hard of hearing (their audiological status, not cultural identity), are nonetheless able to undertake consecutive interpreting tasks.

Historically and even today, Deaf people have asked other Deaf people in the Deaf club or at school to explain English texts (such as correspondence or newspapers) or to translate letters or documents in sign language on their behalf (Adam et al., 2011; Forestal, 2005). A Deaf person might also accompany another Deaf person to important appointments in medical, banking, and legal settings, often to lend moral support and sometimes to lipread for the Deaf person and relate what the hearing person says, sometimes to write down for the hearing person what the Deaf person says, and less often to actually speak for the Deaf person. These are never professionally paid roles but are valued nonetheless.

As highlighted earlier, the situation of the Deaf interpreter is not always accepted by other service providers, including hearing interpreters. According to Egnatovich (1999, 1), "certified Deaf interpreters are only there for deaf people with minimal language skills or whenever I need them." This situation may find parallels in the "welfare colonialism" carried out by hearing people (Ladd, 2003, 17), which entails the "destruction and replacement of indigenous cultures by Western cultures." For example, in the Australian context, the cultures and languages of aboriginal peoples were destroyed when white colonizers tried to replace their way of life with their own. There has been a parallel drawn between the experiences of Australian aboriginal peoples and Deaf people in that sign language and Deaf culture have been devalued by hearing people and, in some contexts, the language and culture have been replaced by spoken language. We suggest that by not accepting Deaf interpreters and the historical basis of interpreting within the Deaf community, hearing interpreters and other hearing professionals demonstrate a welfare colonialism toward Deaf people and Deaf interpreters.

Adam et al. (2011) conclude that "clearly there is a tension between the choices exercised by Deaf people (the choosing of a Deaf person to interpret for them) and institutional control made manifest either in the choosing of non-Deaf people as interpreters (Stone & Woll, 2008) or in the deployment of welfare workers to publicly display their expertise." In that vein Bienvenu and Colonomos (1992, 76) comment that having a Deaf interpreter working with a hearing interpreter is not a sign of a weak interpreter but rather "a disciplined and ethical interpreter. Some situations call for the use of two qualified interpreters—it's as simple as that."

Given that Deaf interpreters come from within the community itself and undertake "pro bono work" in the community, including within the family and at the Deaf club, it is important for the training and registration process for Deaf interpreters to take these factors into account. This is of particular importance with respect to understanding what the Deaf community expects from a Deaf interpreter, let alone a hearing interpreter. Only then can an appropriate definition of a Deaf interpreter be developed.

DEAF INTERPRETERS IN MEDICAL AND MENTAL HEALTH SETTINGS

There has been little research on the use of Deaf interpreters in medical and mental health settings, although this practice is reasonably well established in the UK, the United States, and Canada. Boudreault (2005) makes suggestions about what is appropriate for one-on-one settings, which may be applied to medical and mental health interpreting, particularly with respect to the setup of the room and where the hearing interpreter and the Deaf interpreter sit in relation to the client. The importance of an experienced and fully trained interpreter, Deaf or hearing, in a medical setting cannot be understated (Ebert & Heckerling, 1995) as this results in a better relationship between the Deaf patient and the hearing medical professional. A recent report on malpractice[4] in medical situations suggests that a "competent interpreter" should be used during every encounter between healthcare providers and Deaf clients.

A comparable model for doctor-patient relationships is proposed by Valero-Garcés, (2005) who discusses doctor-patient consultations in dyadic and triadic settings. She investigated three different types of interactions: (1) doctor/foreign language patient; (2) doctor/foreign language patient/ family member; (3) doctor/foreign-language patient/trained interpreter. She found that in type 3 interactions, the interpreter was able to maintain the interpreter role. Similar communication strategies were found in types 1 and 2 interactions where communication strategies (frequent questions, repetitions, reformulations) were used, which ultimately influence the structure of the interaction. With respect to type 2 interactions, which utilized an ad hoc interpreter (e.g., a spouse or family member who often acted as an advocate), similar communication strategies were used as in type 1 interactions because the doctor did not fully comprehend the ad hoc interpreter's level of skill. That is to say that more interaction took place between the doctor and the ad hoc interpreter, specifically as an advocate and a family member. Additionally, the interpreters in type 3 interactions used the first person, as opposed to the third person, giving them a "voice" within the interaction.

Valero-Garcés (2005) has also found that the interpreters in type 3 encounters were able to maintain impartiality and ask appropriately for reformulation or clarification when necessary. Many parallels can be drawn with the Deaf community. Historically, Deaf people were not accompanied by professionally trained interpreters; they were accompanied by family members or hearing friends to appointments, a situation that parallels type 2 interactions. If it is the case that (type 3) spoken language interpreters can share the client's spoken language as a first language or share the same habitus as the client (as noted earlier), then it becomes important to consider Deaf interpreters in this setting. Deaf clients should have the right to a Deaf interpreter, as a Deaf interpreter is more likely to share the same habitus as the Deaf client; the lived experience of being a Deaf person is even more important in medical situations. Appropriately trained Deaf

---

4. http://mighealth.net/eu/images/5/59/Malpractice.pdf.

interpreters can draw upon their lived experience (or ELK, extralinguistic knowledge) while also providing the most appropriate service as detailed in the description of type 3 interactions in Valores-Garcés (2005).

In another study, Elderkin-Thompson, Cohen Silver, and Waitzkin (2001) found that bilingual nurses needed some training to understand their role as nurse-interpreters. This allowed physicians to extract meaning from their rendering without the nurses' adding clinical expectations, slanting interpretations, or using metaphors that were not compatible with Western clinical discourse. These nurses acted as ad-hoc interpreters and did not get involved in discussions between doctor and patient, nor did they allow cultural or language differences or even personal expectations to get in the way of interpreting between the doctor and the patient—because, after training, they understood their roles better.

Liz Scott Gibson, who is president of the World Association of Sign Language Interpreters,[5] also indicates that Deaf interpreters should almost always be assigned in mental health or child protection settings to work with the sign language/spoken language interpreter (personal communication). According to Scott Gibson, if a Deaf person with mental health issues is using language that is atypical in some way (e.g., experiencing a psychotic episode or is echolalic), the native user may identify this aberration, whereas those who have learned a sign language as a second language may not. Second language learners also learn the adult form of the language and are more likely to have used the language with Deaf adults and thus are not well placed to adapt to child language forms. Deaf interpreters are more likely to have a deeper understanding of what the Deaf client is saying not least because they have grown up as a Deaf person and have a broader frame of reference.

Finally, Rudvin (2007) has found that the interpreter's professionalism and adherence to the code of ethics were bound by the interpreter's cultural parameters and the way in which the interpreter positions the "self" in the group. Deaf interpreters and hearing interpreters would therefore, by virtue of the positioning and cultural parameters of the former individuals, have a different interpretation of the code of ethics and the concept of professionalism.

---

5. The World Association of Sign Language Interpreters is an international body that comprises national organizations of sign language interpreters (http://www.wasli.org).

DEAF INTERPRETERS IN MENTAL HEALTH SETTINGS IN THE UK

The Deaf Interpreter Practitioner's Background

As Deaf interpreters have not by and large had their knowledge and skills developed by interpreter education programs, it may well be useful for us to examine our own pathways and how our expertise was developed. Pamela's parents were Deaf; her mother was born in London but was of Scottish descent; her Scottish grandparents were also Deaf, and her maternal grandmother lived with the family for most of her life. Pamela's grandmother attended Donaldson's School for the Deaf in Edinburgh from 1895 to 1909. Her father, on the other hand was Irish, from Dublin, Eire; thus, he used Irish Sign Language (ISL), with its one-handed fingerspelling system. He attended the Cabra School for Deaf Boys in Dublin.

Pamela spent her early years observing her mother and grandmother communicating with each other by using a mixture of the southern and Scottish dialects of BSL and fingerspelling. As with many Deaf children of Deaf parents, she frequently relayed information, conversations, or messages from hearing people to her parents, read letters, and translated from English into sign language and vice versa for them. She also relayed information to her classmates at school: "It became a natural way of life for me. I thought nothing of it."

This is the classic background of Deaf ghostwriters (Adam et al., 2011; Forestal, 2005). They spend their younger years at home with the family or at the Deaf club being asked to undertake regular language brokering tasks by friends, family, and even other classmates in school (Bienvenu & Colonomos, 1992; Boudreault, 2005; Adam et al., 2011).

In the early 1990s Pamela became involved with the Usher's Group under the auspices of Sense (a Deaf-Blind organization in the UK) and was trained to become a Deaf Usher syndrome Volunteer Advocate (DUVA). This training was provided by Sarah Reed, a native BSL user who herself has Usher syndrome. Following the training, Pamela became involved in the Usher syndrome UK's committee meetings several times a year as a relay interpreter, using visual frame (which enables Deaf-Blind persons with limited vision to see an interpreter but with a smaller frame of vision) and/or hands on. The first time the British Deaf Association had Deaf relay interpreting, at its conference in Cardiff in 1994, she worked as a paid Deaf interpreter.

To date there is still no national register for Deaf interpreters, let alone those working as Deaf-Blind relay interpreters. Although the Deaf Usher's group has disbanded, Pamela continues to work with Deaf-Blind clients using the skills learned over the years. It is our hope that by September 2011 registration will be open to Deaf interpreters working between two sign languages and between written English and BSL.

In 1993 Pamela started working in the Deaf in-patients' unit as a health-care assistant with the London-based National Deaf Mental Health Services (NDMHS). Although she had no background in mental health, she quickly acquired a wealth of experience by working with consultant psychiatrists, clinical psychologists, nurses, occupational therapists, and other professionals. She worked her way up within the mental health field by starting from the in-patient unit and moving on to work in the community with Deaf people who used the NDMHS. She took additional training and became a counselor as well, working with the NDMHS for a total of 16 years: "I felt this to be a necessity, being a Deaf professional working within the Deaf community. More importantly, I was working as a relay interpreter with the Deaf Usher UK Group. I felt my clients deserved the best, and that meant that I had to gain this next level."

In 2004 Pamela acquired her Level 4 National Vocational Qualification (NVQ) in BSL, which was a formal language qualification but not an interpreting qualification. There are as yet no opportunities for Deaf people to become qualified interpreters although developments are currently in progress. A Deaf relay course was offered in 2006 by an interpreting service agency, but it was never fully accredited because the awarding body did not consider that it satisfied the criteria of interpreting between two languages: "It got me thinking and discussing with others. This seemed to be an unfair situation for both service providers and users."

In spite of the lack of training opportunities and registration of Deaf interpreters, Pamela continues:

> I feel I have finally found my vocation [as a Deaf interpreter]. I feel that, having been an observer on numerous occasions where clients have not fully accessed the information they are entitled to, often major, life-changing decisions are made about them and their lives,

and they are not fully part of the process. In the worst cases clients have been misrepresented or misunderstood, resulting in catastrophic outcomes to their lives. I get great satisfaction from the positive feedback I receive from clients who say that finally they are understood and listened to and their views are considered fully.

There is a connection between the client and me (when I work as a Deaf interpreter). This connection is one where they can feel to be in a peer (where the client and I share a language and culture) situation where otherwise they would feel isolated, inferior, and inadequate. What would otherwise be a hearing-oriented environment then becomes an environment where they feel engaged, a feeling of belonging, where they can then relax and become familiarized with their circumstances.

However, having spent the best part of her career proving her worth and acquiring the qualifications and recognition that follows from this, Pamela now finds herself in a position that she finds most uncomfortable:

I am as qualified as I possibly can be at this stage. I am also a supporter of ASLI[6] (although I am currently not eligible to be a member). I feel that some of my hearing counterparts do not see me as a peer, and I am therefore not treated the same as other hearing Interpreters in the profession. This leaves me feeling vulnerable. I can fully empathize with some of my clients who prior to having a Deaf Relay Interpreter felt disempowered. I remain hopeful that enough professional, well qualified, Deaf Relay Interpreters will continue to work in the community, slowly helping to change attitudes and that more people will see the real and significant benefits of accessing our services.

Pamela's background as a Deaf interpreter has parallels with Elderkin-Thompson et al. (2005)'s findings that bilingual nurses who were trained as interpreters performed better in that role; Pamela has a background as both a qualified counselor and a highly experienced Deaf interpreter. Drennan and Swartz (1999, 191) find that as different therapies may be performed in mental health settings, different skills and styles of working are required

---

6. Association of Sign Language Interpreters (UK), the national body representing sign language interpreters in England, Wales, and Northern Ireland. For more information see http://www.asli.org.uk.

from interpreters and that one size of interpreting skill or style does not fit all. Only by having a greater awareness of the needs of the individuals and the institutions can the interpreter ensure optimum access, and Pamela ensured that she was able to do that.

Robert, on the other hand, grew up in Melbourne, Australia, and also had Deaf parents. He grew up watching his hearing grandmothers, who were proficient in sign language (one in Australian Sign Language [Auslan] and the other in Australian Irish Sign Language [AISL]), interpret conversations and television programs. Occasionally one of his grandmothers drafted letters on his parents' behalf for them to sign and mail. Later he was asked to draft letters and deliver messages for his parents; because the neighbors were hearing, Robert would go next door and ask them to make phone calls on his parents' behalf. When he grew older and became an adult member of the Deaf community, he would draft newsletter articles, requests for funding, and other correspondence for various Deaf individuals and groups, and he even sat in on Deaf sports club meetings to take minutes. He has also proofread letters, essays, and documents for Deaf people and continues to do this via email even though he does not live in Australia. His first professionally paid interpreting job, like Pamela's, was for a Deaf Usher's group meeting, where he interpreted for Deaf-Blind clients.

Later, as a member of the organizing committee of the XIII World Congress of the World Federation of the Deaf, he performed ad hoc interpreting work between representatives of the Australian Association of the Deaf and the World Federation of the Deaf, between Australian Sign Language and International Sign. This led to working as an international sign interpreter at international events, which includes the International Congress for Educators of the Deaf, the World Federation of the Deaf, and the Deaflympics.

Both Pamela and Robert have come into the Deaf interpreter field through the traditional route; they both started at home and within their Deaf community networks, demonstrating one of the current ways that Deaf interpreters are educated.

Experiences of a Deaf Interpreter Practitioner

We—Pamela and Robert—would like to share some specific examples of experiences that Deaf interpreters confront in their work so that Deaf interpreter education courses can become informed of these actual working experiences. These are not specific to medical and mental health settings, although applications to such situations are given when appropriate. Whatever the setting, these experiences give us insight into some of the situations a Deaf interpreter may face.

Situation 1: A police situation, where two BSL interpreters were working with Pamela, the BSL interpreter (A) relayed information to her for her to relay to the Deaf client; the other BSL interpreter (B) voiced what Pamela signed to the client. This puts the hearing interpreter in a position of power, as there was no one checking the accuracy of BSL interpreter A. There is an inherent assumption that the Deaf interpreter's work is potentially inaccurate and that it would be easier to apportion blame to the Deaf interpreter in the event of the transfer of erroneous information. This may be considered an example of the welfare colonialism that Ladd (2003) refers to—a situation in which the interpreter is unable to relinquish power to the Deaf interpreter and in which the interpreter is unable to trust and depend on the Deaf interpreter. In medical settings, the situation for the Deaf client may become unnecessarily complicated—and even more so in mental health settings, when clinical issues such as paranoia may arise.

Situation 2: Pamela and Robert were booked to interpret at a national Deaf conference. They were the only two Deaf interpreters working all day for two days, while teams of three hearing BSL/English interpreters worked throughout the conference. A similar situation could occur in a long healthcare procedure, such as labor and delivery. It is our experience that, whenever teams are used, there are usually fewer Deaf than hearing interpreters. This may be a reflection of some of the community attitudes toward the work of Deaf interpreters, which some consider low status and easy or something that does not require special skills or training.

Situation 3: Pamela worked with a Deaf client in a meeting with a solicitor, which the BSL interpreter did not attend. She had to write everything that the client said for the solicitor, and the solicitor wrote everything down for her to translate into BSL for the client. At the end both the client and the solicitor were thrilled with the progress and information and with what they were able to achieve in such a short time in comparison to several previous meetings over a period of time. In mental health or healthcare settings Deaf interpreters may enable a greater level of understanding and help prevent unnecessary clarifications and misinterpretations, which may result in fewer appointments.

Situation 4: Robert worked with a hearing interpreter in a mental health setting. A Deaf person had been sectioned and was being treated in a secure mental health facility. This person did not grow up in Australia and did not have Australian Sign Language as a first language. The person was able to discuss his treatment and progress at meetings only when Robert was interpreting. This highlights the importance of having the appropriate interpreting service provision, having access to interpreters with the appropriate language combinations and languages skills, and having access to Deaf interpreters.

Situation 5: In a juvenile court setting, after a number of hearings with a hearing interpreter working on her own, Robert worked with a different hearing interpreter. For the first time, the Deaf client understood that a number of criminal charges had been filed against him. It was not until a Deaf interpreter was assigned that the Deaf client understood the gravity of the situation. This shows how grave the consequences can be in a healthcare setting if the Deaf client is not able to understand what the medical consequences of treatment are. It also speaks to early and appropriate diagnosis of medical and mental health conditions in which the clients' words and the clinical team's observations and medical assessments all contribute to diagnosis and treatment.

Working as a Deaf Interpreter in a Mental Health Setting in the UK

Deaf relay interpreting requires a very clear understanding of professional boundaries, as well as an interpreter who is competent in BSL and has a good grasp of standard English. Deaf interpreters should be able not only to relay information without altering the intended meaning or message significantly but also to draw upon their life experiences as a Deaf member of the Deaf community to ensure that culturally appropriate inferences can be understood. It is important to be able to do this work and at the same time be open to constructive criticism as it is important to continually review and monitor one's performance. As with hearing interpreters, it is important for a Deaf interpreter to be a supportive team player. As Pamela says:

> As a Deaf person whose native language is BSL, I have an instinctive aptitude to tune in to individuals who may not be using generally accepted, "standard," or recognized sign language. I am able to pick up on nuances of a person's visual language. I am also able to use generic visual language to ensure that a client understands the contents without using specific, recognized signs.

In a mental health setting, interpreters must have firsthand knowledge of or training in mental health issues. It is essential to know and understand the technical terms used in the area of mental health. In the UK, Deaf interpreters must have an understanding of the Mental Health Act (1983), as well as relevant policies and legislation, particularly with respect to the "sectioning" of clients. Some mental health assessment methods (e.g., psychometric tests) are not designed for Deaf BSL users; Deaf interpreters should have the knowledge and ability to translate the information into clear BSL without losing meaning or intention. When working with Deaf immigrants and refugees, it is useful to be able to use broader language strategies—gestures and possibly signs from other sign languages—to ensure clarity and maximize the potential for the Deaf client to understand.

In Pamela's experience, it is quite common for Deaf persons who have a mental health illness to experience the following: isolation, institutionalization, low self-esteem, and lack of confidence. They may have poor life skills and social skills or come from a disadvantaged educational background.

According to the Sign Health website,[7] more than 50% of Deaf people have experienced some kind of abuse as children. One in four culturally Deaf people experience a mental health problem at some point in their lives (UK Department of Health). Given that there are an estimated 70,000 Deaf people who use BSL in the UK, this equates to more than 15,000 Deaf people who will eventually experience a mental health problem. On top of this, 95% of Deaf children are born to hearing parents, who may struggle to understand their needs. This highlights a great need for appropriate mental health services for Deaf people, including access to Deaf interpreters.

---

7. http://www.signhealth.org.uk/index.php?pageID=80.

When people have a mental illness, some of the issues that can arise are mood and thought disorders, varying degrees of depression, and language disorders. Distressing issues within these people's lives may cause them to experience disturbing episodes and display symptoms, which can affect their ability to communicate. They may, for example, vary their speed of BSL usage, employ idiosyncratic signs, copy others' signing exactly, and make repetitions. Often, when going through an episode, a client may appear erratic and sign in an exaggerated fashion, which may be due to frustration or fear.

Often Deaf people who are severely ill have poor concentration, lack motivation, or feel exhausted; this may also be due to the side effects of their medication. A Deaf interpreter should have the ability to recognize this and be able to summarize information given without leaving out vital aspects. What may seem like a tic to a sign language interpreter may carry significant meaning and weight. For example, what may appear to be a gesture or a flick of the hand could refer to an actual person or object. Cultural issues may also cause problems in properly assessing an individual's mental health. A client's native language may not be English or BSL, which can create an even greater barrier to making an accurate diagnosis. A good diagnosis needs someone who has excellent communicative and receptive skills and an understanding of a client's mood and emotional state.

WORKING AS A DEAF INTERPRETER IN MENTAL HEALTH SETTINGS

The preceding experiences illustrate the need to rethink the nature of the work of Deaf interpreters. In a study of community interpreters working with minority groups, taking into account how cultural differences are approached, a typology of roles for interpreting has been suggested by Leanza (2005, 186), who proposes four different roles for a community interpreter:

• As a system agent, the interpreter transmits the dominant discourse, norms, and values to the patient. Cultural difference is denied in favor of the dominant culture. Cultural difference tends to be elided or assimilated.

• As a community agent, the interpreter plays the reverse role, [and] the minority norms and values are presented as potentially equally valid. Cultural difference is acknowledged. This role can be played in various ways, more or less nuanced.

• When acting as an integration agent, the interpreter finds resources to help migrants (and people from the receiving society) to make sense, negotiate meanings, and find an "in-between way of behaving." These roles take place outside consultations in everyday life.
• As a linguistic agent, the interpreter attempts to maintain an impartial position (to the extent that it is possible).

This study proposes training not only for interpreters but also for healthcare professionals and other professionals who work with interpreters. Such training should be followed up in healthcare institutions. It raises the question of whether Deaf or hearing interpreters are the appropriate community agent (Leanza, 2005) in the process and whether they should be acting as a cultural informant, a cultural broker, and/or an advocate. It would be interesting to compare the interactions between Deaf and hearing interpreters and the client with those between hearing interpreters and the client to see which role more frequently characterizes these (potentially) different exchanges.

This raises the question of training. For all professions, training is essential and should be required, and this applies to the Deaf interpreter profession. In its working document on competencies of Deaf interpreters,[8] the NCIEC (2010) refers to extralinguistic knowledge, which is firsthand knowledge of the Deaf world. Deaf interpreters can hone this tacit knowledge and professionalize it through interpreter education.

Additionally, even though the generic code of ethics for sign language interpreters is applicable to Deaf interpreters, it has implications for when the Deaf interpreter and the Deaf client share the same habitus. If we accept the statement that the Deaf community and the hearing mainstream have different norms, then this will manifest when following the code of ethics; Deaf and hearing people can behave differently while following the same code of ethics because different communities understand notions (e.g., impartiality) differently.

The discussion of these important differences between trainee Deaf and hearing interpreters would be most helpful. There is not a one-size-fits-all model of interpreter education, and while there is much common ground in the training of Deaf and hearing interpreters, certain aspects of a Deaf interpreter's work require separate training.

---

8. http://diinstitute.org/wp-content/uploads/2010/04/DC_WorkingDoc0410.pdf.

Conclusion

Deaf interpreters are an important consideration in medical and mental health settings because of what they bring to the assignment: a common habitus. Deaf interpreters share the same language and habitus of the Deaf client and can work with appropriately qualified hearing interpreters to provide the best possible service to all clients. The experiences of traditional Deaf interpreters, such as ghostwriters and other language brokers, have much to contribute to the existing knowledge and current training practices in this field. Professional training is essential for Deaf interpreters who do not have the same opportunities as hearing interpreters.

References

Adam, R., Carty, B., & Stone, C. (2011). Ghostwriting: Deaf translators within the Deaf community. *Babel* 57(4), 375–393.

Bienvenu, M J, & Colonomos, B. (1992). Relay interpreting in the 90s. In Laurie Swabey (Ed.), *The challenge of the 90s: New standards in interpreter education, Proceedings of the Eighth National Convention of the Conference of Interpreter Trainers* (pp. 69–80). Pomona, CA: Conference of Interpreter Trainers.

Boudreault, P. (2005). Deaf interpreters. In Terry Jantzen (Ed.), *Topics in signed language interpreting: Theory and practice* (pp. 323–55). Philadelphia: John Benjamins.

Bourdieu, P. (1986). The forms of capital. In J. G. Richardson (Ed.), *Handbook for theory and research for the sociology of education* (pp. 241–58). New York: Greenwood Press.

Carty, B., Macready, S., & Sayers, E. (2009). "A grave and gracious woman": Deaf people and signed language in colonial New England. *Sign Language Studies*, 9, 297–323.

Drennan, G., & Swartz, L. 1999. Institutional roles for psychiatric interpreters in post-apartheid South Africa. *Interpreting*, 4(2), 169–98.

Ebert, D., & Heckerling, P. (1995). Communication with deaf patients: Knowledge, beliefs, and practices of physicians. *Journal of the American Medical Association*, 273(3), 227–29.

Edwards, R., Temple, B., & Alexander, C. (2005). Users' experiences of interpreters: The critical role of trust. *Interpreting* 7(2), 77–95.

Egnatovich, R. (1999). Certified deaf interpreter WHY. *RID Views*, 16, 10.

Elderkin-Thompson, V., Cohen Silver, R., & Waitzkin, H. (2001). When nurses double as interpreters: A study of Spanish-speaking patients in a U.S. primary care setting. *Social Science and Medicine*, 52, 1343–58.

Forestal, E. (2005). The emerging professionals: Deaf interpreters and their views and experiences on training. In M. Marschark, R. Peterson, & E. A. Winston

(Eds.), *Sign language interpreting and interpreter education: Directions for research and practice* (235–58). New York: Oxford University Press.

Hall, N., & Robinson, A. (1999). The language brokering behaviour of young children in families of Pakistani heritage. Retrieved from www.esri.mmu.ac.uk /resprojects/brokering/Pakistani.doc.

Ladd, P. (2003). *Understanding Deaf culture: In search of Deafhood.* Clevedon: Multilingual Matters.

Leanza, Y. (2005). Roles of community interpreters in pediatrics as seen by interpreters, physicians, and researchers. *Interpreting, 7*(2), 167–92.

Napier, J., McKee, R., & Goswell, D. (2006). *Sign language interpreting: Theory and practice in Australia and New Zealand.* Sydney: Federation Press.

O'Rourke, S., & Flynn, C. (2010). *Deafness and the criminal justice system: Can we make a difference?* Paper given at the Eighth European Congress on Mental Health and Deafness. Cambridge, UK, November 2–5.

Rudvin, M. (2007). Professionalism and ethics in community interpreting: The impact of individualist versus collective group identity. *Interpreting, 9*(1), 47–69.

Smith, T. B. (1996). *Deaf people in context.* Unpublished doctoral dissertation, University of Washington.

Stone, C., & Woll, B. (2008). Dumb O Jemmy and others: Deaf people, interpreters, and the London courts in the 18th and 19th centuries. *Sign Language Studies, 8*(3): 226–40.

Valero-Garcés, C. (2005). Doctor-patient consultations in dyadic and triadic exchanges. *Interpreting, 7*(2), 193–210.

Woll, B., & Adam, R. (2012). Sign language and the politics of deafness. In M. Martin-Jones, A. Blackledge, and A. Creese (Eds.), *The Routledge handbook of multilingualism* (pp. 100–114). New York: Routledge.

BRUCE DOWNING AND
KARIN RUSCHKE

Professionalizing Healthcare Interpreting between Spoken Languages

Contributions of the National Council on Interpreting in Health Care

WHILE THE professionalization of sign language interpreting in the United States is well advanced, with academic training and certification of interpreters long established, interpreting between speakers of spoken languages has lagged behind. However, the scene is changing rapidly, and over the last decade many exciting developments have occurred, particularly in the field of community interpreting between English and other spoken languages and the subfield of healthcare interpreting.[1]

This chapter discusses the expansion and professionalization of healthcare interpreting in the United States and emphasizes developments that have taken place in response to continuing immigration, legal mandates, and concerns about access to public services and patient safety.[2] As members of the National Council on Interpreting in Health Care and of its Committee on Standards, Training, and Certification, we emphasize this organization's contributions to the advancement of healthcare interpreting.

---

1. "Community interpreting" is defined as interpreting between providers of public services and their patients or clients, and "healthcare interpreting" as a subarea of community interpreting in which communication focuses on improving the client's health and well-being.
2. An earlier status report on the development of this field is Downing (1998).

209

The Setting and the Need for Community Interpreters in Diverse Languages

Historically, America has been a land of immigrants, and the influx of new residents continues today. In recent years the places of origin of immigrants to the United States have shifted from mainly Eastern and Western Europe, Canada, and Mexico to a much more diverse mix, including large numbers from Central and South America, various parts of Asia, and both East and West Africa. According to the Migration Policy Institute's Migration Information Source, as of 2009, 38.5 million immigrants were living in the United States (12.5% of the total population) (Batalova & Terrazas, 2010).

According to a report on the 2000 census, "the proportion of the population aged 5 and over who spoke English less than 'Very well' [and therefore are considered 'limited English proficient' or LEP] grew from 4.8 percent [of the U.S. population] in 1980, to 6.1 percent in 1990, and to 8.1 percent in 2000" (Shin & Bruno, 2003, 3). This is the population for whom interpreters are needed for critical encounters with providers of healthcare and other services, as well as in the justice system. While Spanish is predominant in most parts of the country, many communities report 30–50 or more different languages whose speakers require interpretation or written translations. Considering that the LEP population has increased steadily in recent decades, it is safe to assume that these numbers will continue to increase in the coming years.

Immigrants who come seeking employment and a better standard of living and refugees from war-torn countries often speak little or no English on arrival. There is considerable distrust and resentment of immigrants in the United States, but, fortunately, there also are advocates for their welfare and service providers ready to offer needed services. In addition, federal law exists to protect their right of access to public services and publicly supported health care (Federal Interagency Working Group on Limited English Proficiency, n.d.).

LEGAL REQUIREMENTS

Recently, a major impetus for improved language services is the more stringent enforcement of the Civil Rights Act of 1964 (U.S. Department of Justice, 2011), which requires institutions that receive federal funds to provide reasonable access to services regardless of one's "national origin." The federal Office of Minority Health (OMH) established enforceable guidelines in 2001, the National Standards for Culturally and Linguistically Appropriate Services in Health Care (CLAS). Standard 4 reads as follows:

> Health care organizations must offer and provide language assistance services, including bilingual staff and interpreter services, at no cost to each patient/consumer with limited English proficiency at all points of contact, in a timely manner during all hours of operation. (Office of Minority Health, 2001)

The federal "guidance" documents that spell out language rights require the translation of certain essential documents and the provision of qualified interpreters in healthcare encounters within specified limits, but they are not precise as to what the qualifications of a competent interpreter are and how qualifications should be assessed (U.S. Department of Justice, 2003). Many states have also passed laws to ensure reasonable access to health care for the limited English population. In addition, The Joint Commission, an organization that accredits hospitals in the United States, recently approved new and revised hospital standards to improve patient-provider communication (2010). It is now widely accepted that effective communication is no longer simply a patient's right or a means to support patient satisfaction but that it is vital to ensuring patient safety.

PROFESSIONALIZATION OF HEALTHCARE INTERPRETING

In the past, interpreting in health care was done in an informal way by patients' friends and family members or by nominally bilingual hospital staff. However, over the past 15 years or so, many institutions and individuals have played roles in developing this field by acting as funders, organizers, trainers, and advocates. One key organization in the development of this field has been the National Council on Interpreting in Health Care (NCIHC). The NCIHC began as an informal working group in the mid-1990s and has grown into a national, multidisciplinary membership organization working for the advancement of the field of healthcare interpreting in the interest of patient health and safety.

At the same time the NCIHC was working to professionalize the field of healthcare interpreting, civil suits and complaints filed with the Office for Civil Rights in a few metropolitan areas around the country (e.g., Seattle, Boston, San Francisco, Chicago) led to the development of more formal interpreter programs, which used bilingual individuals as dedicated interpreters. Over time, healthcare interpreting has grown, and more attention is now being paid to training interpreters, to forming professional associations, to developing models for provision of service, and to incorporating the use of telephone and video technology in providing services.

Today, while some resistance to the cost of incorporating interpreter services into all healthcare interactions with LEP patients still lingers, hospital administrators have stopped asking, "Why do we need to provide interpreters?" and have started asking, "How can we provide language access services in the most cost-effective way?" The expectations for the quality of interpreting have risen, and a new profession is emerging: that of the professional healthcare interpreter.

We can trace the extent of progress along these lines in more detail by reference to two publications that provide developmental guideposts. Holly Mikkelson, an interpreter educator associated with the Monterey Institute of International Studies, has written an important paper on professionalization (1996). In it she calls attention to Roda Roberts's "guidelines for the professionalization of community interpreting," a series of recommended steps for the development of community interpreting as a recognized professional field (Roberts, 1994):

> 1) clarification of terminology . . . ; 2) clarification of the role(s) of the community interpreter; 3) provision of training for community interpreters; 4) provision of training for trainers of community interpreters . . . ; 5) provision of training for professionals working with interpreters . . . ; and 6) accreditation. (Mikkelson, 1996)

We use Roberts's guidelines to organize the following discussion of how the field of community interpreting, and specifically interpreting in health care, has developed in the United States in the years since Roberts's and Mikkelson's articles were published, emphasizing the contributions of the National Council on Interpreting in Health Care and related organizations.

The NCIHC is a nonprofit organization formed in 1998 following a series of annual convenings of a "national working group" that began in

1994. Members of the NCIHC represent a broad spectrum of stakeholders; while many members are interpreters, it is not an interpreter organization, and its goals are broader than the advancement of the interpreting profession. Its officers and committee members work without remuneration. Its mission statement is as follows: "The NCIHC is a multidisciplinary organization whose mission is to promote and enhance language access in health care in the United States" (NCIHC, n.d.).

Even before the NCIHC was formally organized, the Massachusetts Medical Interpreters Association (now the International Medical Interpreters Association) had played an important regional and even national role in uniting the profession, and other organizations have contributed, such as the California Healthcare Interpreting Association, formed in 1996, and various other recently launched statewide and regional organizations of interpreters. However, the NCIHC, because of its mission, its broad membership, and its national focus, has been able to take a leadership role in the professionalization of healthcare interpreting. There is no comparable organization devoted to community interpreting more broadly or to any of its other domains, such as interpreting in governmental or social services, education, or business (although legal interpreting is well represented by NAJIT, the National Association of Judicial Interpreters).

Following Roda Roberts's guidelines for professional development, cited earlier, we now trace the way healthcare interpreting has developed since the NCIHC came into existence in the late 1990s.

Clarification of Terminology

Terminology may appear to be a trivial matter in the development of a profession, but it is important to be clear on basic concepts and terms. The English-speaking public does not understand the difference between "translator" and "interpreter," and at the first meeting of the national working group mentioned earlier—the first-ever national forum on interpreting in healthcare settings—there was no consensus even among the attendees as to the meaning of "interpreter" (Avery, 2001). To establish a common vocabulary for discussion, one of the early projects of the NCIHC was the publication of a glossary of terms used in healthcare interpreting (NCIHC, 2001/2008). The glossary provides definitions of essential concepts such as "consecutive interpreting," "sight translation," and "register." Another terminological contribution has involved clarification of differences between, for example, "dedicated interpreter," "dual-role interpreter," "on-call interpreter," "ad-hoc interpreter," and "bilingual worker" (Downing, 1992; Downing & Roat, 2002).

It may be of interest that spoken-language interpreters use three different modes of interpreting when working in a healthcare setting: consecutive interpreting, simultaneous interpreting, and sight translation, with consecutive (interpreting when a speaker pauses) being the primary mode, in contrast to ASL interpreters, who primarily work in the simultaneous mode.

Sight translation is a mode of communication used by both ASL and spoken-language interpreters in which the interpreter "reads a document written in one language and simultaneously interprets it into a second language" (NCIHC, 2001/2008, 8). Although spoken-language interpreters continue to debate the types of documents appropriate for sight translation, The Joint Commission's standard on what constitutes informed consent indicates that sight translation of a consent form, by itself, is not considered informed consent.[3]

One of the most difficult elements of accuracy is maintaining the speaker's register. "Register" refers to styles of speaking or writing (e.g., intimate, casual, vulgar, formal) or a way of communicating associated with a particular occupation or social group (e.g., slang, criminal argot, medical jargon, business jargon, legal language) (NCIHC, 2001/2008). Both ASL and spoken-language interpreters are expected to match the patient's register regardless of whether the patient is using very formal, educated speech or slang. This helps sensitive providers understand the patient's level of education so that they can adjust their own register and explanations accordingly.

Two additional terms that often lead to confusion within the interpreting profession are "certification" and "certificate." The Institute for Credentialing Excellence says this about certification:

The certification of specialized skill-sets affirms a knowledge and experience base for practitioners in a particular field, their employ-

---

3. "Informed consent is not merely a signed document. It is a process that considers patient needs and preferences, compliance with law and regulation, and patient education" (The Joint Commission, 2009, 327).

ers, and the public at large. Certification represents a declaration of a particular individual's professional competence. (n.d.)

The difference between "certification" and a "certificate of completion" or "certificate of attendance," therefore, is that certificates may be awarded without the testing that would reliably attest to (i.e., certify) the recipient's ability to perform the interpreter role. The current status of certification for spoken-language interpreters is discussed later.

Clarification of the Roles of the Community Interpreter

At the NCIHC working group meetings in the 1990s, certain key questions dominated the discussion on the healthcare interpreter role: the nature and scope of the role and the nature of the interpreter's relationship with both the patient and the provider. The views voiced by participants were oftentimes polar extremes of one another, with one group adhering to the more traditional view of the "neutral interpreter" while others advocated for a more "active interpreter" role.

Participants on the side of neutrality argued that the most critical barrier to communication between two people is a difference in language and that the interpreter's role is therefore to act simply as a channel for communication—no changes to meaning, no adjustment of register, no intervention from the interpreter. The interpreter simply replicates the messages generated by the speakers, allowing healthcare providers to interact with patients who don't speak English as they would with English-speaking patients. This view did not consider that the interpreter may have ties to the patient's community or the healthcare facility where the patient is being seen. These "neutral" interpreters were strongly discouraged from establishing any kind of relationship with the patient.

The opposite of this view is an interpreter who assumes multiple duties beyond simple message conversion. Champions of this view argue that unlike court interpreters, who work in an adversarial setting in which key participants want different and sometimes mutually exclusive outcomes, healthcare interpreters work in a collaborative setting where everyone communicates with the goal of "understanding." "Understanding" in this view does not simply refer to the words themselves but also takes into consideration the cultural context in which communication was attempted.

Culture shapes how we understand and interact with our world, and it reflects the meaning that we place on what happens to us. Language is a reflection of culture and so cannot be separated from it. "In the area of health, culture influences the meaning given to symptoms, the diagnosis of those symptoms, the expectations regarding the course of the related disease or illness, the desirability and efficacy of treatments or remedies, and the prognosis" (NCIHC, 2004, p. 9). Since interpreters often have knowledge of the patient's culture, as well as Western medical culture, they are able to better assess the intended meaning of the message and intervene if a cultural misunderstanding is evident.

Despite these polar views, by 1999 the working group had agreed upon some basic aspects of the healthcare interpreter role:

• Interpreters are to remain faithful to the original message. This is the essence of the interpreter role.
• The interpreter's essential obligation and duty is to support the health and well-being of the patient and family system of supports—a value shared by all healthcare professionals.
• Interpreters are to respect the importance of culture.
• Interpreters are obligated to be transparent, thus ensuring that everyone in the interaction knows what is being said at all times.
• Interpreters only perform those functions for which they are qualified by training and experience.
• Interpreters are required to respect the autonomy of the patient, refraining from influencing the encounter. (Avery, 2001, pp. 12–13)

Discussing, clarifying, and eventually reaching broad consensus on the role of the healthcare interpreter has continued to be a major concern of the NCIHC up to the present.[4] Yet tension remains between advocates of a more limited traditional role similar to that of the conference or court interpreter and, at the other end of the spectrum, a perspective that reflects research on interpreting practice,[5] as well as the concerns of traditional

---

4. For example, a recent publication aims to explain healthcare interpreting and translation services to consumers (National Council on Interpreting in Health Care and American Translators Association, 2010).

5. For example, Angelelli (2004); see also the review of Angelelli's book by Bruce T. Downing (2004/2007).

cultural groups such as Native Americans and many immigrant groups, to the effect that the interpreter should also be a communication participant, adviser, and advocate.

The Standards, Training, and Certification Committee of the NCIHC adopted a long-range plan to build a national framework for the healthcare interpreting profession. The first step, the publication of Avery's paper (2001), was to describe the evolution of the concept of the healthcare interpreter's role. Other steps included developing a single, nationally accepted code of ethics and standards of practice for interpreters in health care; working out standards for healthcare interpreter training programs; and facilitating the development of a national certification process. This program has been vigorously pursued over a decade. At each stage every effort has been made to promote discussion and obtain input broadly from interpreters and other stakeholders through conference sessions, focus groups, and online surveys. The experience and publications of organizations in related fields and other nations have also been considered.[6]

With funding from the federal Office of Minority Health, *A National Code of Ethics for Interpreters in Health Care* was developed by the Standards, Training, and Certification Committee and published by the NCIHC in 2004. With support from The Commonwealth Fund and The California Endowment, National Standards of Practice for Interpreters in Health Care was published in 2005. The NCIHC standards have been endorsed by major interpreter associations and recognized by national- and state-level government bodies. These national standards differ little in essence from those of the International Medical Interpreters Association (IMIA) (IMIA and Educational Development Center, 1995, 2007) and the California Healthcare Interpreting Association (CHIA) (2002), but differing formats and scope make each document valuable for reference.

The Standards, Training, and Certification Committee of the NCIHC has also produced a number of working papers intended to guide practice in the field.[7]

---

6. See, for example, Bancroft (2005).

7. Examples are *Guide to Interpreter Positioning in Healthcare Settings* (NCIHC, 2003) and *Sight Translation and Written Translation: Guidelines for Healthcare Interpreters* (NCIHC, 2010).

Interpreter Training

The obvious next step in the agenda of the Standards, Training, and Certification Committee of the NCIHC was to address the need for guidance that could help ensure the quality and appropriateness of education and training for healthcare interpreters.

Training that focuses on community interpreting or interpreting in health care is a fairly recent development and has consisted mainly of single short courses offered by community service and healthcare organizations (e.g., hospitals, language service agencies, and government-funded Area Health Education Centers). An effort in 1991 to catalogue and describe formal educational programs for community interpreters, which extended from the United States to Canada and Western Europe, found few substantial examples (Downing & Helms Tillery, 1992). Short training sessions supported by government funds or grants from foundations have seldom survived longer than their temporary funding. In 1994 the Cross Cultural Health Care Program in Seattle developed Bridging the Gap, the first basic training for healthcare interpreters to be accompanied by a program to train trainers, so that the course could be replicated all over the United States; this 40-hour course has provided initial training to more healthcare interpreters than any other program and has served as a model for other basic courses intended to provide a modicum of training for interpreters who otherwise have no formal preparation for employment as community interpreters (Cross Cultural Health Care Program, n.d.). Today a number of such introductory courses (some online) are available.[8]

Academic programs in community or healthcare interpreting exist only in relatively few scattered institutions across the country. These are usually longer programs of study, often offering an undergraduate certificate of completion. The Certificate in Interpreting at the University of Minnesota, for example, requires completion of six semester courses, including at least three skills-building courses with separate labs for different language pairs (e.g., English-Somali). Specializations are offered in legal and healthcare interpreting, and all students take at least one semester of translation

---

8. The International Medical Interpreters Association (IMIA) hosts a web page (http://www.imiaweb.org/education/trainingnotices.asp) that lists training programs in the United States and Canada and provides hyperlinks to detailed information on each.

(University of Minnesota, n.d). Academic programs, however, vary greatly in content and scope.

A few academic courses in interpreting are now available on the Internet. As an example, a for-profit organization, the Medical Interpreting and Translating Institute Online LLC, offers a series of medical interpreting courses.

Graduate-level programs are even fewer in number. The University of Massachusetts at Amherst offers a single relevant graduate course, "Medical Interpreting Online" (University of Massachusetts, Comparative Literature, n.d.). The Master of Arts in Bilingual Interpreting at the College of Charleston (devoted to English-Spanish legal interpreting), for many years the only graduate-level degree program that emphasized interpreting in the community, has unfortunately been discontinued (Gladys G. Matthews, personal communication). Recently, a Master of Arts in Interpreting and Translation Studies, "emphasizing the critical area of healthcare delivery" and accompanied by several graduate certificate courses, has been announced at Wake Forest University to begin in the fall of 2011 (Wake Forest University, Department of Romance Languages, n.d.).

The NCIHC Standards, Training, and Certification Committee, with funding from The California Endowment and the Certification Commission for Healthcare Interpreters, has recently completed the next step of its professionalization agenda, the creation of national standards for healthcare interpreter training programs. One valuable model for this work was the *CCIE Accreditation Standards*, created for the accreditation of educational programs for sign-language interpreters, although these are not specific to community or healthcare interpreting (Commission on Collegiate Interpreter Education, 2010). Another resource the committee drew upon was a report titled *Core Competencies and Training Standards for Health Care Interpreters* (Refki, Dalton, & Avery 2009). The committee reviewed these and other relevant publications, existing curricula, and relevant research. Especially helpful was the "job task analysis" commissioned by the Certification Commission for Healthcare Interpreters (2010). In addition, focus groups at regional and national conferences were used to ensure that the eventual standards would be acceptable to the field broadly.

In October 2010 the NCIHC launched an online survey, requesting responses from working interpreters and others to elements of a first complete draft of the standards document. An advisory committee made up of recognized experts in interpreter training was assembled and convened in April 2010 to identify content areas and again in November 2010 to elicit suggestions for the format and final content of the standards.

The resulting *National Standards for Healthcare Interpreter Training Programs* (NCIHC, 2011) provides guidance to language-access professionals in the following three overarching areas:

1. Program content: the essential knowledge, skills, and abilities a candidate needs to competently function as a healthcare interpreter
2. Instructional methods: best practices in training healthcare interpreters
3. General program characteristics: operational policies, program design, entry and screening requirements, instructor qualifications, and student assessment criteria necessary for a successful program of study

As already mentioned, at this time the lengths of training programs offered around the country vary greatly, from 2-hour orientations to certificate programs, and the availability of training programs around the country is limited. Thus, no single program of study currently meets the training needs for interpreters in all parts of this country and in all languages; therefore, it is incumbent upon candidates who wish to enter the field of healthcare interpreting to use various resources available to them to acquire all of the training considered essential for competent independent performance as a healthcare interpreter. The standards therefore address "programs of study"—possibly sequences of programs (rather than individual courses or isolated programs)—that can assist interpreters in acquiring all the knowledge, skills, and attitudes they need to function competently as a healthcare interpreter.

Training for Interpreter Trainers

The next in Roda Roberts's recommended steps for the development of community interpreting as a recognized professional field is the training of trainers. This is only beginning to be addressed in a serious way.

For many years the Bridging the Gap program and some similar programs have offered short trainings that are required of potential new instructors before they can offer the course themselves. The program at the University of Minnesota has offered multiple 2-week intensive Interpreter Trainer Trainings, taught by experienced trainers along with experts in pedagogy from the University's Center for Teaching and Learning. Mikkelson and Neumann Solow have written about the challenges experienced in training community interpreters to teach the University of Minnesota's Introduction to Interpreting course at another college (2002), and the Monterey Institute of International Studies (MIIS) currently offers a noncredit "training of trainers for the healthcare interpreting profession" (MIIS, n.d.). However, until now there have been no academic degree or postgraduate programs targeting the preparation of interpreter trainers. Recently, though, Wake Forest University's Department of Romance Languages announced a Postgraduate Certificate in Teaching Interpreting, to begin in fall 2011.[9] This is clearly a timely development, and more such programs can be expected.

The NCIHC National Standards for Healthcare Interpreter Training Programs lists desirable qualifications that interpreter trainers should have, defined with reference to "individual instructors or teaching teams collectively," which may be expected to encourage more attention to the preparation of interpreter educators (NCIHC, 2011, 24). Some individuals working in the field of spoken-language interpreting have joined the Conference of Interpreter Trainers (CIT), an organization of primarily ASL interpreter educators. In the future perhaps we will see a broadening of the membership and interests of the CIT or the creation of a parallel organization.

Training for Professionals Working with Interpreters

It is abundantly clear that training healthcare providers to work with interpreters and providing guidance for the effective organization of language services that employ interpreters are nearly as important as the proper preparation of interpreters. This aspect of the development of the field has primarily involved local or regional efforts in the form of very brief trainings for hospital staffs and others. Curricula for short trainings, ranging from 1 or 2 hours to a full day, have been developed by several organizations and been offered during staff meetings, grand rounds, and

---

9. Wake Forest University, Department of Romance Languages, *Certificate Courses of Instruction: Postgraduate Certificate in Teaching Interpreting*, (n.d.).

conferences. Minnesota's Interpreting Stakeholder Group, for example, with funding from the Bush Foundation, has produced a set of training materials for "How to Work Effectively with Interpreters," available for use by any qualified trainer (Interpreting Stakeholder Group, n.d.). Some medical schools include practice in working with interpreters in patient interviews as part of the professional training of prospective doctors.

Accreditation

Roda Roberts identified accreditation as the final step in professionalization. In the United States, the usual term is "certification," but credentialing really has two parts: first, a process, usually including performance testing, in which a practitioner's qualifications can be assessed and "certified," and, second, a legal designation that gives special or exclusive status to those who have met this qualification ("licensing"). Thus, federal courts in the United States certify Spanish-English court interpreters through a written and oral examination and also require that, for that particular language pair, only certified interpreters be employed in the federal courts. Many but not all individual states have a similar process for the certification of court interpreters in a number of different languages, as well as rules that at least give priority to interpreters thus certified.

Although certification for sign language interpreters has existed for more than 25 years, and ASL interpreters can be certified at three levels (NIC, NIC Advanced, NIC Master), certification and regulation of healthcare or community interpreters working between spoken languages has not kept pace. In 1995 the Washington State Department of Social and Health Services established the first state certification for healthcare and social service interpreters. Other states have only recently begun efforts to register or otherwise qualify community interpreters. The consensus is that, for the specialty of healthcare interpreting, there should be a national process of certification (with the *practice* of interpreting perhaps regulated by state governments). In 2007, in keeping with a recommendation by the Expert Panel on Community Interpreter Testing and Certification (Interpreting Stakeholder Group, 2007), a National Coalition for Healthcare Interpreter Certification was formed, with broad representation of stakeholder organizations, including the NCIHC, to work toward this goal.

This unity of effort, unfortunately, proved impossible to maintain. Two separate national organizations have come into being since 2007, both of which now offer healthcare interpreter certification for entry-level interpreters: the Certification Commission for Healthcare Interpreters (CCHI) and the National Board of Certification for Medical Interpreters (NBCMI). At this time both offer certification only for Spanish-English, but certification in at least a few other language pairs is planned.

One of the biggest challenges today regarding certification of spoken-language interpreters is the number of immigrant languages spoken in the United States. Certification requires a demonstration of the *ability to interpret* at the level required to perform competently as a healthcare interpreter. However, with more than 149 languages spoken in the country, the financial barrier to designing linguistically and culturally appropriate oral exams for each language, as well as manually scoring each oral exam, is insurmountable.

So how do we ensure the competence of interpreters working in so many diverse languages? One way in which this is being addressed by both certifying organizations is to offer a written exam that tests only interpreters' knowledge, not their skills or abilities. Since this type of exam is offered in English, it is available to speakers of all languages. Upon the successful completion of this exam, the candidate receives a *credential, not* certification. Yet even this written exam presents daunting challenges. In many newly arriving refugee groups, literacy in English or any language is quite low, so even competent interpreters may not respond well to a written examination.

It is worth noting that all certification for spoken-language interpreters in the United States is field specific. Court interpreter certification, state and national, is focused on the language of the courtroom and the protocols of the court setting; the CCHI and NBCMI certification processes include assessment of one's ability to handle specific language elements commonly encountered in healthcare settings. This contrasts with the generalist (not field specific) certification of ASL interpreters, developed and implemented over the years, which is respected and recognized officially in most states as relevant to both legal and medical interpreting (RID, n.d.).

Certification of sign-language interpreters has provided a model and a goal for spoken-language interpreting. However, preparing and assessing interpreters who interpret the diverse languages of immigrant and refugee communities and who very often are members of these communities and intimately associated with many of their clients present their own unique challenges.

FINAL REMARKS

The impact of quantitative research on approaches to bilingual communication in medical settings and of qualitative research on the interpreter role has necessarily been neglected here, given our focus on the contributions of the National Council on Interpreting in Health Care. One relevant activity of the NCIHC, however, has been to help make this research accessible to the field, especially through the compilation of an annotated bibliography of research published in medical journals (Jacobs et al., 2003).[10]

In this chapter we have illustrated what can be and has been accomplished through the largely volunteer efforts of a broad coalition of stakeholders to advance the field of spoken-language community interpreting. Two aspects of this history will be of special interest to ASL interpreters and interpreter trainers: the fact that the NCIHC has always identified itself as a broad stakeholder organization rather than an organization of interpreters and its field-specific focus on healthcare interpreting.

The professionalization of healthcare interpreting has come a long way since those first discussions in the early 1990s. The field will continue to evolve with the rapidly increasing use of telephone and video interpreting of spoken languages—in the legal system and in health care. However, the one element that will remain constant regardless of how the profession develops is that effective communication between patients and healthcare providers is essential to ensure accurate diagnosis and treatment, obtain informed consent, and prevent medical errors. The NCIHC, as a broad stakeholder organization, has worked to advance the professionalization of healthcare interpreting while keeping this underlying principle always in focus.

---

10. An example of relevant quantitative research is Flores et al. (2003). Studies using various qualitative approaches are cited by Vargas-Urpi (2011). Both quantitative and qualitative methods are employed by Angelelli (2004) to explore the active role of medical interpreters as communication participants.

References

Angelelli, C. V. (2004). *Medical interpreting and cross-cultural communication.* Cambridge: Cambridge University Press.

Avery, M. B. (2001). *The role of the healthcare interpreter: An evolving dialogue.* National Council on Interpreting in Health Care. Retrieved July 28, 2011, from http://www.ncihc.org.

Bancroft, M. (2005). *The interpreter's world tour: An environmental scan of standards of practice for interpreters.* Woodland Hills, CA: California Endowment. Retrieved July 28, 2011, from http://www.ncihc.org.

Batalova, J., & Terrazas, A. (2010). Frequently requested statistics on immigrants and immigration in the United States. Migration Information Source. (Migration Policy Institute). Retrieved July 28, 2011, from http://www.migrationinformation.org/USfocus/display.cfm?ID=818#2g.

California Healthcare Interpreting Association. (2002). *California standards for healthcare interpreters: Ethical principles, protocols, and guidance on roles & intervention.* Woodland Hills, CA: The California Endowment. Retrieved July 28, 2011, from http://www.chiaonline.org/?page=CHIAStandards.

Certification Commission for Healthcare Interpreters. (2010). *Job task analysis study and results.* Retrieved July 4, 2011, from http://www.healthcareinterpreter certification.org/images/webinars/cchi%20jta%20report-public.pdf.

Commission on Collegiate Interpreter Education (CCIE). (2010). *CCIE accreditation standards.* Retrieved July 27, 2011, from http://www.ccie-accreditation.org /PDF/CCIE_Standards_2010.pdf.

Cross Cultural Health Care Program. (n.d.) "Welcome to Bridging the Gap." Retrieved July 4, 2011, from http://www.xculture.org/BTGwelcome.php.

Downing, B. T. (1992). The use of bilingual/bicultural workers as providers and interpreters. *International Migration, 30,* 121–30. Special issue: *Migration and Health in the 1990s,* ed. H. Siem and P. Bollini.

Downing, B. T. (1998). Community interpreting and translation in the U.S.A. context. In C. Valero-Garcés and I. de la Cruz Cabanillas (Eds.), *Nuevas tendencias y aplicaciones de la traducción: Encuentros en torno a la traducción,* vol. 3 (pp. 15–33). Alcalá de Henares, Spain: University of Alcalá.

Downing, B. T. (2004/2007). Review of C. V. Angelelli, *Medical interpreting and cross-cultural communication. Language in Society 36*(3) (2007), 474–78.

Downing, B. T., & Helms Tillery, K. (1992). *Professional training for community interpreters.* Minneapolis: Center for Urban and Regional Affairs, University of Minnesota.

Downing, B. T., & Roat, C. E. (2002). *Models for the provision of language access in healthcare settings.* National Council on Interpreting in Health Care. Retrieved July 28, 2011, from http://www.ncihc.org.

Federal Interagency Working Group on Limited English Proficiency. Limited English Proficiency: A Federal Interagency Website. http://www.lep.gov.

Flores, G., Barton Laws, M., Mayo, S. J., Zuckerman, B., Abreu, M., Medina, L., & Hardt, E. J. (2003). Errors in Medical interpretation and their potential clinical consequences in pediatric encounters. *Pediatrics, 111*(1), 6–14.

Institute for Credentialing Excellence. (n.d.) *What Is Certification?* Retrieved July 28, 2011, from http://www.credentialingexcellence.org/GeneralInformation/WhatisCertification/tabid/63/Default.aspx.

International Medical Interpreters Association. *Training directory.* Retrieved July 27, 2011, from http://www.imiaweb.org/education/trainingnotices.asp.

International Medical Interpreters Association (IMIA) and Education Development Center (EDC). (1995, 2007). *Medical interpreting standards of practice.* Retrieved July 28, 2011, from http://www.imiaweb.org/standards/standards.asp.

Interpreting Stakeholder Group. (n.d.) *How to work effectively with interpreters.* Retrieved July 28, 2011, from http://umtia.org/WorkingWithInterpreters.html.

Interpreting Stakeholder Group (2007), *Expert panel on community interpreter testing and certification, final report.* Retrieved July 26, 2011, from http://www.umtia.org/ExpertPanel.html.

Jacobs, E. A., Agger-Gupta, N., Chen, A. H., Piotrowski, A., & Hardt, E. (2003). *Language barriers in health care settings: An annotated bibliography of the research literature.* Woodland Hills, CA: The California Endowment.

The Joint Commission. (2009). Elements of performance RI.01.03.01 #9. In *Hospital Accreditation Standards.* Oakbrook Terrace, IL: Author.

The Joint Commission. (2010*). Advancing Effective Communication, Cultural Competence, and Patient- and Family-Centered Care: A Roadmap for Hospitals.* Oakbrook Terrace, IL: Author.

Mikkelson, H. (1996). The professionalization of community interpreting. In M. M. Jérôme-O'Keefe (Ed.), *Global vision: Proceedings of the 37th Annual Conference of the American Translators Association.* New York: John Benjamins. Retrieved July 5, 2011, from http://www.acebo.com/papers/profslzn.htm.

Mikkelson, H., & Neumann Solow, S. (2002). Report from the front lines: Multilingual training-of-trainers for refugee interpreters. Paper presented at the Conference of Interpreter Trainers (CIT) biennial conference, Minneapolis, Minnesota, October, 2002. Retrieved July 5, 2011, from http://www.acebo.com/papers/report.htm.

Monterey Institute of International Studies. *Translation and interpretation short programs.* Retrieved July 28, 2011, from http://www.miis.edu/academics/short/translation-interpretation.

National Council on Interpreting in Health Care. (n.d.). Retrieved from http://www.ncihc.org.

National Council on Interpreting in Health Care. (2001, rev. 2008). *The terminol-*

ogy of healthcare interpreting: A glossary of terms. Retrieved July 28, 2011, from http://www.ncihc.org.

National Council on Interpreting in Health Care. (2003). *Guide to interpreter positioning in healthcare settings.* Retrieved July 28, 2011, from http://www.ncihc.org.

National Council on Interpreting in Health Care. (2004). *A national code of ethics for interpreters in health care.* Retrieved July 28, 2011, from http://www.ncihc.org.

National Council on Interpreting in Health Care. (2005). *National standards of practice for interpreters in health care.* Retrieved July 28, 2011, from http://www .ncihc.org.

National Council on Interpreting in Health Care. (2010). *Sight translation and written translation: Guidelines for healthcare interpreters.* Retrieved July 28, 2011, from http://www.ncihc.org.

National Council on Interpreting in Health Care. (2011). *National standards for healthcare interpreter training programs.* Retrieved July 28, 2011, from http:// www.ncihc.org.

National Council on Interpreting in Health Care and American Translators Association. (2010). *What's in a word? A guide to understanding interpreting and translation in health care.* Washington, DC: National Health Law Program. Retrieved July 5, 2011, from http://data.memberclicks.com/site/ncihc/Whats _in_a_Word_Guide.pdf.

Office of Minority Health. (2001). *National standards for culturally and linguistically appropriate services in health care: Final report.* Washington, DC: Department of Health and Human Services. Retrieved July 5, 2011, from http://minorityhealth .hhs.gov/assets/pdf/checked/finalreport.pdf.

Refki, D. H., Dalton, A. C., & Avery, M. B. (2009). *Core competencies and training standards for health care interpreters: Research report and recommendations.* Albany, NY: Center for Women in Government and Civil Society, University at Albany and Education Development Center.

Registry of Interpreters for the Deaf. (n.d.). *Education and certification overview.* Retrieved July 5, 2011, from http://www.rid.org/education/overview/index.cfm.

Roberts, R. (1994). Community interpreting: Today and tomorrow. In P. Krawutschke (Ed.), *Proceedings of the 35th Annual Conference of the American Translators Association* (pp. 127–38). Medford, NJ: Learned Information.

Shin, H. B., & Bruno, R. (2003). Language use and English-speaking ability: 2000. *Census 2000 Brief C2KBR-29,* p. 3. Washington, DC: U.S. Census Bureau, 2003. Retrieved July 5, 2011, from http://www.census.gov/population/www/cen2000 /briefs/index.html.

University of Massachusetts, Comparative Literature. (n.d.) Graduate course catalog. Retrieved July 27, 2011, from http://www.umass.edu/complit/courses_cat _grad.shtml.

University of Minnesota, College of Continuing Education, Program in Translation

and Interpreting. (n.d.) Retrieved July 5, 2011, from http://www.cce.umn.edu
/pti.

U.S. Department of Justice. (2003). Guidance to federal financial assistance re-
cipients regarding Title VI prohibition against national origin discrimination
affecting limited English proficient persons. *Federal Register* 68.153. Retrieved July 28, 2011, from http://www.justice.gov/crt/about/cor/lep
/hhsrevisedlepguidance.php.

U.S. Department of Justice. (2011). Federal government's renewed commitment
to language access obligations under Executive Order 13166. Retrieved July 5,
2011, from http://www.lep.gov/13166/AG_021711_EO_13166_Memo_to
_Agencies_with_Supplement.pdf.

Vargas-Urpi, M. (2011). The interdisciplinary approach in community interpreting research. *New Voices in Translation Studies* 7: 47-65. Retrieved July 26, 2011,
from http://www.iatis.org/images/stories/publications/new-voices/Issue7-2011
/article-vargas-2011.pdf.

Wake Forest University, Department of Romance Languages. (n.d.). *Certificate courses
of instruction: Postgraduate certificate in teaching interpreting.* Retrieved July 5, 2011,
from http://www.wfu.edu/romancelanguages/Graduate_program/Certificates
.html.

Wake Forest University, Department of Romance Languages. (n.d.). *MA in interpreting
and translation studies program.* Retrieved July 5, 2011, from http://www.wfu.edu
/romancelanguages/Graduate_program/index.html.

MAYA DE WIT, MARINELLA SALAMI,
AND ZANE HEMA

Educating Sign Language Interpreters in Healthcare Settings

A European Perspective

By COMPARING the United Kingdom, Italy, and the Netherlands, this chapter explores Europe's current and future needs with regard to the education of sign-language interpreters in healthcare settings. We begin with an overview of the current training programs for sign-language interpreters. Then we consider the current work settings and education of sign-language interpreters in relation to healthcare settings. In addition, we discuss the needs of the deaf[1] population for trained sign-language interpreters in healthcare settings. The information in this chapter is based on a review of policies and reports and on personal interviews with interpreters, educators, employers, and service users.

TRAINING IN EUROPE

Still a relatively young vocation, the sign-language interpreting profession has undergone rapid development in Europe in the last two decades (de Wit, 2008). Currently more than 50 educational programs for sign-language interpreting are operational in Europe, ranging from a 2-year associate's degree to a 5-year master's degree. Each country has developed

---

1. In this article we use lowercase "deaf" to refer to any deaf person regardless of community or cultural affinity.

and established its own interpreting program, and the majority of Western European countries have more than one. All of these programs focus on the general training of sign-language interpreters.

No scientific data on the curricula of the various European programs have yet been collected. At the last European Forum of Sign Language Interpreters (efsli[2]) trainers' seminar held in Helsinki in October 2010, the participants expressed interest in developing a standard curriculum for sign-language interpreters throughout Europe. In discussions at the seminar, the content of the educational programs became apparent. All of the credits focus on foundational skills and knowledge, which leaves little room for specialized training such as healthcare.[3] This is also the case in the UK, Italy, and the Netherlands, where no comprehensive education program for interpreters in healthcare settings is available.

SIGN-LANGUAGE INTERPRETERS IN HEALTHCARE SETTINGS

Sign-language interpreters in Europe work in a wide variety of settings from conferences to hospitals. They are not required to have a special degree or certificate to interpret in healthcare contexts.

According to the Free Dictionary (2010), health care is the prevention, treatment, and management of illness and the preservation of mental and physical well-being. In this chapter we define a healthcare setting as one in which a sign-language interpreter interprets the interaction between a patient and a healthcare professional.

Currently, no EU legislation entitles people to either a spoken-language or a sign-language interpreter in healthcare settings. An initial step toward establishing this right is the first EU Directive on the Rights to Interpretation and Translation in criminal proceedings,[4] which was adopted in October 2010 by the EU Council of Ministers. This directive grants

---

2. The lowercase spelling is standard usage for this organization.

3. In this article we use the term "healthcare" settings to mean any medical setting that involves general or specific health care, such as mental health. If relevant, the term "mental health" is mentioned specifically.

4. http://www.consilium.europa.eu/uedocs/cms_data/docs/pressdata/en/jha/116913.pdf (last accessed November 9, 2010).

the right to an interpreter or translator only in criminal proceedings—nowhere else. The European Union of the Deaf (EUD) states that this is a good step forward but points out that it must be extended to healthcare settings as well.

The Netherlands

Dutch law requires healthcare professionals to use the services of an interpreter if the professionals cannot otherwise make themselves understood.[5] In 2003 the Dutch government researched the use of qualified interpreters in healthcare settings.[6] The results showed that family members were used to communicate between the healthcare professional and the patient. In 2008 this resulted in the establishment of national guidelines that indicate to healthcare professionals instances in which a formal interpreter is required.[7] These regulations pertain to spoken-language interpreters but are also valid for sign-language interpreters.

Gosselink and Frederiks (2009) state that the Dutch Ministry of Welfare, Healthcare, and Sports (VWS) needs to look more closely at the language and interpreting needs of deaf patients in healthcare settings, especially with regard to a proposed Dutch law following the 2007 UN Convention on the Rights of With Disabilities.[8]

In the Netherlands all sign-language interpreters are entitled to work in (mental) health settings. They are not required to take an exam or obtain certification in order to work in this environment. Sign-language interpreters do, however, need to have a diploma and be registered in the national registry[9] if they want to be paid for their services by the Dutch government. The registry also shows which interpreters have completed 1,200 hours of continuing education within mental health settings. As of 2010, 10 interpreters have accomplished this.

---

5. Wet op de Geneeskundige Behandelingsovereenkomst (wgbo), Wet Klachtrecht Cliënten Zorgsector (wkcz), de Kwaliteitswet, Wet op de Beroepen in de Individuele Gezondheidszorg (Wet big).

6. Inspectie voor de Gezondheidszorg (2003).

7. Rijksoverheid. Wanneer laten tolken? Veldnormen voor de inzet van tolk in de gezondheidszorg (2008).

8. http://www.un.org/disabilities/convention/news.shtml (accessed November 15, 2010).

9. Stichting Register Tolken Gebarentaal: http://www.rtg.nl.

In the Netherlands several mental health institutions and social support organizations, such as the Riethorst[10] and VIA, the National Center for Mental Health and Deafness, serve deaf and hard of hearing patients and clients. These institutions employ approximately 15 sign-language interpreters. This is unique for the Netherlands since the majority of interpreters work as freelancers. These institutions and organizations also work with freelancers when their own staff interpreters are unavailable. Most of the time the freelancers are selected from a list established by the institution to ensure that interpreters are competent and familiar with working in mental health settings.

The staff interpreters at the mental health institutions are members of the healthcare team. They attend staff meetings, have pre- and post-assignment evaluations with the medical personnel, provide communication advice, and fulfill administrative functions. At some of the institutions the interpreters are the first ones who see a new client. The interpreter does a communication intake, determines the client's mode of communication, and informs the medical team of the findings.

No hospitals or physicians in private practice employ sign-language interpreters. However, one large institution, the Gelderhorst, works with employed interpreters and often deals with healthcare settings.[11] The only facility of its type in the Netherlands, the Gelderhorst is a home for senior citizens who are deaf or hard of hearing. The senior citizens live in semi-independent housing attached to the main building, where daily healthcare services are provided for those who need intensive nursing care. The Gelderhorst works with deaf and hearing staff members, including medical personnel. For many years it hired a variety of freelance interpreters, but the Gelderhorst eventually decided to employ four part-time staff interpreters because the senior citizens in residence preferred familiar interpreters who could deal with their many different communication styles. In addition, the staff saw the need to work with interpreters who are familiar with the names of those living in the home and knowledgeable enough about medical discourse to understand the nursing reports shared at shift changes.

---

10. http://www.degelderseroos.nl/site/Zorgaanbod/Multicomplexe%20zorg/Doven%20en%20slechthorenden (accessed November 15, 2010).

11. www.gelderhorst.nl (accessed November 15, 2010).

The Gelderhorst provides an interpreter at all doctor visits within the facility and at a special interpreting services desk. Deaf people can come to the desk, where an interpreter is available at specific times to assist with interpreting needs. The deaf residents are free to use this service if they wish. Many of the Gelderhorst residents are not used to working with an interpreter because they grew up at a time when sign language was prohibited. However, the continued presence of an interpreter has had a noticeably positive effect on how the older deaf people view the use of one. According to the Gelderhorst's communication department, the use of interpreting services has increased over the years. Of the 72 persons living in the care unit, 69 currently have the right to interpreting services by Dutch regulations. In addition, in the semi-independent housing approximately 89 of the 100 residents use the interpreting services desk during the interpreting hours.[12]

United Kingdom

The relevant laws in the UK are the Equality Act (2010) and the Mental Health Act (1983). The Equality Act replaces the Disability Discrimination Act (1995) and makes it unlawful to directly or indirectly discriminate against a *person with a disability*, and this includes deaf people. Section 20 (5) contains three requirements, the third of which is relevant to the provision of sign-language interpreting in healthcare settings. It states, in essence, that when a person with a disability would, but for the provision of an auxiliary aid, be put at a substantial disadvantage in relation to a relevant matter in comparison with those who do not have a disability, reasonable steps must be taken to provide the auxiliary aid.

A sign-language interpreter is considered to be an auxiliary aid. Thus, where a deaf person would be placed at a substantial disadvantage without a sign-language interpreter in a (mental) healthcare setting, then the general practitioner (GP), hospital, or institution must take reasonable steps to provide one.

---

12. In the Netherlands deaf people have the right to an interpreter in 100% of educational settings, 15% of their employed work time, and a total of 30 hours a year for daily needs, such as doctor visits.

The Mental Health Act (1983 and 2007) covers the assessment, treatment, and rights of people with a mental health condition. The accompanying Code of Practice in section 2 emphasizes the importance of communication and mentions the need for an interpreter:

2.5. Where an interpreter is needed, every effort should be made to identify who is appropriate to the patient, given the patient's gender, religion, language dialect, cultural background, and age. The patient's relatives and friends should only exceptionally be used as intermediaries or interpreters.[13]

A number of institutions provide specialist services to deaf patients and employ sign-language interpreters. The National Deaf Services provides a range of comprehensive mental health services for deaf adults, children, and their families and employs sign-language interpreters in doing so. The National Centre for Mental Health and Deafness provides mental health services for deaf people throughout the north of England, Wales, and Scotland. The National High Secure Deaf Service provides a comprehensive, multidisciplinary team assessment, treatment, and rehabilitation for a maximum of 10 deaf males irrespective of their diagnosis or treatment within a high secure setting. Alpha Hospital has highly specialized services for deaf men and women who require low or medium secure care. Its services offer culturally sensitive treatment for deaf patients. Its staff are highly skilled in British Sign Language, and its services are well known for innovation and development within the field. Alpha Hospital's sign-language interpreting service utilizes both in-house and freelance interpreters.

Interpreters also work for SignHealth, a healthcare charity for deaf people that provides health-related services for all deaf people. This includes SignTranslate, an online interpreting service using a live web-cam link to interpreters, provided by partner interpreting organizations around the country. The service is for deaf people during doctor visits or in hospital emergency rooms and is not a replacement for live interpreters but, given the shortage of interpreters, is an effective use of interpreters' time.

---

13. Department of Health (2008), *Code of Practice: Mental Health Act 1983*. Rev. 2008. http://www.dh.gov.uk/en/Publicationsandstatistics/Publications/PublicationsPolicyAndGuidance/DH_084597 (accessed November 14, 2010).

Interpreters make a distinction between working in general health care and in mental health settings; more interpreters work in the former than in the latter. The reason for this is that interpreters view working in mental health as more specialized and demanding and thus feel the need to undergo additional training for that venue. Steve Powell, chief executive of SignHealth, states that "Mental health settings require even more experience and skill" (personal communication, 2010). Several interpreters in the personal interviews we conducted confirmed this and explained why they chose not to interpret in mental health settings:

"I do not accept mental health bookings as I have no experience in this domain and believe this is a specialist area that requires extra skills and training above and beyond interpreter training."

"I do not work in mental health settings because I do not have enough experience or training yet."

Numerous organizations throughout the country provide generic sign-language interpreting services, including healthcare interpreting. One recent development, however, is the increasing number of spoken-language interpreter agencies that have secured contracts to provide sign-language interpreting services in healthcare settings. This is causing some concern because these agencies are providing unregistered people. Whether this is to keep costs down or because they are not conversant with the current structures of registration is unclear. The national chairperson of the Association of Sign Language Interpreters for England, Wales, and Northern Ireland (ASLI), Sarah Haynes, said the following:

In the current [economic] climate there appear to be pressures and risks in this area. With more procurement exercises giving provision of interpretation to large corporations [nonspecialist], there is a danger that standards that have been established to date, with increasing numbers of registered and trained interpreters being used in the sector, will be sacrificed for financial savings. The position is therefore not necessarily stable, and I perceive it could alter vastly in the next 12–36 months. (personal interview, October 2010)

According to Thompson (2008), "A majority (70%) of practices do not have a quality standard in place covering the standard of interpreters that they book." The actual number of individuals working as sign-language interpreters is not known as there is no requirement to register. In its February 2011 update report, the National Registers of Communication Professionals working with Deaf and Deafblind People (NRCPD) listed 1,000 registered interpreters, but many more are working and are not registered. Due to this and the fact that 70% of medical practices do not have a quality standard in place to regulate the hiring of sign-language interpreters, the quality of service that deaf patients receive varies (Tribe & Thompson, 2008).[14]

Italy

The Italian Constitution, as declared and recognized in article 32, protects health as a fundamental right:[15] "The republic protects health as the fundamental right of the individual and the interest of the collectivity. It guarantees free medical treatments to all indigent people." The Italian National Health Service (Servizio Sanitario Nazionale) was set up in 1978 (law no. 833), and public medical assistance and healthcare services are provided by its health offices and agencies, which are located throughout the country. Maio and Manzoli (2002, 304)[16] describe the Italian National Health Service (NHS) as similar to the model developed by the British National Health Service in providing "universal healthcare coverage throughout the Italian State as a single payer." Recent national legislation has implemented a policy of devolution and changed the NHS accordingly. Uniform and essential levels of healthcare services are still guaranteed by the NHS, but local and regional governments now have a greater political, administrative, and financial responsibility to provide these services.

Although numerous special laws regulate the rights of people with disabilities (and deaf people are included under this definition), the right to

---

14. http://www.bps.org.uk/document-download-area/document-download$.cfm?file_uuid=1A3DE908-1143-DFD0-7E89-7C702AAD2FDA&ext=pdf (accessed November 14, 2010).

15. The original Italian quotes in this article have been translated into English by Marinella Salami.

16. http://www.pharmscope.com/ptjournal/fulltext/27/6/PTJ2706301.pdf (accessed November 14, 2010).

a competent and trained sign-language interpreter to facilitate communication with medical personnel, the patient, and the patient's family in hospitals and emergency rooms is not specifically protected by the Italian law. Article 9 of the framework law for the assistance, social integration, and rights of persons with disabilities (law no. 104, 1992) declares that municipalities and local health authorities can provide services to people with temporary or permanent limited autonomy. Sign-language interpreting services are included. As these services are not mandated, however, local bodies may provide them as their budgets allow. Consequently, the provision of interpreting or communication services can vary considerably from region to region or even from city to city. For instance, a regional law promoting interventions for the inclusion and social integration of people who are deaf (regional law no. 17, 2010)[17] has recently been approved by the regional government of the southern region of Basilicata. Article 4 states that specialized nurses who are able to use sign language to interact with persons who are deaf should be available in hospitals.[18]

The local branches of the Italian Deaf Association (Ente Nazionale Sordi, ENS) are very active in lobbying for accessible services. Sometimes these are set up by private associations in cooperation with local health units. Founded in 2003, Asvomedicalis[19] is an association of deaf and hearing people whose objective is to break down communication barriers in hospitals. It operates at the Bassini Hospital in Cinisello Balsamo near Milan and counts on more than 40 volunteers to communicate with deaf people. Interpreting services are also provided. Another valuable medium shared by the deaf community and sign-language interpreters to make the healthcare system accessible to deaf people is a CD-ROM titled *Quando nasce un bimbo* [When a Baby Is Born], which gives basic information about pregnancy, delivery, and puerperium in Italian Sign Language (with subtitles and voice-over) (Il Treno, 2008).

This is a preliminary overview of deaf Italians' access to interpreters. More research is needed on this topic.

---

17. http://www.consiglio.basilicata.it/consiglionew/site/Consiglio/detail.jsp?sec=107173 &otype=1150&id=106558&anno=2010 (accessed November 14, 2010).
18. We are grateful to Maddalena Catalano, Italian Sign Language interpreter, for this information.
19. http://www.asvomedicalis.org/ (accessed November 14, 2010).

CURRENT EDUCATIONAL STATUS

The education of sign-language interpreters in the United Kingdom, Italy, and the Netherlands is organized differently not only in their basic education but also in the more specialized fields such as (mental) healthcare settings. As mentioned earlier, sign-language interpreters are trained in general sign-language interpreting, which prepares them to work in a variety environments such as work meetings, classrooms, and conferences. This differs from the education of spoken-language interpreters, where students are trained to become community[20] or conference interpreters. The European Union of the Deaf (EUD) notes the risk of having an untrained interpreter in healthcare settings in Europe: "This is then the responsibility of the interpreter in diligently preparing for the assignment" (personal interview, Mark Wheatley, EUD director).

The Netherlands

The Netherlands has only one program for Dutch Sign Language (NGT) interpreters. It is a 4-year, general education bachelor program at the University of Applied Sciences Utrecht (HU). Currently 300 students are enrolled in the sign-language interpreter track.[21] There are no prerequisites to enter the program other than a 5-year high school diploma. In the program the students learn Dutch Sign Language and interpreting. In 2006 the program started with four minors,[22] which are now called "specialty courses." One of the minors, interpreting in (mental) health settings, was developed by experienced professors at the HU because of the great need for sign-language interpreters in that milieu. The HU still has the same minors, and the content of the specialty course in healthcare settings has not changed over the years. In their fourth[23] year, the students must se-

---

20. English has a variety of synonyms for "community interpreting," such as "public service interpreting." Terms like "health," "medical," "healthcare," "mental health," "educational," "social" (or "social service") interpreting are considered hyponyms of "community interpreting" (Mack, 2005).

21. The program also educates teachers in Dutch Sign Language (NGT) and speech-to-text interpreters, as they are called in the Netherlands.

22. A minor is a set of courses that are sufficient to establish proficiency in a discipline without having to take all of the courses required for a major.

23. This is expected to change starting in 2011. The minor will then be moved to the third year.

lect two specialty courses. Interpreting in healthcare settings is the most popular choice. Over the years a total of 60 students have completed the specialty minor.

The specialty course covers a total of 20 European Credit Transfer and Accumulation System (ECTS) subjects,[24] such as anatomy, deaf culture, ethics, NGT vocabulary and usage, interpreting and interactive skills, and both general and mental health settings. The course also includes an internship, which consists of 24 hours each in a hearing mental health setting and a deaf mental health setting.

The HU does not provide continuing education for graduate interpreters. Those interpreters who are working in mental healthcare settings in the Netherlands have set up their own mentoring and continuing education program, which consists of a 1-day meeting four times a year. During the meeting they share new developments, discuss a preselected topic, and listen to a presentation by a guest speaker invited from one of the related mental health institutions. This group of experienced interpreters has also designed a new code of ethics for sign-language interpreters in mental health settings, which was adopted by the Dutch Association of Sign Language Interpreters (NBTG) in 2009.[25] The interpreters believed this new code was required in order to meet the special interpreting needs in mental healthcare settings, such as the requirement for more detailed and specific information about a patient's psychiatric condition prior to an assignment. Another example is the need to occasionally play a more explanatory role when tests are conducted due to the fact that not all tests are designed for deaf sign-language users.

There are no continuing education or specialized classes that sign-language interpreters can attend in the Netherlands to enhance their skills in healthcare settings. In the past, the NBTG organized a 2-day seminar on the topic, and a few additional workshops have been held. If interpreters would like to specialize in the field of healthcare interpreting, they must organize their own education.

---

24. The European Credit Transfer and Accumulation System compares the educational achievement of higher education students throughout the European Union and other collaborating European countries.

25. http://www.nbtg.nl/over-het-beroep/beroepscode-tolken-in-de-GGZ (accessed November 27, 2010).

United Kingdom

In the UK a number of universities offer a range of both undergraduate and postgraduate training programs. The undergraduate programs may run 2–3 years, and the postgraduate programs 1–2 years. These programs are generic in their offerings. At the University of Wolverhampton, Sarah Bown is the senior lecturer in interpreting (BSL/English) and the deaf studies course leader in interpreting (BSL/English):

> The undergraduate program here at the University of Wolverhampton trains students to enable them to achieve either JTI[26] or TI[27] status upon successful completion of the degree. As such, this training encompasses a diverse range of theoretical, linguistic, practical, and professional skills at this level. Health settings are therefore incorporated (generically) within academic discussion; role plays and individually supported at third-year-level work placement through discussion, reflective analysis, and documentation of experiences/observations. These are the foundation skills that can then be built upon postgraduation with more specialized domain training. (personal interview, October 2010)

The view is similar at the Durham University of School of Modern Languages and Cultures, which previously offered a postgraduate diploma program that has now become a master's degree program. The following provides more detail on the content of their program. According to teaching fellow Judith Collins:

> The program is generic as, we believe this is a necessary precursor and foundation before an interpreter is ready to focus and specialize in any specific area. Specifically, we look at medical vocabulary and concepts, the "culture" of the medical profession, discourse structures and medical investigative encounters, translation of medical concepts, and the environment. The knowledge and skills developed is often cross-domain. (personal interview, October 2010)

In addition to the academic programs, some training institutions provide vocationally based development programs. These can be for JTIs or TIs

---

26. Junior trainee interpreters.
27. Trained interpreters.

who have been working in the field and now want to obtain MRSLI (member of the Register of Sign Language Interpreters) status or for individuals who may not have had any formal training but have been working in the field and now wish to undergo training.

A number of short courses and workshops are also offered. These are usually given in response to an identified demand, are aimed at interpreters who wish to learn more about working in these settings, and are often led by experienced interpreters together with a deaf professional.

The Association of Sign Language Interpreters (ASLI) provides a number of short courses as part of its professional development program. The most recent is a 2-day workshop on "Interpreting in Medical settings."[28]

Several organizations provide training in mental health settings. For example, the British Society of Mental Health and Deafness (BSMHD) has provided training in working in mental health settings and in mental health tribunals. Experienced interpreters, together with healthcare professionals, provide this instruction.

Clare Shard (head of Interpreting Services at Alpha Hospitals) runs a 4-day workshop on working in mental health that is very similar to the work Dean and Pollard (2001) carried out in adapting the demand and control schema for sign-language interpreters. This workshop is designed for interpreters who wish to increase their knowledge and understanding of working in mental health settings and emphasizes close working relationships with other mental health professionals before, during, and after the assignment as a means of jointly providing a high-quality service.

Italy

Italy has no state-approved academic training programs, although several institutions currently offer programs around the country. The length and content may vary, though the tendency is to standardize the general curriculum. For this reason, the Association of Italian Sign Language Interpreters (Associazione Interpreti di Lingua dei Segni Italiana, ANIOS) has developed a professional profile that defines sign-language interpreters, describes how they work, and lists skills they must have. These guidelines

---

28. Information on the course content of an ASLI workshop on medical settings is available at http://www.asli.org.uk/interpreting-in-medical-settings-course-information-p282.aspx (accessed November 14, 2010).

should help trainers and training bodies to shape their own programs. The implementation of sign-language courses or interpreter training in some university curricula is encouraging, and the next target is to create a bachelor's degree for sign-language interpreters. Intensive workshops designed as continuing education for certified/trained interpreters have been offered by ANIOS and other associations and institutions throughout the years.

No specialty courses or modules dedicated to interpreting in healthcare settings have been organized or included in the training programs. The "requisites of professional competence" section in the ANIOS profile contains only a generic reference to "jargon," which refers to the terms used by and among practitioners of a certain field. Moreover, ANIOS believes that the deaf community and deaf experts in the field should develop the sign lexicon for medical terminology (personal interviews with several ANIOS board members) and work synergistically with interpreters. The Italian Sign Language interpreters interviewed for this chapter, all of them with some experience in healthcare settings, have confirmed the need for training courses in healthcare interpreting and pointed out that the use of specific terms (for both Italian Sign Language and spoken Italian) is only one of the difficulties they face (as discussed in the next section).

CURRENT EDUCATIONAL NEEDS

Currently the EU offers little training for sign-language interpreters in healthcare settings. There appears to be a need, though, to train interpreters in these venues, as demonstrated by the EU-funded Medisigns project,[29] which has five European partners and focuses on deaf people, medical staff, and interpreters. Its main objective is to develop a specialist training program for interpreters in healthcare settings. The belief of the deaf community and the project consortium is that it is important to provide qualified interpreters who are trained in aspects of health care. Access to and provision of appropriate healthcare are not luxuries but fundamental human rights. Thus, the Medisigns project was initiated.

The need for trained interpreters in healthcare settings was also identified by another EU-funded project, MedInt. The multinational MedInt project was funded by the European Commission as part of the Lifelong

---

29. http://www.medisignsproject.eu (accessed November 9, 2010).

Learning Program. Between 2007 and 2009 the project consortium jointly developed a sample curriculum for healthcare interpreting, designed teaching materials, and concentrated on awareness raising and dissemination initiatives in the partner countries.[30] The project was not designed specifically for sign-language interpreters but does show the need for trained interpreters in healthcare settings.

The European Union of the Deaf emphasizes the need for trained interpreters. In addition, it stipulates that interpreters have at least 10 years of interpreting experience prior to taking on any medical assignment. For the training of sign-language interpreters in healthcare settings the EUD defines five categories: sign language, medical information, people (soft) skills, vicarious trauma, and professional performance. Within these categories the following items are listed:

Sign Language

- Working with the entire range of language use from pure sign language to spoken supported language and with those who use homesigns and those who do not. Knowing how to work and be familiar with the language use of deaf children, persons who are deaf-blind, elderly deaf people, deaf people who have physical conditions that make signs challenging to understand, and deaf people who are refugees or do not know the national sign language
- Correct (in sign language and anatomically) signs of the body and its organs
- Accurate interpreting and appropriate signs in a healthcare setting (e.g., signing to someone who is HIV positive that the person is HIV "plus" is not accurate and can give the deaf person the wrong impression about such a diagnosis)

Medical Information

- Medical terminology, including philosophies (Western and Eastern), approaches, procedures, conditions and diseases, treatments, medications, tests and types of scans

---

30. http://www.jostrans.org/issue14/art_ertl.pdf (accessed November 22, 2010).

- General medical: Understanding the difference between a diagnostic appointment and ongoing consultation/rehabilitation/therapy/treatment
- Mental health: The purpose of cognitive behavior therapy and other therapies, transference and countertransference issues
- General knowledge: Understanding of the human anatomy (and correct signs)
- Awareness of referral processes

People (Soft) Skills

- Respecting people's privacy
- The fine line between empathy and professionalism

Vicarious Trauma

- Interpreters need to be aware of available support systems that can assist them in dealing with matters that affect them once outside of an assignment.

Professional Performance

- Not accepting just any interpreting assignment that is offered simply because one is available. One should also be competent to do the job.

The Netherlands

As mentioned earlier, the only ongoing training in the Netherlands for sign-language interpreters in healthcare settings is the minor within the current bachelor's degree program at the University of Applied Sciences in Utrecht. Interpreters who have completed the minor and are now working as certified interpreters agree that the minor provides a good basis for becoming acquainted with the field of healthcare interpreting. It presents elementary knowledge about general healthcare interpreting assignments and outlines clear differences between them and nonhealthcare jobs. The graduate interpreters describe the many classroom role plays as very informative, especially when not carried out in smaller groups but in a large group under the guidance of a teacher, who can give feedback on the spot. The graduate interpreters stated that the minor should provide more instruction in medical terminology. In addition, they found the limited placement for internships and the short duration (24 hours) of the minor to be major shortcomings. The sign-language interpreters employed at the mental health institutions confirmed this. Since internships are quite limited, students have very little exposure to deaf-related mental health settings. In addition, the interpreters also found that the interns had very little specialized knowledge about the healthcare setting even though they were enrolled in the minor. The interpreters reported a great need to have completed a specialist training, externally and internally, when planning to work in mental health settings.

The Utrecht University of Applied Sciences is now investigating ways to change the minor to better address pressing issues in the field of sign-language interpreting. There is a demand for sign-language interpreters in general healthcare settings but less of one in mental health settings. In addition, since the implementation of the minor in 2006 few changes have been made in the program. The content must be reviewed to reflect current trends and developments.

Surprisingly, the research carried out in 2003 by the Dutch health inspection agency (Inspectie voor de Gezondheidszorg [IGZ])[31] on interpreters in healthcare settings does not mention the education of healthcare interpreters. The report expresses a need for qualified interpreters but makes no recommendations for the type of training that interpreters should undergo.

United Kingdom

Specialist training in health care and mental health care settings is available in the UK as highlighted earlier. In order to identify current training needs, questions were sent to individual practicing interpreters and to interpreter e-groups. A total of 80 responses were received (representing about 10% of the registered population in the UK). Currently, according to this cohort,

---

31. Inspectie voor de Gezondheidszorg (2003).

training programs for interpreting in healthcare settings must focus on the following:

1. Knowledge
   This includes medical terminology, human anatomy, ailments, medical procedures, treatment options, and the overall structure of the healthcare system.
2. Working with deaf people/deaf professionals/deaf trainers
   This includes training in understanding the deaf patient's experience and also the ways in which deaf people understand their condition and treatment so the interpreter can engage them appropriately and effectively. Deaf people have a role to play in developing the interpreters' medical sign lexicon and could also offer training in how symptoms, diagnoses, different conditions, procedures, operations, and treatments are described in sign language.
3. Working with healthcare professionals
   Training is needed in how to develop a better working relationship between sign-language interpreters and healthcare professionals. The latter need to understand the role of the former and their wish to provide an overall better-quality service by closer cooperation.
4. Working with experienced interpreters
   Interpreters would like to shadow, then review and reflect upon their practice with experienced colleagues. This could be done through a mentoring relationship or supervision with peers or within an in-house context: "It would be good to have a training course where experienced interpreters are able to share their knowledge and then have the opportunity within a safe environment to practice."
5. Understanding the dynamics of medical interactions
   Training needs to address a range of other issues, including the following:
   Dealing with the communication dynamic and developing techniques to manage interaction effectively
   Understanding the consequences and intention of apparently simple utterances
   Juggling humanity and professionalism in dealing with emotional aspects, sensitive situations, and disempowered clients and in respecting clients' dignity and privacy
   Understanding ethical implications
   Understanding how to be assertive

Developing good interpersonal skills
Developing coping strategies in the waiting room
6. Learning how to deal with transference (interpreting bad news and the aftermath)

Interpreting in Mental Health Settings

Many of the responses given for interpreting in medical settings were similar to those for interpreting in mental health settings. Therefore, the following findings list only responses or comments that are particular to this setting. According to respondents, a need exists for specialist training in mental health that deals with the following:

Relevant legislation
Mental health services
Mental health conditions, diagnoses, and treatments
Differences in services for deaf people

Additional training in the specific needs of working in therapeutic settings: triadic therapeutic alliances, different ways of working (e.g., eye contact/ clarifying information/boundaries to ensure the therapeutic alliance is maintained). This also involves having an understanding of the therapeutic approach in order to work effectively.

There is an acknowledgement that deaf professionals working in the mental health domain can, in certain circumstances, work in collaboration with a hearing interpreter. This provides a need for training in how the two professionals can successfully work together.

7. The need to develop skill in working into the spoken language
   As many mental health conditions may affect the communication process of a deaf patient, interpreters need to understand how this impacts in order to develop the necessary skills to provide an accurate interpretation.
8. The need for opportunities to be observed and mentored
   A few respondents felt that training could be in the form of observation, particularly of a deaf mental health team.

A few years ago ASLI produced a code of practice[32] for interpreters working in mental healthcare settings and made available a number of

---

32. http://www.asli.org.uk/asli-s-policies-p35.aspx (accessed March 20, 2011).

useful articles and guidelines.[33] The purpose was to develop best practices to enable interpreters to meet the special requirements of working in mental health settings.

Italy

A request for participation in a survey on mental health/general healthcare settings was sent to those on the ANIOS mailing list, which contains 80 email addresses (out of 83 total ANIOS members; 3 interpreters do not use email). Only 6 interpreters responded. A set of questions ranging from work experience in medical settings to training needs was submitted to them.

All of the respondents said that they have had no specific training in this particular field (one added that healthcare issues were addressed when discussing a case study during ethics classes). These responses, although too few to make any official statistics, seem to confirm the data collected from past and present training courses. All of the respondents have some work experience in NHS hospitals (emergency and operating rooms), at doctor's offices, or at private healthcare centers. As mentioned before, the medical terminology in both languages makes the interpreting task more difficult although background knowledge about anatomy, pathology, or other medical disciplines have helped the interpreters to process and transfer information. Doctors are seen as responsible for clarity of language with both hearing and deaf patients.

The most problematic aspect of interpreting in healthcare settings seems to be how to manage emotions:

> It has been a battle between heart and mind in certain situations. It is true that you keep on learning through the years. However, I have refused many assignments if clients were close acquaintances of mine or if I was experiencing an emotional moment of my life at that time.

> I believe that the emotional impact cannot be disregarded . . . Not all of us bear the sight of many things, the smell of strong odors, the sight of people in pain . . . In other words, you really have to think about it before going there.

---

33. http://www.asli.org.uk/guidance-for-members-working-in-mental-health-settings-p23.aspx (accessed March 20, 2011).

> Sometimes there are situations that you are not prepared to face and make you feel torn as a professional and as a human being . . . How to face the death of a person!

Training is considered very important in helping interpreters develop the appropriate technical and decision-making skills. Furthermore, a code of ethics specifically designed for healthcare interpreting would be of help when handling ethical issues, a challenging aspect that is also identified by Kaufert and Pusch (1997, 7, cited by Angelelli, 2003, 7). The Italian Sign Language interpreters who took part in the survey expressed a need for more training in healthcare settings in the following areas:

theoretical instruction in medical disciplines

theoretical training in a variety of medical settings and contextual dimensions (e.g., the difference between working in an operating room and working at a doctor's office for a patient's routine checkup)

vocabulary instruction (medical terms in both Italian Sign Language and Italian)

management of emotions and psychological aspects

interpersonal dynamics required for a successful partnership between interpreters and professionals

interpersonal dynamics required for a successful partnership between interpreters and deaf/hearing clients and their deaf/hearing relatives

Working in mental health settings is even more demanding, and interpreters try to cope with the lack of training by seeking close cooperation with doctors and the medical staff. Deaf professionals also have high expectations of the quality of interpreting. Again, appropriate training is seen as the key to successful interpretations:

> In the past I worked with an interpreter, but she was not able to interpret effectively. She used to get emotionally involved very easily and interfered in my work with my own patient. She could not keep professional distance, and if my patient wept bitterly, she would move (I could see a teardrop falling from her eye). . . . I have been in therapy myself for almost five years with a hearing therapist who cannot sign. I proposed bringing an interpreter, but she refused because she does not trust interpreters. Alas, maybe she is right because

there is no specific interpreter training in psychological fields. (deaf psychologist, personal interview)

The individual interpreters in the UK and Italy mentioned earlier the need for knowledge about how to deal with end-of-life care. Norris et al. (2005) identify a framework for interpreters with basic professional skills and qualities that interpreters considered important for both physicians and interpreters in language-discordant settings, such as honesty and compassion. They provide some specific recommendations on how spoken-language interpreters can improve communications about end-of-life care in language-discordant encounters. Schapira et al. (2008) also confirm the need for physicians to establish collaborative practices with interpreters and provide further recommendations on working with medical interpreters.

Educational programs for sign-language interpreters could review the recommendations in these studies with spoken-language interpreters and determine how they could be implemented in new training programs for sign-language interpreters.

Needs and Views of the Deaf Population

In 1990 Jones and Pullen carried out one of the very first European surveys to focus on deaf signers in 11 countries of the former European Community in order to discover their views on health, employment, education, training, and interpreting provision. The health section tackled three issues:

deaf people's access to healthcare delivery
means of communication used when utilizing health services
access to health information and health promotion

Although 20 years have passed since this report was first published, many problems the deaf interviewees raised are still unsolved and being debated today, including poor communication in medical settings and with professionals in particular, limited or no access to information, lack of or very few trained interpreters. The report also gives a general picture of the provision of interpreting services at that time:

Communicators in the health service were mainly family or friends. In Italy in particular there seemed to be an informal arrangement with friends based on the exchange of drinks and meals in return for interpreting, whereas in Holland more official interpreters were used. In the UK it was often social workers, which sometimes caused problems. (Jones & Pullen, 1990, 53)

In November 2010 the European Union launched the new Disability Strategy 2010–2012[34] for a barrier-free Europe. This strategy spells out how the EU and the national governments can empower people with disabilities to fully exercise their rights. It is an important step forward in promoting accessibility for deaf people in Europe, which was emphasized by EU commissioner Viviane Reding and Ádám Kósa, the first deaf member of EU parliament, at the EUD–EU conference on the implementation of sign-language legislation (Brussels, November 18, 2010).

The Netherlands

No research has yet been carried out in the Netherlands on the use of sign-language interpreters in healthcare settings. Some studies have concentrated on spoken-language interpreters in medical settings (Bot, 2005; Vonk, 2001). The little available research on sign language discusses communication between healthcare professionals and deaf persons. For example, Smeijers and Pfau (2009) investigated communication problems between hearing physicians and their deaf or hard of hearing clients in the Netherlands. They found that significant communication problems occur in these interactions and propose the use of interpreters to reduce the language barriers. Therefore, they plan to further investigate the role of interpreted interactions with physicians.

To improve communication between hearing healthcare professionals and deaf and hard of hearing patients, a project was carried out in 2008–2009 by the Utrecht University of Applied Sciences, Gelderse Vallei hospital, the Gelderhorst, and the Gelderse Roos. The project findings, among others, were that healthcare professionals seldom arranged for an interpreter and that 40% of all deaf patients never requested an interpreter. Of those patients, 34% said that an interpreter was not needed, and 50% preferred to bring a family member along for communication purposes.

---

34. http://ec.europa.eu/social/main.jsp?langId=en&catId=89&newsId=933&furtherNews =yes (accessed November 25, 2010).

One solution to some of the basic communication issues between healthcare professionals and deaf patients has also been provided by the International Federation of Medical Students Associations (IFMSA), which organizes courses on sign language and the lives of deaf people for students at medical facilities throughout the Netherlands.

For many years Dovenschap, the Dutch Deaf Association, has lobbied to have interpreters high on the list of priorities when it comes to medical assignments. Tolknet,[35] the only government-funded referral agency in the Netherlands, experienced difficulties fulfilling this request because of the lack of interpreters (de Wit, 2008). Due to an increase in the number of interpreters this has become less of a problem, but deaf patients may nonetheless still find that no interpreter is available for their medical appointment.

In addition, Dovenschap finds that if the current training programs do not provide sufficient training in working in healthcare settings, then continuing education must be offered to certified interpreters to enhance their skills. The requirements, according to Dovenschap, are an adequate knowledge of medical terms and related signs, as well as social and interaction skills.

United Kingdom

In the UK a number of reports have looked at deaf people's experiences with the healthcare system.[36] The most important aspect for deaf people is

35. www.tolknet.org (accessed November 27, 2010).

36. Department of Health (1997). "A Service on the Edge: Inspection of Services for Deaf and Hard of Hearing People." http://www.dh.gov.uk/prod_consum_dh/groups/dh_digitalassets /@dh/@en/documents/digitalasset/dh_4065702.pdf (accessed November 14, 2010).

Royal National Institute of the Deaf (RNID) (2004). "A Simple Cure: A National Report into Deaf and Hard of Hearing People's Experiences of the National Health Service." http:// www.rnid.org.uk/VirtualContent/84923/asimplecure.pdf (accessed November 14, 2010).

Royal National Institute of the Deaf (RNID), Royal National Institute for the Blind, Sign Community (British Deaf Association) (2010). "Is It My Turn Yet? Access to GP Practices in Northern Ireland for People Who Are Deaf, Hard of Hearing, Blind or Partially Sighted." http://www.rnid.org.uk/VirtualContent/95457/ 3603_research_report.pdf (accessed November 14, 2010).

SignHealth (2007). "Deaf People and Suicide." http://www.signhealth.org.uk/documents /suicide_leaflet_v8.pdf (accessed November 14, 2010).

SignHealth (2008). "Why Do You Keep Missing Me? A Report into Deaf People's Access to Primary Health Care." http://www.signhealth.org.uk/documents/Why_report.pdf (accessed November 14, 2010).

to be able to communicate. When no sign-language interpreter has been provided, they have to find alternative forms of communicating, which makes for an unsatisfactory experience. Deaf people's experiences are improved when a sign-language interpreter is provided; however, an untrained person who lacks skill and ability may put the deaf person at greater risk through misinterpretation (Timehin et al., 2006).

Avril Hepner of the British Deaf Association (BDA) (2010) states the following:

> There is a lack of BSL/English interpreters in these settings. There are more deaf people who have mental health and healthcare needs in the UK, and the demand is not fully met. There are lots of funding issues that prevent full access to deaf people in these settings because of the insufficient availability of interpreters. I am worried about the current statistics on canceled appointments because there are no interpreters available. This can affect the mental health of the clients, which can be very sensitive. The unavailability of interpreters should not delay the appointment when a person needs it. I have seen on a number of occasions that the interpreters working in those settings do not have the necessary skills. Who should be monitoring them and decide if they are suitable? Should there be an organization or body to oversee the interpreting work in those settings? (personal interview, Avril Hepner, BDA, 2010)

When asked to list the priorities for increasing the availability of sign-language interpreters, the BDA mentioned the following:

More specialist training in this field

More community placements training in this field, preferably with experienced interpreters

Funding for specific training in this area

NHS Health Advisory Service (1996). "Mental Health Services Forging New Channels." http://www.deafinfo.org.uk/policy/ForgingNewChannels.pdf (accessed November 14, 2010).

Department of Health (2005). "Mental Health and Deafness: Toward Equity and Access." http://www.dh.gov.uk/prod_consum_dh/groups/dh_digitalassets/@dh/@en/documents/digitalasset/dh_4104005.pdf (accessed November 14, 2010).

Royal National Institute of the Deaf (Cymru) (2008). "The National Assembly for Wales (Legislative Competence) (no. 6) Order 2008 (Relating to Provision of Mental Health Services)." http://www.assemblywales.org/mh_29_-_rnid_cymru_.pdf (accessed November 14, 2010).

Compulsory recruitment of deaf relay interpreters to work with interpreters to translate for deaf clients. Often many interpreters do not translate properly for deaf people who have mental health issues, so the translations are best coming from a deaf native user of the language

More training and workshops on the terminology of this field to develop signs for actual use

Provision of full-time jobs for interpreters in mental health and healthcare settings

Interpreters should not accept assignments if they are not fully confident of their ability to carry them out satisfactorily.

Interpreters need to mix more with deaf people in this field to gain more knowledge before accepting assignments. Interpreters must be fluent and have many years of experience before accepting assignments.

Interpreters must be qualified and registered with an organization or association like SASLI/ASLI.

SignHealth (2010) believes that qualified, experienced interpreters are vital in healthcare settings. However, the reality is that the limited number of such professionals requires that we look at provision. The minimum provision should be online support, and with better use of interpreters, enhanced provision is feasible: "To improve provision you either have to train more interpreters or change their working conditions. Training, as we know, will take many years, but an alteration to the terms and conditions under which they operate is quicker."

Italy

Italy and other European countries have witnessed progress, and today practitioners and the deaf community are much more aware of the importance of having trained, skilled interpreters working in the field of health care. Nevertheless, the old practices sometimes continue. When sign-language interpreters are not available for whatever reason, family members and friends still act as communication helpers. Viglione (2008) reports an interview with a young deaf Romanian woman admitted to the burn center of a hospital in Rome after a domestic accident. With the help of the woman's husband, also a Romanian and able to understand both Italian and sign language, the interviewer felt the woman's sense of loss and loneliness in a medical environment with barriers to effective communication:

What frightened and upset her the most was not only her not being understood but also the fact of not being able to follow the course of her condition. And not being able to understand what the administered drugs were for, what the urinometer or the saturometer were for. In order to access basic information she had to wait for her husband or a friend to arrive. (39)

Alternative communication strategies are another option. A deaf doctor described how deaf people are welcomed at the hospital where she works:

As far as I know, deaf people are treated like other patients. Generally speaking, I believe the medical staff act with sensitivity. Even if they cannot sign, they try to speak as clearly as they can. A hearing relative is almost always there. I must say that I have never seen an interpreter during clinical activities. (personal interview, October 2010)

To rely on relatives or members of one's language community to communicate with doctors and nurses seems to be a common practice also with hearing immigrants who cannot speak any language except their own, though different rules might apply if interpreters become permanent staff of the healthcare units. Delli Ponti and Forlivesi (2005), spoken-language interpreters employed at the hospital in Rimini, point out that friends or uncertified interpreters are allowed to assist patients with their communication needs only in exceptional situations, and, in any case, they are almost always supported by one of the interpreters on the Rimini hospital team. Immigration laws and policy plans promote cultural mediation activities for the integration of immigrants and foresee the use of "cultural mediators" who will often act as community interpreters.

A compromise solution might be utilized during emergency situations or when dealing with patients who are speaking an unknown language or using sign language. Delli Ponti and Forlivesi report that sometimes interpreters have to rely on the doctor's knowledge and experience and on their own "talent for improvisation": "[H]aving to deal with some deafmute [*sic*] Poles, the interpreters helped out with a bilingual dictionary, big gestures, and a lot of good will for many days" (2005, 198). A shortage of sign-language interpreters in the Rimini area, emergency treatments, or lack of general information about deaf communication needs might also have led to this solution.

The sign-language interpreters interviewed reported that in most cases they are appointed and paid by deaf people. If the hospital does not provide an interpreting service, deaf patients might decide to hire a professional sign-language interpreter, depending on their personal budget,[37] especially if long treatments are required:

> I have rarely been to the hospital, but once I had to face a serious situation being diagnosed with cancer. My partner acted as my interpreter. I could not afford an interpreter for the whole duration of radiotherapy or when I needed to talk to the head physician. Perhaps the hospital should at least have provided me with an interpreter. (Italian deaf man, personal interview, October 2010)

CONCLUSION

Relatives and friends of deaf people have traditionally served as the communication link between the deaf and the hearing worlds. Healthcare settings have been no exception. The process of professionalization, mostly carried out by training, has radically changed this situation although interpreting services are not completely regulated by professional principles. As a matter of fact, the diverse community of sign-language interpreters in Europe comprises trained, certified, and registered interpreters, as well as untrained, uncertified, and unregistered ones. While the majority of interpreters are educated and have passed qualification tests, people who have no training or certification are continuing to work as interpreters, particularly in medical settings.

In general, sign-language interpreters view the general healthcare setting as distinct from that for mental health care. A number of generic training programs provide a good foundation, but additional training that focuses on medical and mental health settings is also needed. In Italy today, the fragmented training situation does not help. Sign-language interpreters are required to find resources and develop tools by themselves. Any possible cooperation among interpreters, the deaf community, and health professionals has always produced positive results, especially at a local level. As a consequence, a general awareness of the necessity of specialized education in healthcare settings is rapidly growing. Although there is a need within the deaf and interpreting community, the Netherlands offers limited train-

---

37. Deaf people are provided with a monthly allowance from the state to meet their communication needs (law no. 508, 1988). In 2010, the amount given was 239.97 per month.

ing for healthcare settings only within the existing BA program and in sporadic workshops for graduate interpreters. In the UK, training organizations seem to recognize the need and have responded by running a number of short courses or workshops and making these available to practicing interpreters in healthcare or mental healthcare settings, as well as helping them assess their readiness to start working in these venues. Where these courses are not available, sign-language interpreters have expressed the desire to be specifically trained to better meet their clients' needs.

Individual sign-language interpreters from the UK, the Netherlands, and Italy have indicated that more specialized training in healthcare milieux is needed. They have identified in detail the current shortcomings in their education that leave them insufficiently prepared to work in healthcare settings. They feel they cannot guarantee that they will be able to meet the special demands of healthcare settings. Training institutes can improve this state of affairs by designing specialist short courses and workshops in the future. With regard to this, the British Deaf Association has expressed concern but also notes that there may be trained and registered interpreters who do not yet have the skills to work in these settings. Interviews with deaf individuals from the Netherlands and Italy confirm this point of view.

The call for detailed, specialized training in healthcare contexts was confirmed by the European Union of the Deaf. The involvement of deaf people in interpreter training is particularly needed in teaching signed lexicon for specific healthcare terminology and instructing interpreters in how best to describe symptoms, diagnoses, conditions, and treatments. In addition, interpreters need to be trained in how deaf people understand their condition.

On the basis of personal interviews with deaf people, interpreters, and educational programs, this chapter shows the need for the development of specialized training for sign-language interpreters in healthcare settings in three European countries. As practitioners ourselves, we strongly recommend more structured research projects involving interpreters, the users of sign-language interpreting services, and the healthcare profession, and we urge the implementation of specialty courses in mental health and healthcare settings. The current developments in the European Union with regard to new strategies for increasing accessibility for people with disabilities further confirms these needs. The national organizations of sign-language interpreters and national deaf organizations must lobby to ensure inclusion of trained sign-language interpreters and accessibility for deaf people in the new EU strategies.

ACKNOWLEDGMENTS

We would like to express our gratitude to our interpreter colleagues from our respective countries for their time in responding to our questions. Our sincere thanks also go to the associations who have contributed to this chapter by sharing their views and information (in alphabetical order): Alpha Hospitals, ANIOS, ASLI, BDA, Bristol University, British Society for Mental Health and Deafness, City Lit, Dovenschap, Durham University, efsli, EUD, Gelderhorst, National Deaf Services, Riethorst, SIGNAMIC, SignHealth, University of Wolverhampton, Utrecht University of Applied Sciences, and VIA.

REFERENCES

Angelelli, C. (2003). The visible co-participant: The interpreter's role in doctor-patient encounters. In M. Metzger, S. Collins, V. Dively, & R. Shaw (Eds.), *From topic boundaries to omission: New research on interpretation* (pp. 3–26). Washington, DC: Gallaudet University Press.

Bogaerde, B. van den, de Lange, R., & Vorrink, S. (2009). *Help, een dove cliënt.* Paper presented at the final conference of SIA RAAK Public Project "Oog voor Communicatie." December 8. Utrecht: University of Applied Sciences.

Bot, H. (2005). *Dialogue interpreting in mental health.* Amsterdam: Radopi BV.

Buonomo, V. (2008). Il profilo professionale dell'interprete LIS. *OPPInformazioni, 105,* 41–44.

Dean, R., & Pollard R. (2001). *Application of demand-control theory to sign language interpreting: Implications for stress and interpreter training.* New York: Oxford University Press.

Delli Ponti, A., & Forlivesi, K. (2005). Il lavoro dell'interprete all'interno di una struttura ospedaliera. In R. Mariachiara and G. Mack (Eds.), *Interpretazione di trattativa* (pp. 195–201). Milan: Hoepli.

Gosselink, R., & Frederiks, B. (2009). De rechtspositie van dove patiënten in de gezondheidszorg: De kwaliteit van (het recht op) communicatie in het geding? *Medicine, Tijdschrift voor Gezondheidsrecht, 33*(4), 306–308.

Inspectie voor de Gezondheidszorg (IGZ). (2003). *Kortschrift: Tolken in de gezondheidszorg.* Retrieved July 5, 2011, from http://www.ggdkennisnet.nl/kennisnet/uploaddb/downl_object.asp?atoom=19684&VolgNr=2.

Jones, L., & Pullen, G. (1990). *Inside we are all equal: A social policy survey of Deaf people in the European community*. European Community Regional Secretariat of the World Federation of the Deaf. London: DoCOM.

Mack, G. (2005). Interpretazione e mediazione: Alcune riflessioni terminologiche. In R. Mariachiara and G. Mack (Eds.), *Interpretazione di trattativa* (pp. 3–17). Milan: Hoepli.

Maio, V., & Manzoli, L. (2002). The Italian Healthcare System: W.H.O. ranking versus public perception. *Pharmacy and Therapeutics, 27*, 301–308.

Norris, W. M., Wenrich, M. D., Nielsen, E. L., Treece, P. D., Jackson, J. C., & Curtis, J. R. (2005). Communication about end-of-life care between language-discordant patients and clinicians: Insights from medical interpreters. *Journal of Palliative Medicine, 8* (November 5), 1016–24.

Schapira, L., Vargas, E., Hidalgo, R., Brier, M., Sanchez, L., Hobrecker, K., Lynch, T., & Chabner, B. (2008). Lost in translation: Integrating medical interpreters into the multidisciplinary team. *Oncologist, 13*, 586–92.

Smeijers, A., & Pfau, R. (2009). Toward a treatment for treatment: On communication between general practitioners and their deaf patients. *Sign Language Translator and Interpreter 3*(1), 1–14.

Timehin, E., Odell, E., Woodcock, J., Kitching, S., & Mancktelow, B. (2006). *Communicating with Deaf and hearing impaired patients: Audit report 2006*. Retrieved from http://www.stgeorges.nhs.uk/docs/about/EHR/DeafAwarenessAudit.pdf.

Il Treno. (2008). Soc. Coop. Soc.le ONLUS. *Quando nasce un bimbo: Guida sulla gravidanza, parto, e puerperio in LIS e Italiano*. CD-ROM. Rome.

Tribe, R., & Thompson, K. (2008). *Working with interpreters in health settings: Guidelines for psychologists*. Leicester: British Psychological Society. Retrieved July 5, 2011, from http://www.ucl.ac.uk/clinical-psychology/traininghandbook /sectionfiles/Appendix_6_BPS_guidance_on_working_with_interpreters.pdf.

Viglione, D. (2008). La sordità: Indagine sui problemi di comunicazione tra non udenti e il personale infermieristico di un DEA. Tesi di Laurea 2006–2007. In S. Maragna and B. Marziale (Eds.), *I diritti dei sordi* (pp. 38–39). Milan: Franco Angeli.

Vonk, M. (2001). *Accreditation of interpreters and translators in the Netherlands*. Paper presented at the Critical Link 3 Conference: Interpreters in the Community Conference. Montreal, Canada, May 22–26.

Wit, M. de, (2008). *Sign language interpreting in Europe*. Baarn: Author.

INDEX

Figures, notes, and tables are indicated by f, n, and t following page numbers.